The Wood Finisher's Handbook

Sam Allen

Drawings by
Bob Steimle

Sterling Publishing Co., Inc.
New York

Library of Congress Cataloging-in-Publication Data

Allen, Sam.
The wood finisher's handbook / Sam Allen.
p. cm.
Includes index.
ISBN-13: 978-1-4027-3037-5
ISBN-10: 1-4027-3037-3
1. Wood finishing—Handbooks, manuals, etc. I. Title.

TT325.A45 2006
684'.084—dc22

2006004777

10 9 8 7 6 5 4 3 2 1

Published by Sterling Publishing Co., Inc.
387 Park Avenue South, New York, NY 10016
This edition is based on material found in *Wood Finisher's Handbook* © 1984 by Sam Allen

Distributed in Canada by Sterling Publishing
c/o Canadian Manda Group, 165 Dufferin Street
Toronto, Ontario, Canada M6K 3H6
Distributed in the United Kingdom by GMC Distribution Services
Castle Place, 166 High Street, Lewes, East Sussex, England BN7 1XU
Distributed in Australia by Capricorn Link (Australia) Pty. Ltd.
P.O. Box 704, Windsor, NSW 2756, Australia

Printed in China

Sterling ISBN-13: 978-1-4027-3037-5
ISBN-10: 1-4027-3037-3

For information about custom editions, special sales, premium and corporate purchases, please contact Sterling Special Sales Department at 800-805-5489 or specialsales@sterlingpub.com.

Acknowledgments

The material in this book is based largely on the experience I have gained during my career as a woodworker, so I would like to acknowledge those that have helped me gain that experience.

My wife, Virginia, who is an accomplished woodworker in her own right, has helped me with many projects. Without her help in preparing the manuscript this book would not have been possible. My sons, Paul and John, helped with many of the photos. Their hands appear throughout the book.

I would also like to thank my mother, Betty Allen. Her encouragement early in my life enabled me to pursue a career in woodworking, and she helped in preparing this book. Her knowledge of chemistry was a valuable resource in preparing the chemical stain section.

Marcella and Mel Van Orman gave me my first set of tools when I was a boy, and I appreciate their encouragement.

Roger Roylance, who has been my friend since grade school, worked with me on some of my first projects; we developed our skills together. He has always encouraged me to strive for better quality work.

I would like to thank all of the dedicated shop teachers that helped to instill a love for wood in me. The instructors and professors in the woodworking department at Brigham Young University, where I received my formal training, are very knowledgeable and I appreciate the instruction I received from them.

I am particularly grateful to the foremen and crews that I have worked with for sharing the knowledge they have gained over the years.

I would also like to thank the following companies who have provided information during my research and material that has been used as a basis for some illustrations in this book: Minwax Co. Inc.; Bassett Furniture Industries, Inc.; Parks Woodworking Machine Co.; Shopsmith, Inc.; 3M Industrial Abrasives Division; Great Neck Saw Mfrs., Inc.; Garrett Wade Co., Inc.; Norton; General Wood Works Co., Inc.; DeVilbiss; and Watco-Dennis Corp.

Contents

Introduction

Wood finishing is an art as well as a craft. Before you can practice the art of creative wood finishing, you must become proficient at the craft of wood finishing. There are many basic skills to be mastered before you can consider yourself an expert wood finisher, but along the way to becoming an expert you can produce many beautifully finished pieces **(i–1)**. Some finishes can be effectively applied even by the most inexperienced beginner.

Modern techniques and equipment not only make it easier than ever for the beginner to achieve good results, they allow the advanced finisher more freedom to exercise creativity in finishing.

The first section of this book covers the basics of wood finishing from wood preparation through the finish coat. If you have never applied a wood finish before, this section will lead you step by step through the entire finishing process. Those of you who already have experience finishing will still find the first section useful because it includes some of the most up-to-date techniques, along with traditional methods that still provide results other methods don't. For example, the chapter on wood preparation covers the newest form of wood surfacing, abrasive planing, as well as one of the older forms of smoothing wood, scraping.

The second section of the book covers advanced techniques that give the experienced finisher more options and creative control over the finishing process. Topics covered in this section include mixing your own stains, chemical stains and wood graining, along with many others. Once you have mastered the basics covered in the first

i-1

A piece of fine furniture deserves a fine finish. In this book, you will learn how to create a finish worthy of your best projects.

section, the topics discussed in the second section will open up new areas for you to explore. Many of the processes discussed in the second section are traditional techniques that have been largely forgotten during the past few years because of the easy-to-use new finishes, but some of the effects created by these traditional methods are hard to duplicate by any other means. For example, chemical stains color the wood without obscuring any of the natural beauty of the wood. They actually change the chemical composition of the wood, altering its color without covering the surface with a coating of pigment.

About Wood

Wood is a complex material with a wide range of characteristics. To fully take advantage of the finishing process, you need to understand a little about the character and unique properties of the wood you are working with.

Wood is composed of elongated cells that vary in length from 1/8 inch to 1/25 inch depending on the species of wood. In a living tree these cells are filled with fluids. When a tree is cut and dried for lumber, the cells dry out and become hollow. The cells are connected to each other by a natural glue called *lignin*. Wood's fibrous properties are a result of these long cells that are all connected by lignin **(i–2)**.

A tree grows by forming new cells in a layer just below the bark called the *cambium*. The grain pattern that gives wood its desirable ornamentation is formed in the cambium as the cells are formed. Periods of rapid growth in the spring create cells that are large and less dense, while the slower growth of summer produces cells that are smaller and more dense. Together the spring growth and the summer growth produce an annual ring. One ring is formed for each year of the tree's life. When a log is cut into lumber, many annual rings are cut through. The grain pattern is formed by the angle at which the saw cuts through the cells that make up the ring.

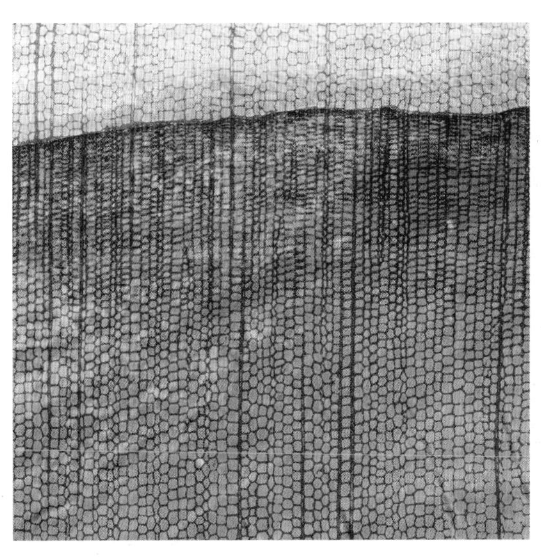

i-2
A cross section of western red cedar, greatly enlarged.

There are three general ways that lumber can be cut, and each produces a different type of grain. *Plain sawing* is the most economical way to cut solid lumber, so it is the most prevalent. Plainsawn lumber is cut so that the saw blade passes almost tangent to the annual rings. The grain produced is called a *flat grain* and is the familiar series of long arcs or parabolas (**i–3**).

i-3
The difference between plainsawn lumber and quarter-sawn lumber is a result of how the blade intersects the annual rings. In plainsawn lumber, shown here, the saw blade cuts through the rings at an angle of 45 degrees or less.

i-4 *The angle between the blade and the rings approaches 90 degrees in quartersawn lumber, producing the grain pattern shown here.*

i-6 *Rotary cutting produces a distinctive grain pattern. Rotary-cut oak is frequently used for doors or plywood.*

i-5 *This illustration shows the anatomy of a log and how the angle that the saw blade intersects the annual rings determines whether the wood is plain sawed or quartersawn.*

Quartersawn lumber is cut so that the saw blade passes at about a 90-degree angle to the annual rings. The grain produced is called a *vertical* or *edge grain*. It is characterized by a long parallel grain pattern (**i–4**).

If a log is placed in a stationary position for cutting and left in that position throughout the cutting process, both plainsawn and quartersawn lumber will be produced. As the first cuts are made, the blade will be tangent to the annual rings, producing plainsawn lumber. As the cutting proceeds through the log, the angle of the annual rings in relation to the blade will become closer to 90 degrees as the blade moves towards the center of the log, producing quartersawn lumber. After passing the center and moving towards the other side of the log, the boards will again be plainsawn (**i–5**). It is possible to maximize the production of either plainsawn or quartersawn lumber by repositioning the log during the sawing.

The third way of cutting lumber is used only for producing veneer or plywood. It is called *rotary cutting*. In this method the log is placed in a giant lathe and rotated; a knife blade peels a thin slice of wood from the surface of the log. The cutting all takes place parallel to the annual rings. This produces a very widely spaced grain pattern because the knife only cuts across the annual rings at a very shallow angle as it spirals in to the center of the log.

Some species of wood exhibit a very wild grain pattern when they are cut by the rotary method. The familiar wild grain of fir plywood is a good example. However, not all woods exhibit this wild grain when rotary cut. Birch plywood is almost always rotary cut and the grain produced is pleasing. Rotary-cut oak is frequently used for doors or plywood and its grain is not objectionably wild (**i–6**). The major advantage of rotary cutting is that long wide pieces of veneer are produced. A sheet of plywood can be made without any joints in the face veneer when rotary cut veneer is used.

Veneers can also be flat sliced, which is the equivalent of plain sawing, or they can be quarter sliced. Both of these methods produce veneer of varying widths depending on the diameter of the log it was sliced from. The piece of log that the veneer is cut from is called a *flitch*. Veneer cut from the same flitch will match closely, especially if the veneer is used in the same sequence as it was cut (**i–7**).

In the growing tree, fluids must be transported from the roots to other areas of the tree. To accomplish this, many small channels or pores are formed in the wood. In some species, such as oak, the pores are large. Wood in this category is called *open grained* because the surface of a board cut from this type of tree will have a distinct texture created by these pores. Other species like birch have pores that are much smaller and less noticeable. This type is called a *closed grain* wood.

Another type of fluid channel is called a *medullary ray cell*. It is a long passageway that radiates out from the center of the tree to the edges. In some woods it is very pronounced and forms a prominent grain feature. Oak is a prime example of a wood that exhibits prominent rays. In plainsawn oak, the rays appear as small dark lines running parallel with the grain, but when the wood is quartersawn the rays show up as large irregularly shaped markings that run across the grain (**i–8**). Quartersawn oak that has a lot of ray marks is sometimes called *tiger oak*.

At the center of the tree is a small-diameter area of soft, usually dark-colored wood called *pith*. This is the wood that was first formed when the tree was a sapling. Surrounding the pith is the *heartwood*. This area

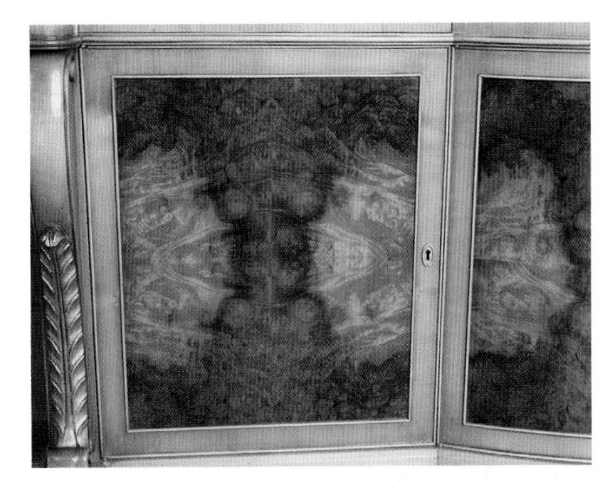

i-7

This door is veneered with burl veneer cut from the same flitch and put together in a book-matched pattern.

i-8

This quartersawn oak exhibits prominent ray marks.

makes up most of the diameter of the tree. The heartwood is essentially dead. The sapwood surrounds the heartwood; it is composed of the most recent annual rings of the tree. In some trees there is a variation in color between the sapwood and the heartwood. For example, the heartwood of the walnut tree is dark brown, while the sapwood is a light cream color.

Knots are formed where a branch connects to the main trunk of the tree. The annual rings are displaced around a knot, creating a variation in the grain. In plainsawn lumber, knots usually appear round or oval. Knots in quartersawn lumber frequently appear as long dagger-shaped defects that run across the grain, called *spikes*.

Wood is classified as either hardwood or softwood depending on the type of tree it came from. This classification has nothing to do with the actual hardness of the wood; softwoods are those from needle-bearing trees, while hardwoods are from leaf-bearing trees. The actual hardness of the wood varies according to the species and the rate of growth. Generally, slow-growing trees produce harder wood than trees that grow rapidly. Hardness is of importance to the wood finisher because it plays a role in how stains and other finishing materials are absorbed.

i-9 *Chemicals and trace minerals incorporated in the structure of wood give each wood its characteristic color. By applying a chemical that will react with chemicals present in the wood, a variety of color effects can be produced.*

There are many chemicals and trace minerals incorporated in the structure of wood. These elements are what give each wood its characteristic color. *Tannin* is a chemical that is present to a varying degree in most woods; it can create a large number of different color effects in combination with other chemicals. The finisher can take advantage of the natural chemical composition of wood to produce colors that are not natural for that species. By applying a chemical that will react with chemicals present in the wood, a variety of color effects can be produced (**i–9**).

As you work with woods, you will begin to recognize the different characteristics described here and you will soon realize that each piece of wood has its own character that will affect the final appearance of any finish applied to it. It is this variability that gives wood its charm, but it also presents a challenge to the wood finisher. You can decide whether to accentuate the character of the wood or de-emphasize some feature. The creative finisher can use the individual characteristics of a piece of lumber to create an unusual effect or mask the character of one board so that the entire project will harmoniously blend together.

Safety First

The process of finishing wood is inherently somewhat hazardous, but if you follow some commonsense safety precautions, working with finishing materials can be safe and enjoyable. Many liquids used in finishing are flammable; don't smoke while using them. Use flammable liquids in a well-ventilated area away from pilot lights, arcing motors, and switches or any other source of ignition. Always store flammable liquids in sealed containers, preferably the one originally supplied with the liquid or one approved for the storage of flammable liquids. Dispose of rags that have flammables on them in a tightly covered metal container to avoid spontaneous combustion.

Airborne dust from sanding or the overspray of spray equipment can pose a health hazard. To avoid inhaling harmful fumes, open all windows and doors to ensure adequate ventilation. Turn on a fan and wear a dust mask or respirator when performing operations that produce dust or fumes.

There are three main types of masks available. Each has a specific use, and if the correct one is not used you will not be protected. The first type is the *dust mask*. This is simply a filter that fits over your nose and mouth; it will filter solid particles out of the air you breathe. It will not remove harmful vapors. The dust mask is sufficient protection from the dust produced by sanding.

The next type of mask is the *organic vapor filter*. This type uses a chemical cartridge to remove the vapors released by common finishing materials; many also incorporate a dust filter. This is the type most often used when spraying common finishing materials in a well-ventilated area (**i–10**).

i-10 *The dust mask in the front of this photo is sufficient protection from the dust produced by sanding, but it will not remove harmful vapors. The two masks at the rear are the organic vapor type. They use a chemical cartridge to remove the vapors released by common finishing materials. They may also incorporate a dust filter. This is the type most often used when spraying common finishing materials in a well-ventilated area.*

The third type of mask is the *air-supplied respirator*. This can be either a mask or a hood that covers your entire head. Fresh air is supplied by a hose to the respirator. This type is recommended when extremely toxic fumes are present or where adequate ventilation cannot be provided. The hood type has the advantage of protecting your eyes as well.

Eye protection is another important safety consideration. Goggles or a full face shield should be worn whenever caustic or irritating materials are being used. Eye protection is also necessary whenever there is a chance that a particle of wood or metal could be thrown into your eye; power sanding and tool sharpening are examples of this.

Protective gloves should be worn whenever your hands will come in direct contact with a finishing liquid or chemical stripper (**i–11**). Some of the solvents used can be very irritating to the skin. The more volatile solvents such as lacquer thinner are prone to remove the natural oil from your skin, causing painful cracks to develop. There are several types of protective gloves available made of vinyl, neoprene, or nitrile. Some types are more resistant to certain solvents or chemicals than others, so check the recommended uses on the glove package and choose appropriate gloves that will protect your hands from the materials you are using.

Chemicals, especially acids, have special precautions that should be followed. Safety procedures for chemicals are fully discussed in the chapter on chemical stains.

Because of the increased awareness of health problems posed by strong solvents, many new finishing products are being developed with a water base. These products are easy to use and provide good results.

Keep safety on your mind as you work and your enjoyment of wood finishing won't be marred by an accident.

i-11 *Lightweight vinyl gloves (left) will keep your hands clean when you are working with mild finishing materials, but they won't protect you from harsh solvents and chemicals. For more protection, use protective gloves made of neoprene (center) or nitrile (right).*

Understanding the Terms on Labels

Finishing products are labeled with specific cautions and warnings. Here is a description of what these terms mean:

Poison These materials are toxic. Wash your hands thoroughly after use and don't get any material on food preparation surfaces. Avoid inhaling the vapors. Don't get any of the material in your mouth, eyes, or nose.

Harmful or fatal if swallowed. These materials are highly toxic. Wash your hands thoroughly after use and don't get any material on food preparation surfaces. Even the vapors can be harmful. Don't get any of the material in your mouth, eyes, or nose.

Use only with adequate ventilation. Products with this label may be flammable, toxic, or both. Adequate ventilation means that the vapor concentration isn't any greater than it would be if the product was used outdoors. This is hard to achieve in an enclosed area. Opening a window or door won't ventilate the area adequately. You would probably need to use large fans to provide adequate ventilation. The best precaution is to only use these products outside or in a professionally designed finishing room with power ventilation. Some vapors are heavier than air, so strong accumulations can accumulate near the floor even if you don't notice them at face level. This can be especially dangerous with explosive materials, because pilot lights may be located near the floor.

Combustible This material and its vapors will burn or ignite when exposed to a source of ignition such as a spark, pilot light, or flame.

Flammable This material and its vapors are more easily ignited than products labeled combustible. It will burn or ignite when exposed to a source of ignition such as a spark, pilot light, or flame.

Extremely Flammable This material and its vapors are more easily ignited than products labeled flammable. It will burn or ignite when exposed to a source of ignition such as a spark pilot light or flame. Use extreme caution.

Wood Preparation

Working with New Wood

The first and one of the most vital steps in producing a fine finish on wood is wood preparation. If the wood is not smooth and free from blemishes, it will not finish well. Preparing wood to accept a finish begins as soon as the project is started **(1–1)**.

One of the first steps in building any project from new wood is squaring and surfacing the stock. If this procedure is not correctly done, the project is already doomed to have a second-rate finish. As work on the project proceeds, other operations are performed that will have an effect on the final appearance of the finish. Assembling the pieces with glue is one operation that has a very derogatory affect on the final finish if it is not done carefully. Glue spots on the wood are difficult to remove and cause light areas in the finish that don't accept stain evenly. Sanding is another procedure that can make or break a fine finish.

1-1 *Preparing wood to accept a finish begins as soon as the project is started. This table has been planed and sanded in preparation for other finishing steps. If the wood is not smooth and free from blemishes, it will not finish well.*

Planing

Wood comes in several categories based on the degree of surfacing and jointing (preparation of the edge) that has been done at the mill. *Rough wood* hasn't been planed at all; it is just the way it left the saw. It may vary in thickness and the edges are neither square with the face nor parallel with each other. Wood that has been planed on the faces is called *S2S* (surfaced two sides). It is uniform in thickness and both faces are parallel. The faces are smooth; all of the rough texture left by the saw has been removed. A board that has been jointed on both edges, as well as having the faces surfaced, is referred to as *S4S* (surfaced four sides). The edges are square with the face and parallel to each other.

In addition to the above types, there are the following less commonly used varieties: *S1S* (surfaced one side), *S1S1E* (surfaced one side one edge), and *S1S2E* (surfaced one side two edges).

All of the above terms apply to solid lumber only. Plywood is available with the faces sanded or unsanded. Cabinet grades of plywood always come sanded and no further surfacing is required. Sanded plywood is ready for finish sanding as it comes from the mill.

The type of lumber you choose to use depends largely on what tools you have available. The more surfacing that is done by the mill the more you will have to pay for the lumber, but to use rough lumber you need a surface planer and a jointer.

A commercial-grade surface planer is one of the more expensive woodworking tools and will be found only in shops that do a large volume of work; but there are many smaller surface planers available that are relatively inexpensive and designed for small shops (**1–2**). A jointer is almost a necessity in a serious woodworking shop. A jointer is all that is required to work with S2S lumber, so you may find that using S2S is a practical way to save on lumber costs.

1-2 *A small surface planer like this one is affordable enough that it is practical for small shops and hobbyists.*

SURFACE PLANING In addition to saving on the cost of lumber, surfacing your own lumber has several other advantages. First, you can vary the thickness of the lumber to suit the application. Second, if you keep your machine in good adjustment and use it carefully you can achieve a smoother surface then is common on most mill-surfaced lumber. At a mill, operations must be performed at the fastest speed that will produce satisfactory results. With both surfacing and jointing a slower feed speed will produce a smoother surface so the mill must compromise, but you don't have to.

As a wood finisher, your objective when using the planer is to achieve the smoothest possible surface on the lumber being planed. A planer that is sharp and in good adjustment will produce good results if you feed at the proper speed and take grain direction into account. The cutting knives of a planer are set into a cylindrical head that rotates against the direction of feed. The cut made by the knives will be trough-shaped because of the circular cutting motion. If the feed is slow enough, the troughs will be small and close together making them practically invisible and easy to remove. When the feed is too fast, the troughs will be large and easily discernible, creating a washboard effect. These marks are called *mill marks*. When this occurs, it is much more difficult to achieve a smooth surface in later finishing steps. Roughing cuts to bring the stock close to the desired thickness can be made at a faster speed and cutting about 1/8 inch at a time. For the final finishing cut, slow the feed down and only take a 1/16-inch cut.

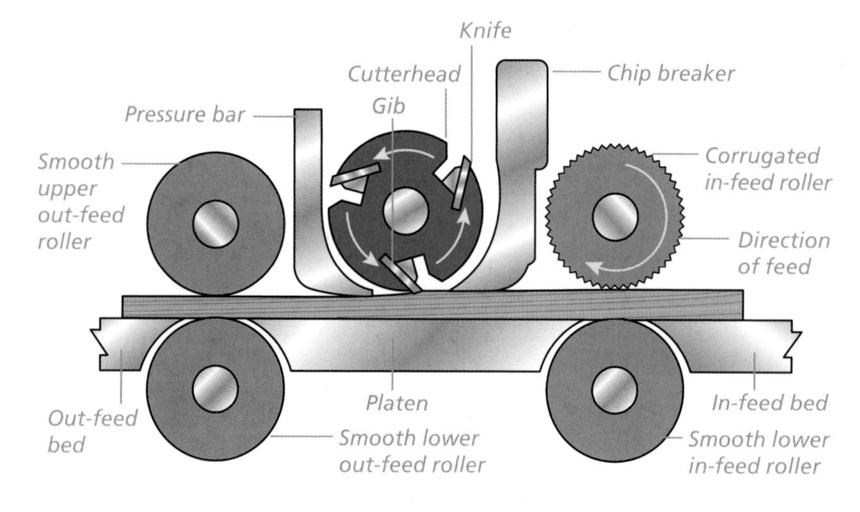

1-3 *The major internal parts of the surface planer.*

If the grain in the board you are planing angles up into the direction of the cutter rotation, small chips or tears may appear in the surface of the stock. If you notice this occurring on the first rough cut, turn the board end for end, so it is feeding in the opposite direction for all of the subsequent cuts. Sometimes the grain direction will change part way through a board; this is especially true around knots. If the full length of the board isn't needed, cut it at the point the grain changes so that each piece can be fed in the proper direction. If this is not practical, take very shallow cuts at a slow feed to reduce the chipping.

You should achieve good results by following these directions if the planer is operating correctly. If you don't get a smooth surface, then the fault is probably in the adjustment or maintenance of the machine. There are five parts of the planer that commonly produce an unacceptable surface when they are not maintained or adjusted properly. They are the in-feed rollers, the chip breaker, pressure bar, out-feed rollers, and the cutter head (**1–3**).

The in-feed rollers feed the stock into the machine; the upper in-feed roller is serrated to grip the stock. These serrations scar the wood, but since the planer removes the top surface of the board as it travels through the machine, it doesn't matter. Some machines use a rubber roller instead of a serrated metal one (**1–4**).

The chip breaker presses against the surface of the board directly in front of the cutter head. If the chip breaker were absent, the cutting knives would tear long chips out of the surface of the board. The chip breaker breaks the chips before they have a chance to tear.

1-4 This planer is designed to eliminate many of the adjustments necessary on most machines. It uses rubber feed rollers that don't require any adjustment, and there are no lower feed rollers; instead, the table is made of polished stainless steel.

The pressure bar is positioned directly behind the cutter head and holds the stock firmly against the bed.

The out-feed rollers help to pull the board through the machine. They are most necessary when the end of the board has passed the in-feed rollers. Both out-feed rollers are smooth because they press directly on the planed surface. If a recurring defect appears in the same general location evenly spaced along the surface of the board, look for a nick or accumulation of pitch on the out-feed rollers.

The cutter head houses the cutting knives. They must be kept properly sharpened and jointed or poor results will occur.

One of the most common problems that improper adjustment may cause is a snipe at one end of the board. A *snipe* is an area of the board that has been cut deeper than the rest of the surface. If the snipe occurs at the end that was fed into the planer, the most likely cause is a chip breaker that is set too high. Other likely causes are a lower in-feed roller that is too high, a pressure bar that is set too low or with not enough spring tension, or an upper in-feed roll that is set too high. A snipe at the end that fed through the planer last is usually caused by a pressure bar that is set too high. When the lower outfeed roller is set too high or the upper outfeed roller set too low, a snipe will also result.

Chips, scars, and marks left by the planer are a more serious problem to the wood finisher. At least snipes can be cut off and discarded before the board is put to use, but some scars left by an improperly sharpened or damaged blade run the entire length of the board.

A raised line running with the length of the board indicates a chip or nick in the blades. It may also indicate that the blades have been improperly sharpened in the past. If the blades were allowed to burn during the grinding process, they will lose their temper and nicks will form easily. This type of blemish is fairly easy to correct in later finishing operations since it is raised above the rest of the surface.

A nick that is gouged below the surface is much more difficult to remove later, so it should be corrected immediately at the source. A gouge running parallel to the length of the board may be caused by a dragging pressure bar or by an accumulation of wood chips stuck between the out-feed roller and the bed.

Irregularly shaped dents that occur at random spots on the board are caused by wood chips that are pressed into the surface

1-5 An abrasive planer uses wide sanding belts instead of knives to smooth the lumber's surface. The opposing heads on this machine surface both sides of the board at once.

1-6 This abrasive surfacer uses sanding drums instead of belts. It won't remove large amounts of wood, but it's great for giving the final surfacing to a board.

by the out-feed rollers. To correct this problem, check the exhaust system. If it is clogged, it won't remove all of the chips and some will fall back to the surface of the board.

Regularly spaced dents that seem to be in a line along most of the length of the board are caused by accumulations of pitch or wood chips mixed with pitch that are stuck to one of the out-feed rollers or the lower in-feed roller, or by a defect in the surface of one of these rollers.

A burn mark across the width of the board indicates that the board stuck at that point momentarily. This may have been caused by taking too heavy a cut or it may mean that the in-feed or out-feed rollers don't have enough tension.

Chips or areas of raised grain may indicate that the blades need to be sharpened and jointed. Also, if a washboard effect occurs even when the feed speed is set correctly, dull blades may be the cause.

USING AN ABRASIVE PLANER Most of the problems associated with machine planing can be eliminated by using an abrasive planer. An abrasive planer is basically a wide belt sander with a feed mechanism similar to a planer. Industrial models have opposing heads that smooth both sides of the lumber at once (**1–5**). Smaller models are available that surface one side at a time and use sanding drums instead of belts (**1–6**). This type is affordable enough for small shops and individuals to consider using. They aren't meant to remove large amounts of wood, but they are great for giving the final surfacing to a board after you have brought it close to the desired thickness on a standard thickness planer.

Since the wood is sanded away rather than cut, grain direction and knots don't create the problems that they do with a conventional planer. This fact has made abrasive planing popular in industry because it cuts down on waste. Another factor that makes abrasive planing attractive in an industrial setting is that maintenance is much simpler, decreasing downtime. The fact that more mills are switching to abrasive planing is a boon to wood finishers because the lumber produced requires much less preparation. Mill marks, raised grain, tear-outs, snipes, and gouges are practically absent from lumber surfaced with an abrasive planer (**1–7**). If you use abrasive planed lumber, you can usually go directly to the finish-sanding operation.

1-7 *The board on the left was planed with a conventional planer. Notice the mill marks, raised grain, and chips around the knot. The board on the right, surfaced with an abrasive planer, is free of them.*

THE JOINTER The jointer's main function is to produce a smooth square edge on a piece of lumber (**1–8**). It can also be used to surface one face of a board as long as the cutter head of the jointer is wider than the board. A jointer is useful for surfacing a face because it will remove slight twisting and warping while a planer won't.

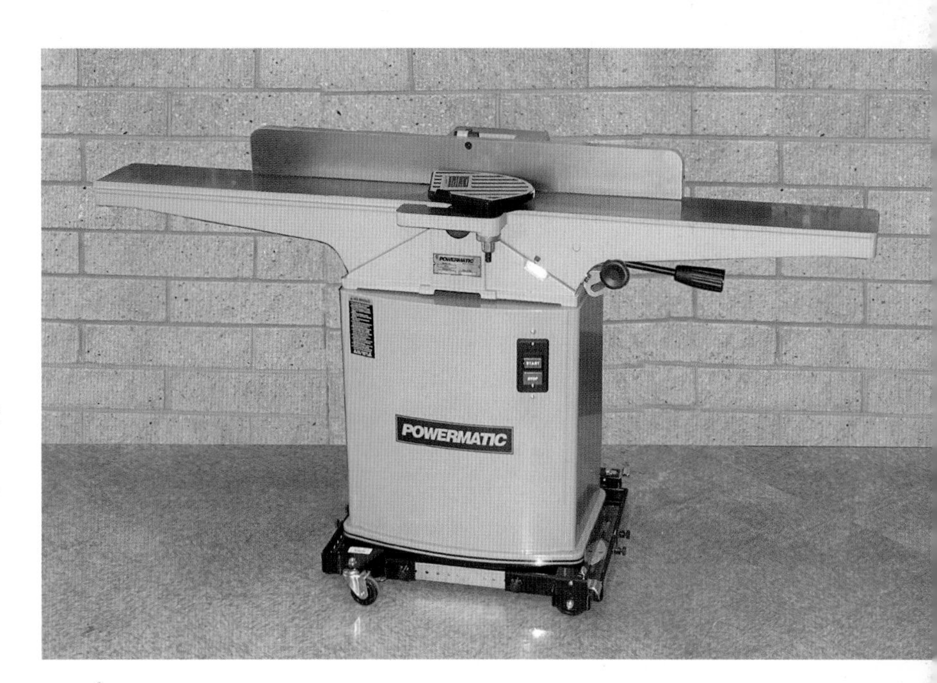

1-8 *A jointer.*

Surface defects caused by an improperly adjusted or maintained jointer are similar to those found with the planer. A washboard effect is caused by too fast a feed. Since there is no feed mechanism on a jointer, the feed is controlled solely by how fast you push the board across the cutter. If the edge is not smooth enough, simply push slower. You can even vary the speed that you push the board to accommodate defects and changes in grain direction.

A nick in the blade crates the same characteristic raised line that was described for

1-9 *Pictured from left to right: metallic jack plane, metallic smooth plane, wooden smooth plane, and wooden block plane. The plane in the rear is a wooden jointer plane.*

the planer. Dull blades will cause chipping and raised grain.

A snipe at the end of the board is caused by the out-feed table being adjusted too low.

HAND PLANES Any board that has been surfaced with a conventional power planer or jointer, no matter how well adjusted the tool was, will have a slight washboard surface. This is unavoidable with a rotating cutter head. So whether you buy lumber that was surfaced at the mill or surface it yourself, you will have to remove these mill marks.

A hand plane is the best way to remove mill marks; however, a belt sander can also be used on board with only slightly apparent marks. A belt sander requires less skill than a plane, so it is the best choice for a beginner; however, in the hands of an experienced user a hand plane will produce superior results. A plane shaves a thin slice of wood off the face of the board. Since the bottom of the plane is very long in relation to the width of one of the troughs left by the planer cutter head, it spans many of the marks, riding only on the peaks. This means that the blade is kept at a uniform depth, creating a smooth surface free of the washboard ridges caused by the rotating cutter.

Hand planes come in many sizes, ranging from the short block plane to the very long jointer plane (**1–9**). Planes are available in both metallic and wooden types. Both types produce good results. For more complete information on planes, see my book *Plane Basics*. All of the sizes serve useful purposes in woodwork, but for the purposes described here, a jack plane, which is from $11\frac{1}{2}$ inches to 15 inches long, or a smooth plane, which is 7 inches to 9 inches long, will work best (**1–10**).

The blade should be sharp and slightly rounded at the corners. The corners are rounded to prevent them from digging into the wood. Don't go overboard when rounding the corners or a noticeable dip in the board will be produced; slightly rounded means that the rounding is difficult even to see. Set the plane iron cap to $\frac{1}{32}$ inch from the tip of the blade and adjust the plane for a very shallow cut; use the lateral adjusting lever to set the blade square in the slot.

Place the board on a bench with its end against a bench stop or a bench hook with the grain facing away from you. You will be planing "with the grain" to avoid chips and roughening. It is important to plane with the grain; if you plane against the grain, the chances of tear-out are increased. Tear-out occurs when the wood fibers split along the grain ahead of the plane iron. This will leave a chipped section that will stand out after the wood is finished. At the first sign of a change in grain direction, reverse the plane and plane into the new grain direction.

Planing with the grain is sometimes called *planing uphill*. When viewed from the side, the grain looks like the slope of a hill. When you are planing in the proper direction, the plane is traveling in the uphill direction. Stock that is straight-grained and free of knots is easy to plane. The shavings will come off in long unbroken curls. Problems occur when the grain direction changes in the board. This is particularly a problem around knots, but it can occur anywhere in the board.

On highly figured wood, it may be impossible to avoid tear-out; in that case, use a belt sander to remove mill marks.

Place the toe of the plane on the end of the board opposite the bench stop and turn the plane about 10 degrees in relation to the length of the board. Now apply gentle pressure to the toe and advance the plane into the work. When the blade has cleared the end of the board by about an inch, slightly increase the downward pressure on the plane. Continue along the entire length of the face in a smooth, even stroke. When the blade clears the end of the board, release downward pressure but continue forward motion for another inch or two before lifting the plane. Go back to the other end of the board and begin another pass slightly overlapping the first. Continue in this manner until the entire face has been planed (**1–11**).

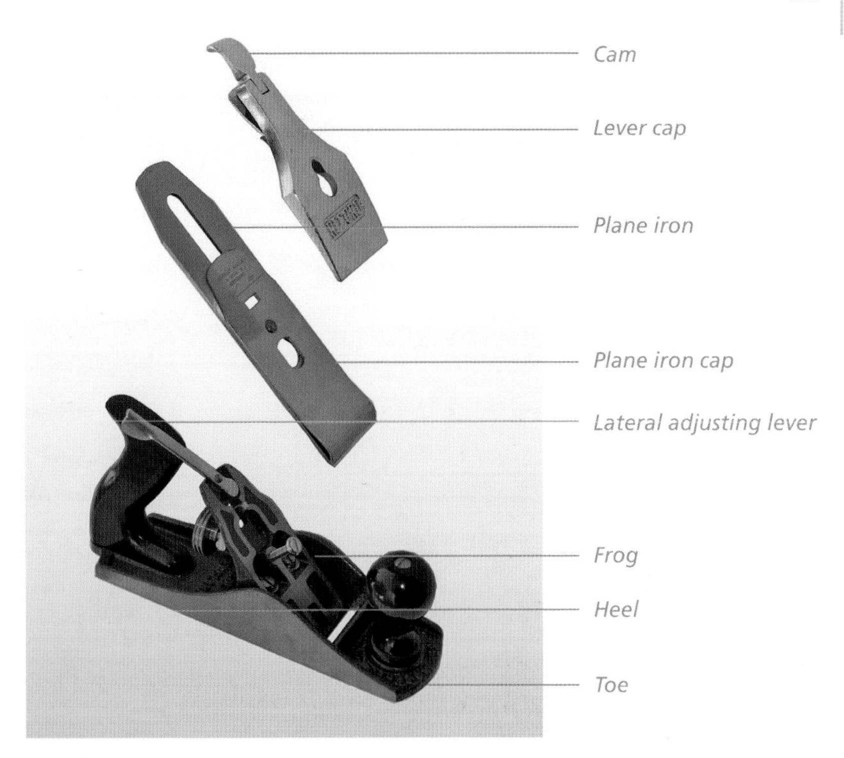

1-10 *Plane, exploded view.*

1-11 *Using a plane to remove mill marks.*

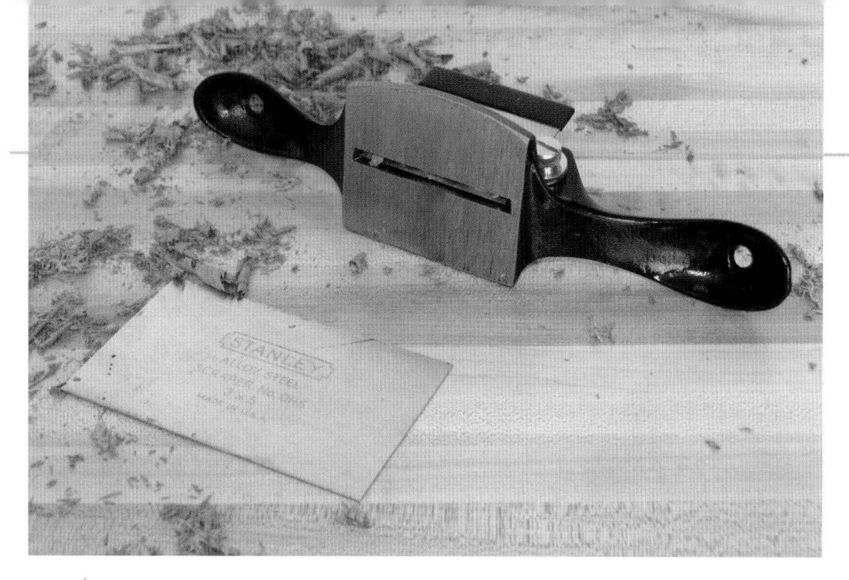

1-12 Front, hand scraper. Rear, cabinet scraper.

Note: A hand plane works best on even grained wood without many knots. Knots or a wild grain will cause the plane to dig in and chip the wood. In that case, the planing is causing more harm than good. Problem boards are best handled with a belt sander.

SCRAPERS It's a sad fact that scrapers have fallen into general disuse lately. Many new woodworkers have never seen or used one. Even though they may be difficult to

Sharpening a Plane Iron

An important step in sharpening that is often neglected is to hone the back of the iron. A cutting edge is formed by the intersection of two honed surfaces. To hone the back of the iron, place it flat on a medium whetstone *(1–13)*. Hone the iron in this position until all of the visible scratches left from the iron's manufacture are removed in the area, starting at the cutting edge and going up the iron about two inches.

Now, switch to the fine stone and hone the same area. Once you have done this, it is not necessary to do it each time you sharpen the iron. The purpose of this step is to remove the grinding marks left on the back of the iron from the surface grinder used at the factory. Next, sharpen the bevel. Examine the cutting edge; it should be straight and free from large nicks. Check it with a square to make sure that it is straight and square. If you need to square it up or remove large nicks, use the grinder.

The bevel should be ground to an angle between 25 and 35 degrees. The plane will cut softwoods better when the iron is ground to a low angle. When you are working with highly figured hardwoods, an iron with a high angle will better avoid chipping. A good average angle for most work is 30 degrees. If the cutting edge is straight and square, doesn't have large nicks, and the angle is correct, there is no need to grind it; proceed directly to the medium whetstone.

1-13 To hone the back of the iron, place it flat on a medium whetstone.

There are two bevels on the cutting edge of the plane iron. The *primary bevel* is the one made by grinding the bevel. The *secondary bevel* is made during the honing process. The secondary bevel is a very narrow band that forms the actual cutting edge. Hone the primary bevel on the medium stone. Place the iron bevel-down on the stone and rock it back and forth until you can feel that the primary bevel is resting flat on the stone. Now, hold the angle of the iron constant as you move the iron in a straight line back and forth across the full length of the stone *(1–14)*. This step will prevent the secondary bevel from getting too wide. After a few strokes, look at the secondary bevel, it should be a narrow band just barely visible behind the cutting edge.

Next, switch to the fine stone and hone the secondary bevel. Place the iron bevel-down on the stone. Rock the iron until you feel the primary bevel resting flat on the stone. Now, rock the iron up about five degrees. Hold this angle constant as you move the iron back and forth on the stone. When a small burr or wire edge forms on find, a good cabinet scraper and a hand scraper will be a wise investment for anyone serious about producing a topnotch finish (**1–12**).

A sharp scraper in the hands of an experienced worker can produce a surface so smooth that it's difficult to duplicate even with very fine sandpaper. Scrapers work best on hardwoods. They can also be used on softwoods, but their cutting action is not as consistent. A lot depends on the board; on some boards, you can get as smooth a surface as produced on hardwood, and on others the scraper will dig in and chatter.

It's important to keep a scraper sharp; a dull scraper doesn't work at all. The procedure for sharpening a scraper seems a bit strange to someone who has never seen it done before, but once you've learned how, it's not difficult.

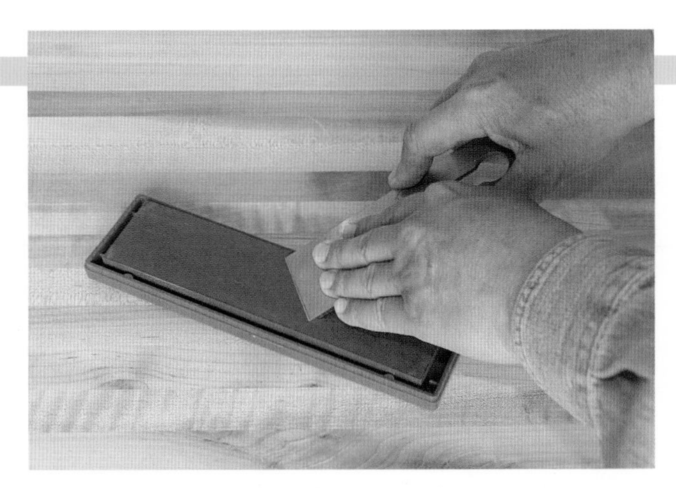

1-14 ***To hone the bevel, hold the angle of the iron constant as you move the iron in a straight line back and forth across the full length of the whetstone.***

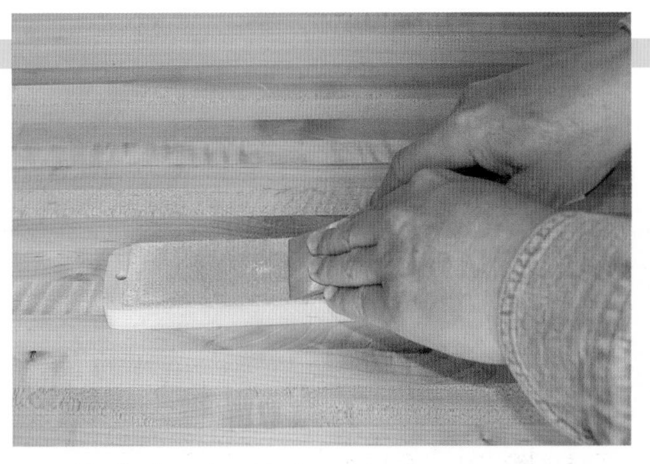

1-15 ***The final step in achieving a very sharp edge is to strop the plane iron on a leather strop.***

the back of the cutting edge, you have honed the secondary bevel enough. The *wire edge* is a small hook of steel that is bent over when the secondary bevel intersects the back of the iron. You may not even be able to see it, but you can feel it by pulling your fingernail across the edge. If your fingernail catches at the edge of the iron, then the secondary bevel is honed sufficiently.

Now, back-off the iron. This procedure will remove the wire edge. Place the back of the iron flat on the face of the fine whetstone and rub it back and forth a few strokes. Now use your fingernail to feel for the wire edge. If it is gone from the back of the iron, feel for it on the front of the bevel. Usually the wire edge will bend over to the front. Turn the iron over and hone the secondary bevel again as described above, but make only two or three strokes. This should be enough to remove the wire edge completely. If the wire edge has not been removed, repeat the backing-off procedure.

The final step in achieving a very sharp edge is to strop the edge on a leather strop. To strop a plane iron, use a piece of leather about the same size as the whetstones and glue it to a flat piece of hardwood. The leather should be impregnated with a very fine abrasive powder. Jeweler's rouge, silicon carbide paste, or polishing compound can be used.

Apply the abrasive to the leather and rub it in. Place the iron on the strop and use the same procedure described for backing-off the iron *(1–15)*. Make sure that all of the strokes are made pulling the iron rearwards. If you push the iron forward, it will cut into the leather. You now have a sharp iron that will leave a smooth surface suitable for a fine finish.

1-16 Apply thumb pressure to the center of the hand scraper to give the blade a slight bow.

1-17 Using a cabinet scraper.

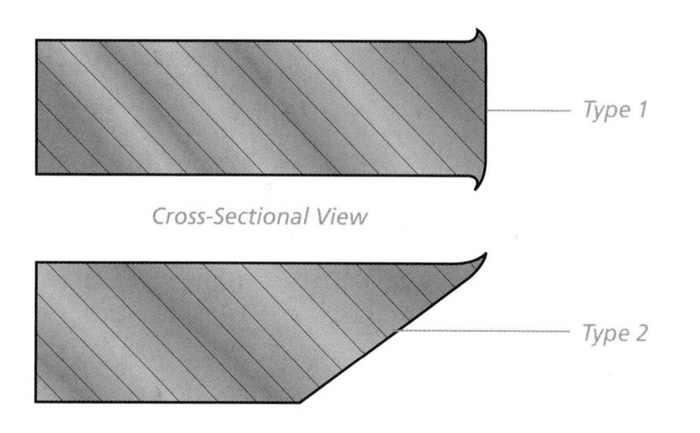

1-18 The cross-sectional views at the top show the difference between a hand scraper blade (Type 1) and a cabinet scraper blade (Type 2).

In use, a scraper blade should have a slight bow sprung into it. With the cabinet scraper, this is accomplished by turning an adjustment screw that presses against the center of the blade while the edges of the blade are held secure by the frame. With a hand scraper, you must bow the blade with your hands. Grasp the blade with both hands. Position your fingers around the edges and thumbs, pressing against the middle of the blade. Press in with your thumbs to give the blade a slight bow (**1–16**).

The bowed-out center of the blade should cut first; this means that you must push a hand scraper away from you, pushing mostly with your thumbs. The cabinet scraper can be either pushed or pulled, but always keep the blade facing so that the bowed out center cuts first (**1–17**).

To adjust a cabinet scraper, loosen all three screws and place the scraper sole-down on the flat surface of a board. Let the scraper blade rest on the board and tighten the two outside screws. The thumbscrew in the middle adjusts the bow of the blade. The amount of bow determines the depth of cut. Start with only a slight bow and increase it slightly until you reach the desired depth of cut.

The scraper will produce a very thin shaving, not dust as sandpaper will. Always work the scraper with the grain. Overlap strokes as you proceed across the face of the board. As soon as the scraper shows signs of becoming dull, resharpen it.

The actual cutting edge of a scraper is a small burr that is formed on the edge of the blade (**1–18**). To prepare the blade to accept a new burr, place the blade in a vise whose jaws have been padded with wood blocks. Remove the old burr by filing across the face edge. Next, draw a smooth mill file across

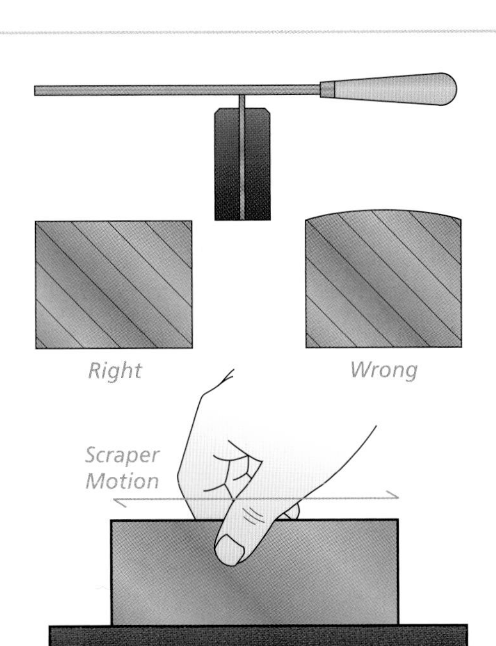

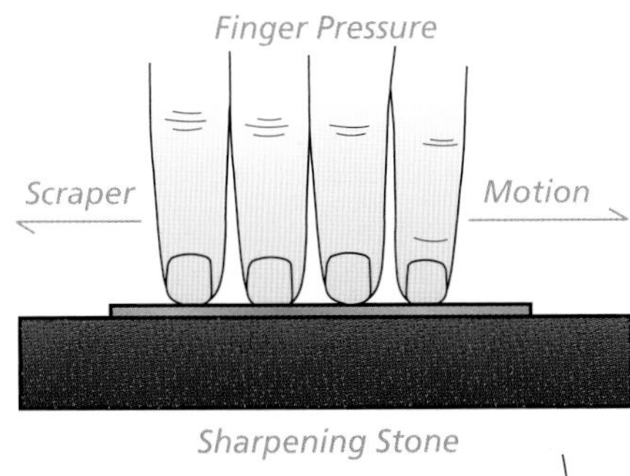

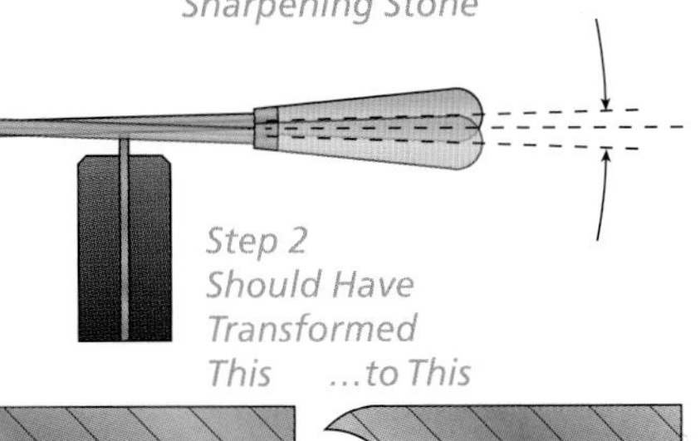

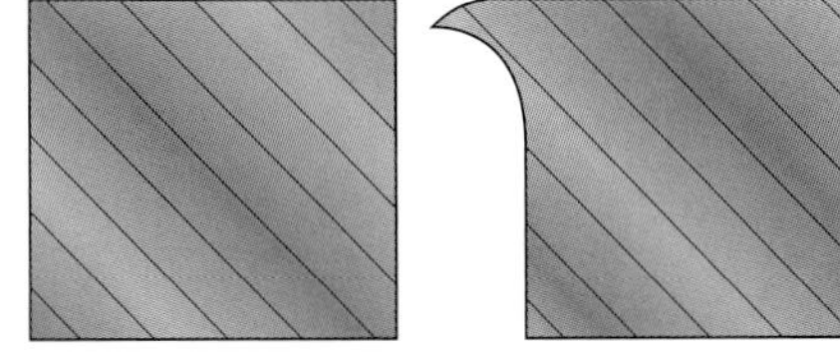

1-19 *Step 1 in sharpening a scraper is to file the edge square. Whetting the edge on a sharpening stone is step 2. Forming the burr with a burnisher is step 3.*

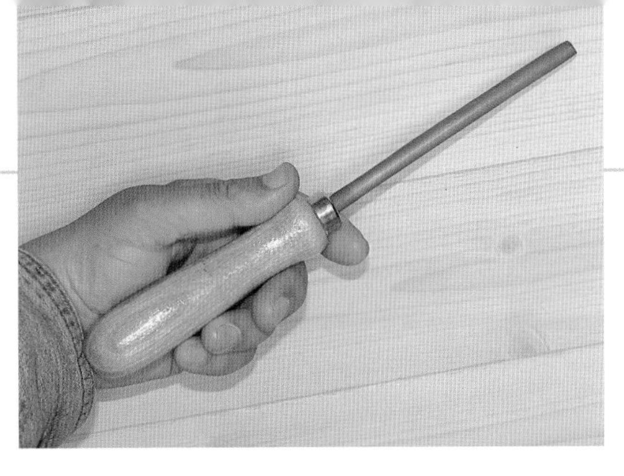

1-20 *A burnisher.*

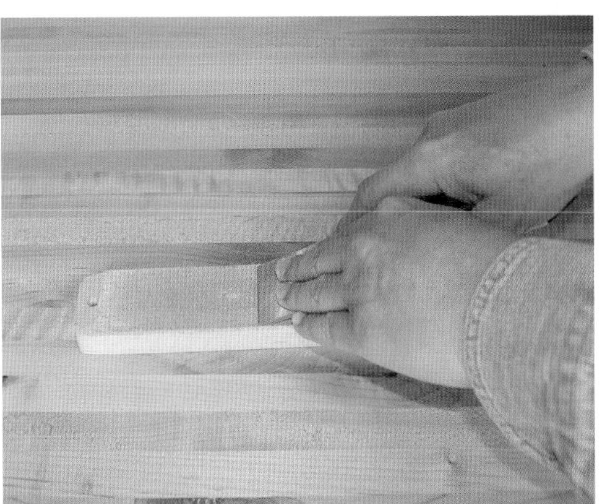

1-21 *This type of burnisher is mounted in a wooden stock that guides it. The knob on the side adjusts the angle.*

the edge, holding it perfectly flat and square on a hand scraper and holding it at the same angle as presently exists on a cabinet scraper blade (approximately 45 degrees). Slightly round the corners.

Next, use a whetstone to whet the edge. Hold the blade of a hand scraper square with the stone; hold the beveled side of a cabinet scraper blade against the stone as you would to sharpen a plane iron. Turn the blade on its side, holding it flat against the surface of the stone, and rub it back and forth several times to remove the burr left from whetting the edge (**1–19**).

To form the cutting burr, you will need a burnisher (**1–20**). There are tools made specifically for this purpose, but any hardened tool steel object can be used. A lathe gouge or an awl will work well. There are also burnishers that are mounted in a wooden stock that guides them (**1–21**).

Place the blade in a padded vise (**1–22**) or on a table with the cutting edge protruding about 1/2 inch past the table edge (**1–23**). Put a drop of oil on the burnisher and rub it over the entire surface. Holding the burnisher flat against the surface of the blade, draw it along the edge about four times.

1-22 *Using a burnisher to form a burr with the blade in a padded vise.*

1-23 *Using a burnisher to form a burr with the blade on a table with the cutting edge protruding about 1/2 inch past the table edge.*

For the hand scraper, the next step is to position the burnisher so it is square with the face of the blade riding along the edge. Draw the burnisher towards you once and then tilt the burnisher slightly and draw it across the edge again. Take about three or four more strokes across the edge, tilting it a little more each time until the final stroke is made with the burnisher held at about 85 degrees to the face of the blade.

To burnish a cabinet scraper blade, start by holding the burnisher at about 45 degrees and increase the angle on each subsequent stroke until an angle of about 75 degrees is reached. After several light strokes, check the burr with your fingernail. When your fingernail catches on the edge, it is time to stop.

When the blade becomes dull, it is not necessary to file and whet the edge every time; simply repeat the burnishing process. When you can't get a good burr by burnishing alone, then file and whet the edge.

Scrapers also are useful for smoothing a shaped edge. You can purchase a ready-made

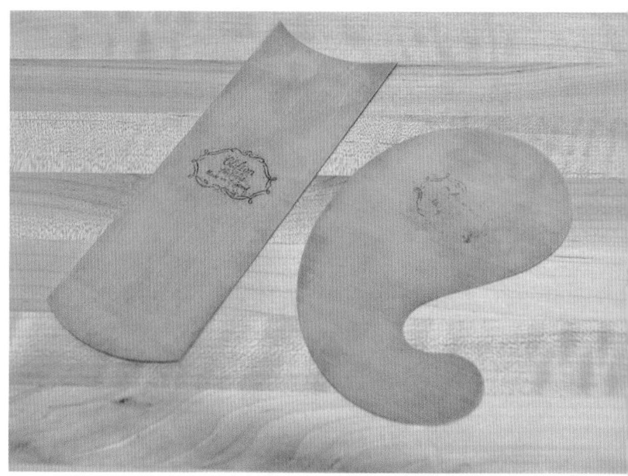

1-24 *Curved scrapers.*

scraper that is shaped so that different areas of the edge will fit the contours of various size coves (**1–24**). If there is a particular shaped edge (a roman ogee for example) that you encounter frequently, you can grind one corner of a hand scraper to fit that shape. As you grind, take small cuts and keep the blade cool by frequently dipping it in water; otherwise, the blade will burn and lose its temper.

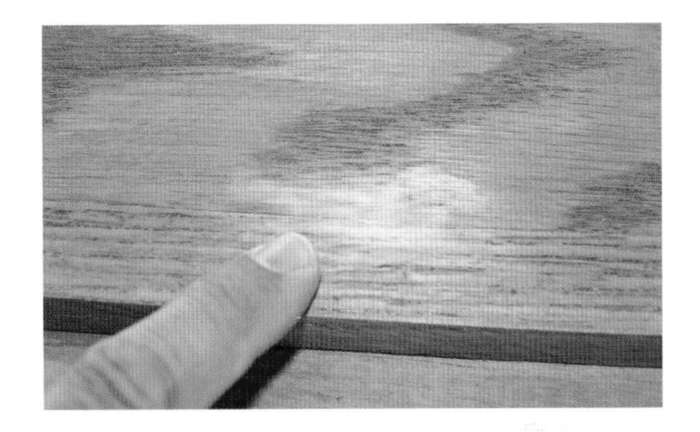

1-25
After stain was applied, this glue spot showed up as a lighter-colored blemish.

1-26
This black stain was caused when the iron clamp bar was left touching the wet glue.

Gluing

Assembling the parts of a project with glue can affect the finish because glue acts as a sealer that will prevent subsequent finishing materials from penetrating into the wood. If glue is smeared on the face of a board and not completely removed, a lighter-colored blemish will appear in the finish (**1–25**).

The best way to avoid glue spots in the finish is to prevent glue from ever coming in contact with the surface of the work. Careful assembly can eliminate most problems. Practice gluing scraps until you are able to gauge how much glue to spread on a joint. For a strong joint, there should be just enough glue so that a tiny bead of glue is formed all along the joint when it is clamped tight. If you use too much glue, it will drip and ooze over the face. If too little glue is used, the joint will be weak, so it is important to use just the right amount of glue.

Many people create further problems when they are trying to wipe off wet glue. If you don't wipe it completely, you may just spread the glue around and force it deeper into the pores of the wood. To completely remove the glue, use a damp rag to wipe it off and be sure to wipe the area several times with clean rags to remove as much of the glue as possible. If the glue hasn't spread over a large area, it is much better to scrape off the glue after it is starting to set using a sharp chisel or scraper. If you have used the right amount of glue so that a very small bead squeezes from the joint, it can be easily and completely removed by this method. Always remove glue before sanding; the heat generated by sanding tends to soften glue marks and spread them around. What started as a small glue mark can turn into a large dirty looking smudge if it is sanded before the glue is removed. White glue (polyvinyl acetate) is especially apt to smear when sanded.

Care must also be taken in the way you clamp a joint. Always use a pad of wood or cork between the clamp and any wood surfaces that will receive a finish. The bare clamp can dent the wood and leave stains. When wet glue comes in contact with an iron clamp, a black stain appears on the wood (**1–26**). This type of stain is very difficult to remove because it is actually a chemical change in the wood itself; the only effective way to remove it is to scrape, plane, or sand the wood away until the stain is gone.

Dents caused by clamping without pads can sometimes be removed by applying a little water to the dent. If that doesn't work, wet the area again and apply a hot iron to the area. Don't keep the iron in one spot too long or it will burn the wood. Dents must be removed in this manner or they will cause trouble later. If, for example, you choose to plane the edge to remove the dent, the area that is dented will expand later when a finish is applied and cause a raised area. This is because the wood fibers in the dented area are compressed while the surrounding fibers are not. If you plane off the surrounding wood to the same level as the dent, the dented area actually contains more wood fibers than the surrounding wood. Of course, if you can take off a lot of wood without affecting the project, you can plane out a dent; just make sure that you plane deep enough to remove all of the compressed fibers.

Filling Nail Holes and Defects

Whenever possible, it's best to avoid having any nail holes in a visible surface, but when it's unavoidable the nails should be set about 1/8 inch below the surface and the hole filled. Small cracks and knotholes should also be filled (**1–27**).

Fillers for this use come in two basic types: solvent-based and water-based. The solvent-based fillers are commonly called plastic putty or wood dough. This type shrinks slightly as it dries, so you should leave it slightly bumped up when you apply it. Solvent-based putty will seal any wood that it touches, so it will leave a mark similar to a glue mark. For this reason, you should be very careful how you apply the putty or there will be unsightly marks around the nail holes. Use a small straight-blade screwdriver or the point of a pocketknife (**1–28**) to push a small amount of putty into the hold. Try not to smear any of the putty on the surrounding wood.

1-27 *Small cracks and knotholes should be filled before finishing. Use a putty knife to apply the putty.*

1-28 *When filling nail holes, use the tip of a pocketknife to apply the putty.*

1-29 *You can use a filler stick to fill nail holes after the finish has been applied.*

When the putty has dried, sand it flush with the surrounding surface. Plastic putty is available in several colors that match different varieties of wood. It is important to use a color that will match the intended finish, because this type of putty won't accept stain very well; so even if the bare wood is light-colored, use a dark-colored putty if the final finish will be dark.

The other type of putty is water-based. It will accept a stain better than plastic putty. Sometimes it will absorb the stain so well that it will be considerably darker than the wood around it. In that case you may have to use a small artist's brush to apply a small drop of shellac to the putty before applying the stain. Apply it in the same manner described for plastic putty. It won't cause as noticeable a mark if it gets on the wood surface but you should still try to avoid smearing it around.

Nail holes can also be filled after the finish has been applied. To do this, you use colored putty that is designed to be applied after the finish or with a product called a filler stick. Filler sticks are similar to a fat crayon in appearance and are made of a colored waxy substance. Choose a stick that closely matches the color of the finish; if you can't get an exact match, a filler that is slightly darker will be less noticeable than one that is lighter. Rub the point of the filler stick over the nail hole until the hole is filled (**1–29**); then polish the surrounding surface with a clean rag to remove the putty that was deposited on the surface. This method is easy and fast but the putty will always remain soft, so it should only be used in small holes that are located inconspicuously.

Sanding

Sanding is probably the most familiar form of smoothing a wood surface. Sanding smoothes the wood by using sharp pieces of grit to cut the wood fibers. Just as a broken piece of glass has a sharp edge that can be used as a wood scraper, so do the abrasive particles. They are made of substances that fracture like glass. When they are crushed to the proper size they fracture, producing the sharp edges that cut the wood. When you use sandpaper, you are in effect using thousands of tiny scrapers at one time (**1–30**). Many times the sanding operation is overused because the preceding steps were overlooked or done poorly. When the wood has been properly planed and scraped, sanding will be neither laborious nor time-consuming.

1-30 *This close-up of a flint particle shows how the fractures form sharp cutting edges.*

Abrasives are used to smooth the wood before a finish is applied, to prepare the finished surface for additional coats, and polish the surface of a finish. The most common types of abrasive products used in wood finishing are sandpaper, steel wool, synthetic steel wool, and finishing pads.

Coated abrasive is the proper name for all products that consist of an abrasive material bonded to a backing. Technically speaking, the term sandpaper only applies to flint paper; however, it has commonly come to mean any coated abrasive with a paper backing. In this book, the term sandpaper will be used to describe all coated abrasives with paper backing regardless of the abrasive used. Coated abrasives with a cloth backing are referred to as "abrasive cloth."

TYPES OF ABRASIVES There are two major classifications of abrasives used in woodworking: *natural* and *man-made* (**1–31**). The natural abrasives are flint, garnet, emery, pumice, and rottenstone. The man-made abrasives are aluminum oxide, silicon carbide, and ceramics. Flint has been used for sandpaper longer than any of the other abrasives. It is a naturally occurring mineral that looks like yellowish-white

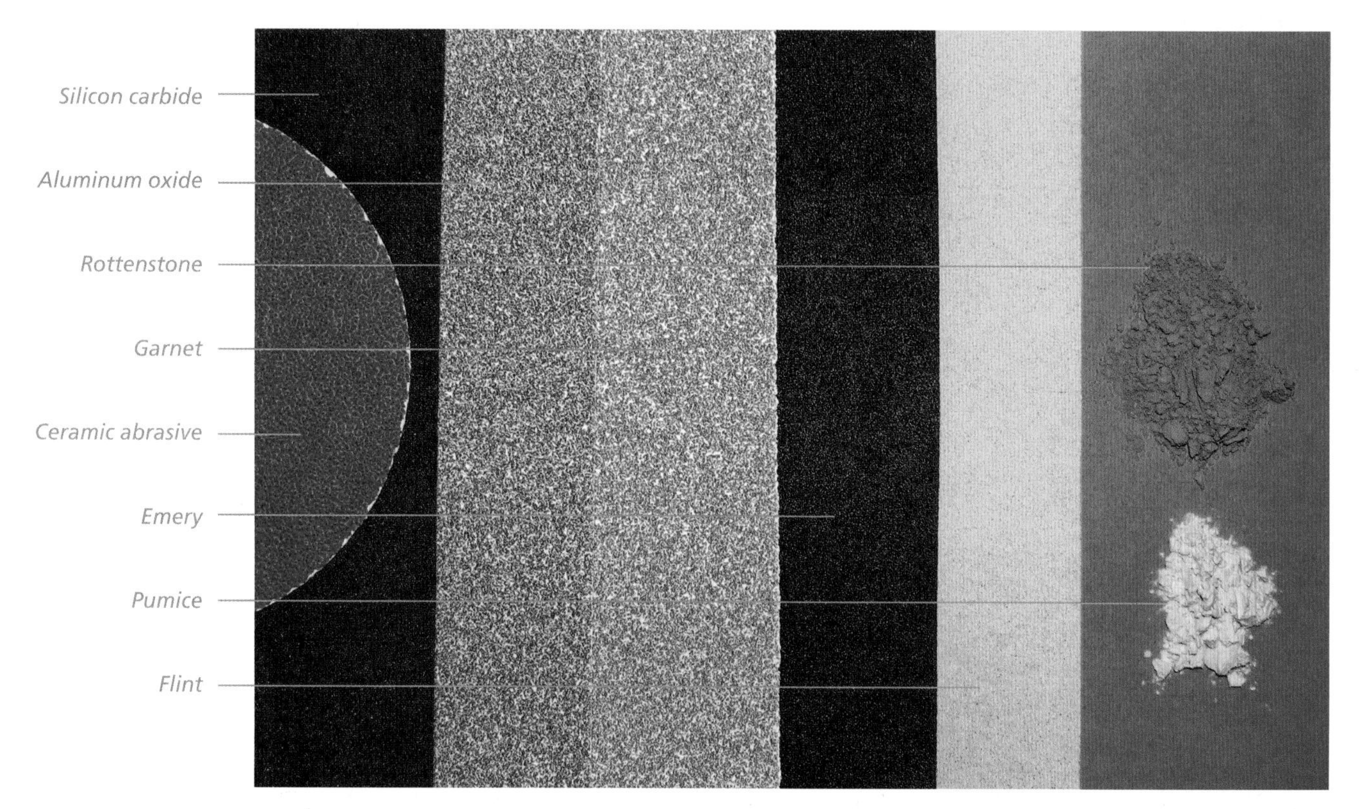

1-31 *Man-made and natural abrasives. The natural abrasives are on the right. Pumice is a white powder, and rottenstone is dark. The next abrasives are shown in sheet form. Flint is a yellowish color. The black abrasive next to it is emery, which is followed by garnet. The remaining abrasives are man-made. Aluminum oxide is light brown, and silicon carbide is black. The blue disc is an example of ceramic abrasive.*

sand. Flintpaper is usually less expensive than any other type of sandpaper, but it also wears out faster than any other type.

Garnet is another natural abrasive. It is much harder than flint, so it can keep cutting longer. You can recognize garnet by its reddish yellow color. Garnet won't last as long as synthetic abrasives, so it's not as useful for removing a lot of wood; however, for the final steps in preparing wood for a finish, garnet is probably the best abrasive. Because it is softer than the synthetic abrasives, garnet will produce a smoother finish. When used on an orbital sander, there will be fewer swirl marks.

Garnet tends to burnish wood as you sand; this can be an advantage or a problem depending on how you look at it. A burnished surface absorbs less stain, but it absorbs more evenly; so if you want a very even stain color and don't mind that it will be a little lighter, use garnet for the final grade of sandpaper before staining. On the other hand, if you want the darkest possible stain application, use aluminum oxide paper before staining.

Emery usually comes on a cloth backing. The flexible cloth backing makes it useful for smoothing contoured surfaces. It is harder than garnet, but because it doesn't fracture as easily, it won't renew its cutting surface like some of the other abrasives. You can recognize emery by its black color.

Aluminum oxide is a man-made material. Aluminum oxide lasts longer than garnet. It stays sharp because it is friable. This means that as you sand, the grit constantly fractures to expose new sharp edges. Because of its long life and good cutting properties, aluminum oxide is probably the best all-purpose abrasive for woodwork. Even though it is more expensive than flint or garnet, it is well worth the cost.

Most companies use a trade name for the man-made abrasives rather than the generic name. This can make it a little confusing when you are looking for aluminum oxide paper. Some common trade names are: Adalox, Aloxite, Imperial, Metalite, Production, and Three-M-ite.

Silicon carbide is even harder and sharper than aluminum oxide. For wood finishing, it is primarily used in only the finest grades to sand between coats of a finish. Silicon carbide paper is a blue-black color. It is more expensive than aluminum oxide and it tends to dull faster than aluminum oxide when used on wood. This is because wood is too soft to fracture silicon carbide, so even though silicon carbide is friable when used on hard material like metal you won't get the benefit of friability when using it on wood. Silicon carbide is sold under the following trade names: Durite, Tri-M-ite, Fastcut, Powerkut, and Wet-or-dry.

Ceramic abrasives are the most aggressive abrasives available. The are extremely tough, but they are also more expensive than the other abrasives. Because they are so aggressive, they are usually only used on coarse grit sanding belts and discs. They are a very good choice for shaping and removing a lot of wood. They are also useful for removing tough finishes. Some ceramic abrasive trade names are: Norzon, Dynakut, and Regalite.

Table 1-1

Abrasive Grit Grading Systems

Note: equivalents are approximate

USE	NAME	CAMI / ANSI	P-SCALE	JIS	MICRON (μ)	AUGHT
Polishing and rubbing out finish top coats		1200	-		5	
	Micro-		2500	2000	8	
	Abrasive	1000	-		9	
			2000	1500	10	
		800	-		-	
		-	-	1000	15	
	Ultra-Fine	-	1200		-	
		600	-		-	12/0
Smoothing between finish coats		-	1000		-	
				800		
	Super-fine	500	-		-	11/0
		-	-		20	
		-	800			
		400	-			10/0
		-	600	600		
		360				
		-	-		30	
			500		-	
			400	400	-	
	Extra-fine	320	-		-	9/0
		-	-		40	
		-	360		-	
		280	-	320	-	8/0
		-	-		45	
	Very fine	-	320		-	
Sanding before applying finishing materials		-	-	280	50	
		-	280		-	
	Fine	240		240		
			240		-	7/0
		220	220	220	60	6/0
	Medium	180	180	150	-	5/0
		150	150	120	80	4/0
		120	120	100	100	3/0
		100	-		-	2/0
Stripping old finishes and shaping wood	Coarse	-	100		150	
		-	-	80	180	
	Extra	80	80			1/0
	Coarse	60	60	60		1/2
		50	50	50		1
		40	40	40		1 1/2
		36	36	36		2
		30	30	30		2 1/2
		24	24	24		3
		20	20			3 1/2
		16				4

GRIT SIZES There are six systems of designating grit size **(Table 1-1)**. The first system gives a name to the different degrees of fineness, starting with coarse and preceding through medium, fine, very fine, and extra fine. The finest grit sizes are generically called *micro-abrasives*. This system is not very precise, because one term, such as *medium*, may actually refer to several grit sizes within the medium range. Normally this system is used in conjunction with one of the other systems to give someone unfamiliar with the more precise systems a general idea of the grit size; however, in the case of flint paper, many times the fineness name will be the only designation given.

The second system is the *aught system*. It is so called because most of the grades are designated by a number of zeros or aughts. This system is practically obsolete. Most grades useful for wood finishing are designated by several zeros (aughts); the more zeros, the finer the abrasive. Grade 0 (also written 1/O) corresponds to a medium grit, 00000 (5/0) is very fine. Coarser grits are designated by numbers that get larger as the grit gets coarser. Grade 1 is coarse and Grade 2 is very coarse.

The other systems are the most versatile, because they allow for more grades than the first two. The *US standard abrasive grading system* is regulated by the Coated Abrasives Manufacturing Institute (CAMI). and American National Standards Institute (ANSI). In this system, a number designates grit size. The higher the number, the finer the grit. Grit sizes usually used in woodwork range from 50 as the coarsest to 600 as the finest.

The European abrasive grading system is called the *P-scale*. It is regulated by the Federation of European Producers Association (FEPA). The P-scale is very similar to the CAMI scale, and for wood finishing the differences are probably insignificant until you get to grades finer than 220. P-scale abrasives are labeled with a "P" followed by a number. The P-scale has tighter tolerances than the CAMI scale, so the individual pieces of grit will be more uniform in size. In grades below 220 this isn't a major factor, but in finer grades used to polish finishes, more uniformity can result in fewer noticeable scratches.

P-scale grade numbers finer than 220 don't correspond to CAMI numbers. For example, the same grit size graded 600 in the CAMI system is graded 1,200 in the P-scale. See the accompanying chart for corresponding sizes.

The Japanese grading system, *JIS*, is regulated by the Japanese Standards Association (JSA). It is approximately equivalent to the CAMI system up through grade 240. In wood finishing it is most useful in the higher grades used for polishing finishes. Usually sandpaper marked with a grit number higher than 1200 without a "P" prefix is JIS.

The most accurate grading system is the *micron system*. This system designates the size of the grit in microns (one thousandth of a millimeter). The Greek letter mu (μ) designates micron-graded abrasives. This system takes some getting used to because it works exactly the opposite of the other systems. The larger the number, the coarser the abrasive. In the micron system, 180μ corresponds to 80 in the CAMI system and 15μ corresponds to 800 in the CAMI system. The micron system has the tightest tolerances of all, so the grit is extremely uniform. This makes it very useful for polishing finishes. Micron-graded coated abrasives can be used instead of pumice and rottenstone to rub out a finish.

Throughout this book, sandpaper grades will be given in the CAMI system unless otherwise noted.

COATING Sandpaper can clog with gummy varnish, glue, or resins from the wood. Clogging decreases the useful life of the sandpaper considerably. For this reason, sandpaper is available in closed and open coats as well as with a special non-clog coating.

Closed-coat means that the entire surface of the paper is covered with grit. This is the fastest cutting type of paper if you are using it on bare hardwood.

Open-coat sandpaper has spaces of bare paper around each grit. This type is much slower to clog than closed-coat paper, so even though there are fewer granules of grit it will cut faster and last longer when you are sanding finished surfaces or softwoods.

Some companies offer a special coating that reduces clogging. This anti-loading coating keeps the paper from clogging up when you are sanding between finish coats. The older type of anti-loading sandpaper used a stearated compound that sometimes caused adverse reactions like fisheyes in subsequent finish coats. Today most manufacturers offer anti-loading sandpaper that is compatible with most finishes, including waterborne finishes.

While sanding, occasionally slap the sandpaper against a hard surface to remove the accumulated dust from between the grit. When sanding a finished surface, small circular accumulations of the finish will stick to the paper; remove them with your fingernail or a knife blade as soon as they form. If they are not removed, they can scar the surface. They also reduce the cutting efficiency of the paper.

BACKING Coated abrasives are applied to several types of backings. Paper comes in several weights. The weight of the paper is designated by a letter of the alphabet, with A being the lightest weight paper. The weights usually used in wood finishing are A, C, and D. Sometimes paper with an A weight backing is referred to as *finishing paper*, while C and D weight papers are called *cabinet paper*. The heavier stock is not very flexible, but it will withstand heavy use. Unless you special-order your sandpaper in large quantities, you will have to settle for the weight of paper that the manufacturer has decided is best for most jobs in each particular grit size. Generally, coarse grits come on heavier paper.

Cloth is another popular backing. It comes in several weights. Jeans (J) and Drills (X) are the most commonly used for general woodwork. Most sheets come with a Jeans backing; it is strong and flexible. Sanding belts usually are made of Drills. Heavier weights like Y and M are used for abrasive planer belts.

Cloth-backed abrasives are useful for sanding irregular surfaces and getting into small crevices. Cloth backing is very useful in power sanding because it resists tearing.

Screen-backed abrasives offer the ultimate in non-clogging. The abrasive is applied to fiberglass screen. Both sides of the screen are coated so you can turn it over for a fresh surface.

Plastic film backing is strong, flexible, and waterproof. It also makes the abrasive cut better. With paper- and cloth-backed abrasives, some of the abrasive particles get pressed into the backing, where they are not effective, and some are higher than the rest, resulting in scratches. With plastic film, all of the abrasive particles are evenly positioned on the surface, where they will cut most effectively and more evenly. Plastic film abrasives will leave fewer scratches, because the grit is more even. Most plastic backing is a type of polyester or Mylar.

Discs and drums are made of a fiber backing that is similar to very strong cardboard.

Arrow indicates the lengthwise direction of the belt, roll or sheet.

NO FLEX: *No mechanical flex. The unflexed or stiff construction is furnished as standard in items such as sheets, in fine grade paper products for hand or machine sanding where added flexibility is not desirable or necessary.*

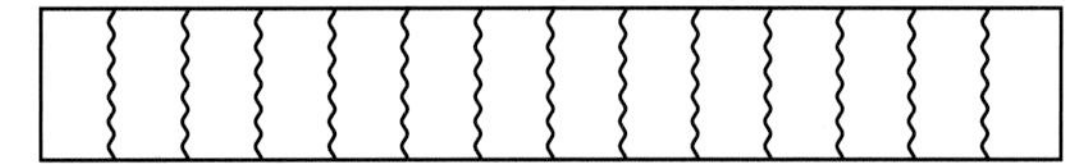

SINGLE FLEX: *A single mechanical flex which createes flex lines at 90° to the edge or running direction of the material. This flexing provides a minimum handling flex and the necessary conformability to run over even small diameter pulleys and contact wheels.*

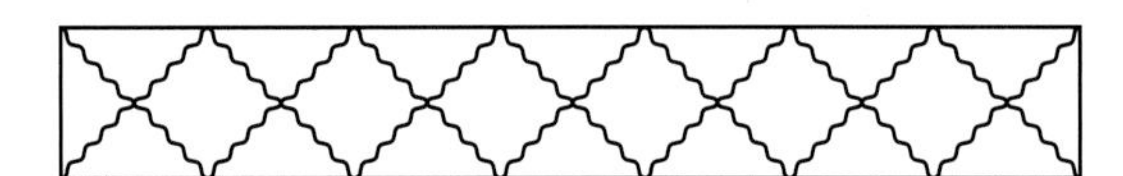

DOUBLE FLEX: *(Two 45° angle flexes). Two mechanical flexing operations which make the material moderately flexible in all directions.*

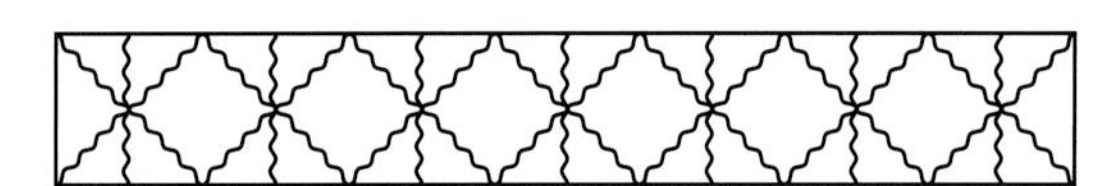

FULL FLEX: *(Two 45° angles and a 90° angle flex). Three mechanical flexes resulting in a product that is soft and flexible, regardless of the direction in which it must bend or conform.*

1-32 *Types of flexes.*

WET-OR-DRY PAPER The adhesive used to attach the grit to the paper is usually not waterproof in standard types of sandpaper. Wet-or-dry paper uses a special waterproof adhesive as well as a waterproof backing paper. This allows you to sand a surface that is wet. This feature is very useful in wood finishing when sanding finish coats. For example, when sanding the final coat of a lacquer finish in preparation for rubbing, a little water will lubricate the surface and also prevent the sandpaper from clogging.

FLEX In the past, hide glue was usually used to attach the abrasive to sandpaper. Hide glue is flexible, so the sandpaper that uses hide glue conforms to the surface well, but hide glue is not waterproof or heat-resistant. Most modern coated abrasives are attached to the backing with two coats of urea or phenolic formaldehyde resin. The first coat of resin, called the *make coat,* is applied to the paper before the grit is applied. After the grit is on the backing, the second coat, called the *size coat,* is applied to firmly attach the grit to the backing.

The modern resins used to attach the abrasive to the backing are hard and inflexible. When the backing is bent, the resin will crack. For sanding disks that should remain flat and inflexible, this stiffness is an advantage; but for sanding belts or sandpaper that needs to flex to conform to an irregular surface, the resin needs to be cracked slightly. Its best for these cracks in the resin to be uniformly spaced and oriented for the most flexibility and long life. For this reason, a coated abrasive should be preflexed. For sheets, this operation is performed by the user.

To flex the paper, place it grit side up on the edge of a table and pull it down across the edge. Turn it one quarter turn and repeat. This process forms many small cracks in the resin that holds the grit on. This way you prevent large cracks from developing in the glue as you sand, increasing the life of the paper.

Abrasive belts are mechanically flexed at the factory in the following patterns (**1–32**):

No flex: No mechanical flex. This unflexed or stiff construction is furnished as standard in items such as sheets, in fine-grade paper products for hand- or machine-sanding where added flexibility is not desirable or necessary.

Single flex: A single mechanical flex which creates flex lines at 90 degrees to the edge or running direction of the material. This flexing provides a minimum handling flex and the necessary conformability to run over even small diameter pulleys and contact wheels.

Double flex: Two 45-degree flexing operations make the material moderately flexible in all directions.

Full flex: Three mechanical flexes (two 45 degrees and one 90 degrees) make this product soft and flexible, regardless of the direction in which it must bend or conform.

STEEL WOOL Steel wool is an abrasive material composed of long, fine steel strands that is used to smooth wood and finish layers. Steel wool is good for smoothing coats of finish (**1–33**). There

1-33
Steel wool is good for smoothing coats of finish, but should not be used with water-based products.

are two reasons for this: Steel wool won't clog like sandpaper, and, because it is flexible, it will conform to surface irregularities. Steel wool leaves small steel particles on the surface after use; these particles must be removed by brushing, vacuuming, or rubbing with a tack cloth before applying another coat of finish. Steel wool shouldn't be used with water-based finishes, because the small steel particles it leaves can react to water-based finishes, producing discolored areas in the finish.

Steel wool comes in grades based on the size of the steel strands. The coarsest grade usually used in wood finishing is #2. It is used to remove finishes with stripper. A finer grade that is used to remove the residue left after stripping an old finish is #O. For smoothing a finished surface between coats, use #00 or #000. The finest grade is #0000. It is used to buff the top coat of a finish to give it a smooth satin luster.

SYNTHETIC FINISHING PADS Synthetic finishing pads are a plastic substitute for steel wool. They last longer than steel wool, and because they won't shed steel particles on the surface, they can be used with water-based finishes. They can be used in almost every instance where steel wool can be used.

One type is a direct replacement for steel wool. It comes in a roll and is composed of soft fibers coated with abrasive (**1–34**). The other type is shaped into stiffer flat pads (**1–35**).

Synthetic finishing pads come in several grades. The coarsest is called a *stripping pad*; it is equivalent to #0 steel wool. It is used to remove residue from the surface of wood when using a chemical stripper. There are finer grades that are equivalent to #00, #000, and #0000 steel wool. Use the finer grades for smoothing a finished surface between coats.

If a finishing pad becomes clogged with finish residue, you can wash it out with water and reuse it after it dries.

1-34 *This synthetic abrasive wool performs like steel wool, but it is safe for water-based finishes.*

1-35 *Synthetic finishing pads can do the same job as steel wool and they can be used with water-based products.*

SANDING TECHNIQUE Scraping and planing will usually leave small ridges that must be removed before a finish can be applied. These ridges are removed by sanding. If you have properly planed and scraped the lumber, the sanding operation won't be too difficult.

In the first phase of sanding, your goal is to flatten out any irregularities left in the surface of the board. To do this, you need to use a nonflexible sanding block. A piece of hardwood works well. If you tear a sheet of sandpaper into quarters, you can use a sanding block that is 3/4 inch thick x 3 inches wide x 5 inches long. This size allows the paper to slightly overhang lengthwise and fold over enough so you can get a good grip on the paper. The face of the block should be flat and free of any irregularities. To achieve this, lay a piece of 100-grit sandpaper, grit up, on a surface that is machined flat, such as a saw table. If you don't have a machined surface, the best substitute is a plastic laminate tabletop. Hold the sandpaper stationary with one hand and run the sanding block across the paper until all surface irregularities have been removed.

The first grade of sandpaper to use depends on the condition of the surface to be sanded. If you have planed and scraped the surface, don't use anything coarser than 100. If you've done a very good job of scraping, you can start with 180. If the surface is rough or has noticeable mill marks, start with 80. The main idea is to use the grade that will remove the remaining defects effectively without causing too much damage to the smooth parts of the surface already achieved through scraping.

1-36 *A hardwood block used with the first grade of sandpaper will help to remove any remaining surface irregularities. Notice that the folded edge of the sandpaper faces the direction of travel. This helps to prevent the edge of the sandpaper from catching on the wood and tearing.*

When you have decided what grit size to use, fold the sheet into quarters and then tear along the fold lines. Next, flex the paper, place it grit side up on the edge of a table, and pull it down across the edge. Turn it one quarter turn and repeat. This process forms many small cracks in the glue that holds the grit on. This way, you prevent large cracks from developing in the glue as you sand, thus increasing the life of the paper.

Fold the paper around the block and grip the edges with your thumb on one edge and your fingers on the other. Position the block on the board so that the folded edges are at a 90-degree angle to the direction of travel. This helps prevent tearing the paper (**1–36**). Apply moderate pressure to the paper and sand with the grain of the wood. Apply equal pressure on both the forward and back strokes. Some people tend to apply the most pressure on the forward stroke and release the pressure on the back stroke. This tends to comb down the wood fibers in one direction. Later as the finish is applied, these combed-down fibers can raise up and create a rough or fuzzy surface. By sanding in both directions, the protruding fiber will be cut off flush with the surface, so there will be less fuzzing when the finish is applied.

Be careful while you are sanding with the hardwood block; if any particles of wood or grit accumulate between the sandpaper and the block, they can cause that area to sand deeper than the rest. You should avoid sanding across the grain because this will cut the fibers of the wood. When stain is applied to the wood, the cut ends of the fibers will absorb more than the surrounding wood and show up as dark scratches.

1-37 *This solid-rubber sanding block is useful for sanding flat surfaces.*

1-38 *A sanding block with a soft backing is used to follow any remaining surface variations.*

Sometimes it is necessary to sand across the grain; this is especially true with turnings. In that case, start with a finer grade sandpaper than you would normally use. The last grade you use should also be finer than normal. This will minimize the scratch marks, but they will still be visible upon close examination. Remove all defects in the board with the coarsest grit you are going to use; all of the subsequent sanding is to remove the scratches left by the preceding grit, not to remove defects.

When you are satisfied with the surface, you can switch to the next finer grit. Taking small jumps in grit size is actually faster than trying to go from a coarse grit to a much finer one in one step, because a grit that is only slightly smaller than the preceding one will cut much faster than one that is a lot smaller. For example, if you start with 100 you will have better results if you go to 150 before you use 180.

After you have removed all defects with the first grade of paper, you should use a flexible sanding block for the subsequent grades. You can use a commercially available block or make your own by padding a wood block with cork or felt. There are several reasons for using a padded block. First, the padding protects the surface you have already smoothed from being damaged by any particles that get wedged between the paper and the block. Second, the flexible backing allows even pressure to be applied to the surface even if there are some irregularities left. A padded block also protects the sandpaper, making it last longer.

1-39 A flexible hand pad is best for touch-up sanding odd-shaped objects.

There are many types of commercial blocks; some are deigned for specific purposes. A block with a solid backing and only a moderate amount of padding is best for sanding flat surfaces. A solid rubber block works well (**1–37**). A block with a softer backing is useful when using the finest grades of sandpaper. Use a plastic or wood block cushioned with foam rubber (**1–38**). The flexible cushion allows the paper to contact the entire surface even if there are slight dips or bumps. For touch-up sanding and sanding irregularly shaped objects, a hand pad with a soft flexible backing is best (**1–39**).

As you sand with the finer grades, your only objective is to replace the larger scratches left by the preceding grade with smaller ones made by the grade you are using. Once you have achieved this, switch to the next finer grade.

When to stop sanding depends on what type of final finish you are after. If the surface will be painted, you can stop with 150. Most surfaces to be varnished or lacquered should be sanded with 220. If you are after the ultimate finish, you may want to go to 320 or 400, but keep in mind that grits finer than 220 tend to give the wood a burnished effect that is desirable in some cases but not in others.

You should take the type of finish to be applied into account when you sand the wood. The burnished surface produces a beautifully polished look when a penetrating oil finish is used. But in some cases the burnishing will make the wood take stain unevenly, so be sure to try a sample if you want to use the finer grades of sandpaper. The burnished surface is more apparent when using a power sander, so you can usually use a finer grit when hand sanding than you could use with a power sander.

If you will be using a water-based stain, you need to perform one additional sanding step. Wipe a wet sponge over the wood surface; then, using wet-or-dry paper one grade finer than the paper you used last, sand the surface smooth. Instead of sanding directly with the grain, sand at about a five-degree angle to the grain direction. This slight deviation from the grain direction won't create cross-grain scratches and it will cut off the fibers better. Wet the surface again and sand it. This process will smooth off the fibers that rise up when they get wet, so when you apply the stain the surface will dry smooth.

A finishing pad can also be used for this process; the pad acts like a sponge, so you can use it to wipe on the water and smooth the surface in a single step. As you apply the water, small fibers will rise from the wood's surface; as this happens, rub the surface with the finishing pad. This will remove the fibers, leaving a smooth surface for the next finishing steps.

Finally, after all other sanding is complete, use fine sandpaper to remove the sharp edge from the corners. Don't round the corners unless the design calls for it; just pass the sanding block along the edge once or twice to get rid of the sharp corner. Removing the sharp edge will make the finish last longer on the edges. If it is not removed, the finish will quickly wear off at the corners, leaving a visibly lighter line.

1-40 *Belt sanders use a continuous belt made of cloth-backed abrasive.*

1-41 *A belt sander is a very efficient way to sand, but you must use it correctly to prevent it from damaging the surface. Hold the sander with two hands. Apply even pressure to the base and don't tilt it. Keep the sander moving; don't let it remain in one place.*

POWER SANDERS Although power sanders are one of the safer power tools, you still need to exercise the same caution you would with any other power tool. Don't wear loose clothing or dangling sleeves, and if you have long hair, tie it back. If your clothing or hair gets caught in a rotating parts, it will draw you into the machine. For the same reason, you should avoid wearing loose gloves around power equipment. Power sanders kick up more dust than hand sanding does, so whenever possible connect the sander to an exhaust system or shop vacuum. Wear a dust mask to avoid inhaling the dust, and protect your eyes with goggles. Whenever you change the abrasive, disconnect the sander from the power source.

There are several types of power sanders available to make the job of sanding easier. Each has advantages and disadvantages.

The *belt sander* has the advantage of removing a lot of wood quickly and producing sanding marks that are parallel to the grain. Its major drawback is that it may remove the wood too quickly and cause irregularities in the surface if it is not used carefully.

Belt sanders use an abrasive belt that varies in length and width according to the type of machine. Portable belt sanders are the most common, but stationary models are available. The portable belt sander uses a belt between about 14 and 30 inches in length and three and five inches in width. The belt travels over two rollers, one at each end of the machine. One of the rollers is connected to the motor to move the belt; the other is spring-loaded to tension the belt (**1–40**).

To use a portable belt sander correctly, you must always keep it flat against the work and apply even pressure to it without tilting the base. Always move the sander with the direction of the grain (**1–41**). If possible, sand the whole length of the board before moving side to side. Occasionally reverse the direction of sanding to cut off any combed down fibers.

If you are careful with it, a belt sander will produce very good results; however, it takes practice to get the feel of one, so start on scrap wood to learn how to handle it. The major problem novices have with a belt sander is they leave it in one spot too long, creating a dip; or they tilt it, causing one side of the belt to cut deeper than the other, creating a gouge. For this reason, even a seasoned pro should be careful when using a belt sander on an important surface. Because a belt sander cuts so fast, don't use it to sand plywood or veneers until you are thoroughly sure of how to operate the machine. It's very easy to sand right through the face veneer without even knowing it.

As was stated earlier, a belt sander can be used to remove the mill marks left by a planer. Use a coarse 50- or 60-grit belt. Be sure to remove all of the marks before changing to a finer belt.

One type of belt sander that is very useful for sanding intricate shapes is the *scroll sander* (**1–42**). The scroll sander uses a very narrow belt. The belt extends vertically from the table and passes over a small roller that is supported several inches above the table. This type has the capability of sanding inside of openings. Another type of sander that is used similarly is the *band saw sanding belt.* This is a belt that fits on a band saw the same as the band saw blade. It is useful for edge sanding intricately cut parts, but it cannot be used to sand inside of an opening as the scroll sander can.

1-42 *A scroll sander is useful for sanding edges. Its design permits it to be used to sand the inside edges of cut-out areas.*

1-43 *Shaped edges can be sanded using a special belt sander and a mold block that is made to fit the contour of the edge.*

A type of stationary belt sander that can rival hand sanding for ease of control and quality of work is the *hand block belt sander.* The hand block belt sander uses a very long belt (several feet long). The work is placed on a movable table and the belt is directly over the work. A block similar to a hand sanding block is pressed against the back of the belt to bring the belt in contact with the work. The position of the block and the pressure applied can be varied as easily as with hand sanding. A variation on the hand block sander uses shaped blocks to contour the belt. This type is used to sand moldings and shaped edges (**1–43** and **1–44**).

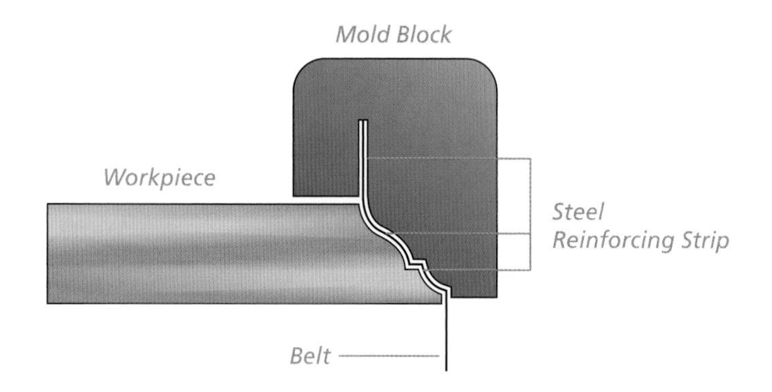

1-44 *This cross section shows how the mold block shapes the belt to fit the contours of the edge. Steel reinforcing strips protect the block from wear.*

The *backstand sander* has one roller exposed. All sanding takes place on this roller. This type is used for freehand sanding of curved parts like chair legs (**1–45**).

One very specialized form of belt sander is the *drawer sander* (**1–46**). This type will usually only be found in shops that produce a large number of drawers. The drawer sander is useful for fitting drawers that have a face that extends past the side. The belt must make a sharp 90-degree turn to sand the square inside corner of the drawer. This sharp turn is very hard on the belt and the platen that supports it. The edge of the platen is made of a special ceramic material that can withstand the friction and wear generated when the belt rubs over it.

Another type of sander that will sand a shaped edge is the *spool and belt sander* (**1–47**). A spool that is shaped to fit the edge serves as one of the rollers for the belt. The belts used with this type must have the ability to stretch to conform to the spool. If the stretch available from a J-weight belt is not enough, there are special bias weave belts available.

The *orbital sander* uses standard sheet sandpaper, usually one-fourth of a sheet, or specially made self-adhesive paper that is precut to the correct size and shape. The sandpaper clamps to the base of the machine. The sanding motion of an orbital sander is circular; the base travels in a small orbit. Older models of orbital sanders had a bad reputation because they left large, highly visible swirl marks on the work, but the new models have been greatly improved.

The best type of orbital sander is called a *random orbit sander*. Its base travels much faster and in a random orbit, so the swirl marks are barely visible. Of course, they are still there, so for the highest quality finish at least the final sanding should be done with a sander that has a straight line motion or by hand.

Orbital sanders don't cut as fast as belt sanders but they are light and easy to handle. They are especially useful for sanding joints where the grain direction changes because grain direction is not important when using an orbital sander (**1–48**).

1-45 *Backstand sanders are used for freehand sanding of curved surfaces.*

Always start and stop an orbital sander with it lifted from the work; the base must be at full speed while in contact with the work to keep swirl marks to a minimum. For this reason, you should also avoid applying too much pressure to the sander as this will slow down the base. Move the sander in a back and forth motion with the direction of the grain. Remove any accumulations from the sandpaper as soon as they appear or they will cause swirl marks.

Oscillating sanders are similar to orbital sanders in general operation and appearance, but they have one major difference: the base oscillates back and forth in a straight-line motion rather than orbiting. For this reason, oscillating sanders are preferred for the final sanding operations. The only major disadvantage of oscillating sanders is that they cut slower than orbital ones. Due to the popularity of orbital sanders, there are not very many oscillating sanders on the market today. The ones available are usually expensive professional models. For most finishers a good orbital sander will be sufficient.

1-46 *A drawer sander is for sanding inside corners.*

Drum sanders are useful for sanding edges. They use an abrasive coated cylindrical cardboard drum mounted on a rubber mandrel. Tightening a screw at one end of the mandrel expands the rubber, holding the drum in place. The drum can be

1-47 *Spool and belt sanders use a flexible belt and a shaped spool to sand complex edge shapes.*

1-48 *A modern orbital sander is capable of producing a very smooth surface free of discernible swirl marks. Orbital sanders are especially useful for sanding joints where the grain direction changes, because grain direction is unimportant with orbital sanding. This particular sander has a dust collection feature; holes in the base collect the dust. Precut self-adhesive sandpaper makes changing paper easy.*

mounted in a drill press or in a special machine. Some machines move the drum up and down as it rotates so the entire surface of the drum is utilized; this type is usually called a *spindle sander* (**1–49**). The drum sander is most useful for sanding curved edges because its cylindrical shape will follow the contours of the work. It's best to use the sander before assembling the pieces.

A *disc sander* consists of a backing disc to which a disc of coated abrasive is adhered. The disc is connected to the motor shaft. Stationary disc sanders have the disc mounted vertically and a horizontal table holds the work (**1–50**). Portable disc sanders use an angle drive to connect the disc to the motor, or, in the case of very small versions, a shaft that fits into the chuck of a portable drill.

Disc sanders are used mostly for shaping rather than smoothing. The marks left by a disc sander are usually cross grain and semicircular. Portable disc sanders are likely to leave an irregular surface.

One of the most useful functions of a stationary disc sander is to sand the edge of a board that has been cut to shape with a band saw or a jig saw. A disc sander cuts very fast, so you can use it to bring the board to its final shape, smoothing out any irregularities left by the sawing operation.

Portable disc sanders are used mostly for metal work, although they can perform some shaping operations in woodwork. They are not well-suited for smoothing the surface of a board.

One unique type of disc sander that is useful in wood work is the *jointer sander*. This is a disc sander that mounts in place of the blade on a tilt arbor table saw. The disc is slightly thicker in the center than at the edges, making it a very squat cone. The tilt arbor of the saw should be set for a two degree angle; this compensates for the angle of the cone, so the sanding surface is square with the table. Because of its unique cone shape, the sanding marks left by the jointer sander are straight and parallel to the grain direction.

1-49 *A spindle sander is especially adapted for sanding the inside edge of a circular cutout.*

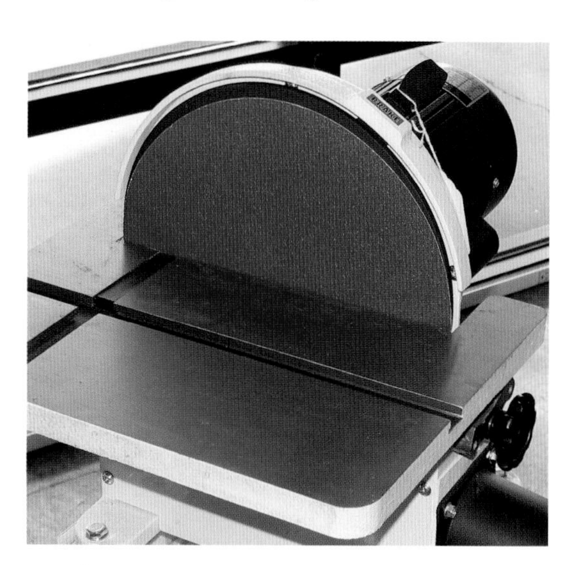

1-50 *A disc sander.*

As its name implies, the jointer sander is used to produce a smooth square edge on a board. To use the sander, the table saw fence is set to the width of the board and the wood is fed through the machine similarly to the way it is when sawing to width. The amount of stock removed in one pass must be kept small, about 1/32 inch. This type of sander is an excellent way to remove mill marks from the edge of a board.

Flap sanders are made from flaps of cloth-backed abrasive that are connected to a central shaft; the shaft is usually mounted on a stationary grinder or in the chuck of an electric drill (**1–51**). Sometimes the flaps are slit into smaller sections and some types use brush bristles to hold the flap straight.

Flap sanders are most useful for sanding oddly shaped objects; for example, the concave interior of a carved bowl or the carved legs of French provincial furniture. Don't use a flap sander on intricately carved surfaces because it will flatten out the detail. Flap sanders are less aggressive than other types of power sanders. The scratch pattern produced by any given grade of flap sander will be about the same as the scratch pattern produced by a sanding belt that is one or two grades finer.

1-51 *Flap sanders will automatically conform to the surface of an irregularly shaped object.*

Flap sanders can be made of die-cut flaps that are pre-cut to a specific shape. This type is useful in production runs where the same shape will be sanded repeatedly (**1–52**).

Most flap sanders must be entirely replaced when the grit becomes dull or worn off, but some types have replaceable sections or they have a roll of abrasive cloth in the hub that can be rolled out to renew the cutting area.

In order for the flaps to best conform to the shape of the object, J-weight cloth is usually used. For longer life and more aggressive cutting, X-weight cloth is sometimes used. When X-weight cloth is used, it is usually slashed into strips for better conformability. The arbor speed of a flap wheel plays a role in its conformability, because centrifugal force makes the flap seem stiffer at faster speeds. Generally, flap wheels run at between 1200 RPM and 1800 RPM.

1-52 *Die-cut flap sanders are used in production runs where the same shape will be sanded repeatedly.*

Decreasing the speed increases the sander's ability to conform to the shape of the object, while increasing the speed will make the sander remove wood faster, but it won't conform to the shape as well, so some of the details will be flattened out.

REMOVING DUST The final step in wood preparation is removing all of the accumulated dust from the surface and pores of the wood. Coated abrasive specialists don't like to use the word "dust" to describe this stuff—they call it *swarf*. The reason they make this distinction is that under a microscope, swarf looks more like plane shavings than dust. Abrasives are really cutting tools on a microscopic scale. The sharp edges of the abrasive particles cut shavings of wood like tiny plane irons. However most woodworkers still call it sanding dust, so I'll call it dust in this book. Any dust left on the wood will show up in the final finish as small bumps. To remove the large quantities of dust left from sanding, a bristle brush works well; brush with the grain to get the dust out of the pores (**1–53**).

A vacuum cleaner fitted with a brush attachment is an excellent way of removing the dust. Compressed air can also be used to blow the dust from the wood, but it has disadvantages. Whenever you blow dust off it will be spread throughout the shop and will settle on other projects you are working on. This is especially bad if you use the same area to apply varnish or other finishes. Another disadvantage is that airborne dust poses a health hazard. So, if you use compressed air to remove dust, do it in a well-ventilated area and use a low pressure setting.

After most of the dust has been removed using one of the above methods, use a tack rag to get the last traces of dust off. A tack rag is a piece of cheesecloth that has been treated to make it attract dust. They aren't very expensive and can be purchased at any paint store. Rub the tack rag over the surface until all of the dust has been removed. When one part of the tack rag becomes excessively coated with dust, unfold the rag and refold it so that a fresh surface is exposed.

1-53 *Dust removal is vital to producing a smooth finish. A brush will reach into the pores of the wood to get out the dust that has accumulated there.*

Whitewood Inspection

Before any finish is applied to wood, it is said to be "in the white" (**1–54**). Operations performed on the wood at this point are called *whitewood operations*. After all the wood preparation steps are complete, perform a whitewood inspection to make sure they were all done correctly. Here are the major steps in wood preparation:

1. Plane the surface to remove mill marks. Keep the blade sharp and set the plane iron cap 1/32 inch away from the tip of the blade. Adjust the plane to take a very shallow cut.

2. Scrape the surface with a hand scraper or a cabinet scraper. Keep the blade sharp. It should produce fine shavings. If it produces dust, it needs to be resharpened.

3. Fill all nail holes and other defects. Sand the filler smooth with the surrounding surface.

4. Sand the surface with aluminum oxide sandpaper. Use a hardwood block initially to back up the sandpaper. Continue sanding with the first grade of sandpaper and the wood block until all high spots and scratches have been removed; then switch to a padded sanding block for all subsequent grades of sandpaper.

5. Remove all dust from the wood. Use a brush or vacuum to remove most of the dust; then wipe the surface with a tack rag to get the last traces of dust off.

When you perform your inspection, check to see that all of the above operations were performed satisfactorily. Check for any remaining mill marks or other surface defects. Look carefully at the results of the sanding operation. Are there any cross grain scratches? Is the surface smooth and free from fuzzy wood fibers? Are there any swirl marks left as a result of orbital sanding?

Check around glue joints to see if there is any remaining glue on the surface. Also examine nail holes and other area that have been filled: are they all filled flush with the surface or has the putty shrunk and left a depressed surface? Is there any putty smeared around the hole? Has the putty been adequately sanded?

Any problems found in the whitewood inspection should be corrected before proceeding to other finishing steps. At this point they are easily remedied, but later they will become more noticeable and harder to correct as the finish is applied.

1-54 *Before any finish is applied to wood, you should perform a whitewood inspection to make sure that all of the wood preparation steps were done correctly.*

Working with Previously Finished Wood

When working with wood that has been previously finished, you must decide whether to attempt to repair and revitalize the existing finish or remove the finish and start over. This decision is based on two factors: the condition of the existing finish and whether or not the existing finish is aesthetically pleasing to you. If you like the present finish but it is dull and lifeless, the solution may simply be a good cleaning with a finish rejuvenator. Minor damages can easily be repaired, but major damage to the finish usually necessitates removal of the finish.

1-55 Sometimes you can revive a dull damaged finish by wiping on a finish restorer.

Cleaning, Restoring, and Repairing the Finish

Note: *All of the products and techniques described here can potentially damage some types of finishes. Before you use the product or technique on a valuable piece of furniture, be sure to test it in an inconspicuous location.*

CLEANING AND REJUVENATING FINISHES When a finish looks dull and lifeless but is otherwise in good condition, you can usually bring it back to life by cleaning off the years of accumulated wax and grime. A product called *wax and silicone remover* or *wax and grease remover* contains special solvents that are well-suited for this job. Work in well-ventilated area, because the fumes are flammable and toxic. Apply the solvent with a rag. Thoroughly wet a section of the finish with the solvent; then use a clean rag to buff it dry. Refold the rag frequently to expose a clean surface; otherwise, you will simply smear the deposits around instead of removing them. This type of solvent won't harm most finishes, so if the underlying finish is in good condition, all that is needed is a coat of paste wax to bring out its beauty.

If the finish is still dull after cleaning, the top surface needs to be restored. You can polish it with pumice and rottenstone as described in Chapter 7 or you can use a finish restorer (**1–55**).

Finish restorers combine special solvents with tung oil to dissolve a thin layer of the old finish and replace it with tung oil. Most companies market several strength products. The first type contains a high concentration of tung oil and very few solvents. It is used almost like furniture polish to add a layer of oil without removing any of the old finish. The second type of product is usually referred to as a *cleaner*. It contains stronger solvents that dissolve the accumulated grime from the surface along with an extremely thin layer of the finish. As the cleaner is buffed off, a layer of tung oil is left on the surface.

The third type is sometimes called a *finish restorer* or *rejuvenator*. It contains strong solvents similar to the type used in strippers. This product should only be used on finishes that are in need of major restoration. Before applying any product of this type, read the directions on the container thoroughly because application techniques can vary from one type to another.

Danish oil is another product that can be used to rejuvenate a finish. The type that contains a mixture of oils and solvents rather than pure tung oil is best for this application. First clean the finish with wax and silicone remover, and then apply a thin coat of Danish oil with a rag and immediately buff it out with a dry rag. Start in an inconspicuous spot to make sure the oil is compatible with the existing finish.

The liquid wax that Danish oil manufacturers market for use with their finishes also makes a good finish rejuvenator. It contains solvents that clean the surface while you are applying the wax. It is available in colors to match the existing finish so it also hides small defects in the finish. Apply a wet coat with a rag and thoroughly clean the finish by rubbing vigorously while it is still wet. Wipe this coat off while it is still wet to remove the grime you have loosened; then apply a thin coat with a fresh rag and let it dry. Finally, use a dry cloth to buff the surface to the desired luster.

If the original finish is shellac, you can bring it back to a beautiful luster by applying a thin coat of shellac using the French polishing technique described in Chapter Four. Practice the technique before using it on the final project because you can cut through the original finish if you are not careful.

CRAZING As a finish ages, it sometime becomes brittle and many hairline cracks develop; this defect is called *crazing*. You can sometimes repair a crazed surface by applying a solvent to dissolve the finish and then letting it harden. This is an unpredictable process, so you should only attempt it if you are prepared to refinish the piece anyway if the process should fail.

Thoroughly clean the finish with a wax and silicone remover. If the old finish is shellac, use denatured alcohol as a solvent; if the finish is lacquer, use lacquer thinner. If the old finish is varnish or if you aren't sure of the finished used, buy a special solvent called *amalgamator*. Apply the solvent to the finish by spraying, padding, or brushing; spraying is best. Use enough solvent to completely wet the surface. The solvent will slowly dissolve the finish and the cracks will flow together. Let the finish dry as if it were a freshly applied top coat. If the process is successful, the finish will look like a new top coat has been applied. You can use steel wool or pumice and rottenstone to polish the surface to the desired luster.

WATER MARKS Finishes vary in their resistance to water; when water is left on the surface of a finish that is not water resistant, a white discoloration occurs. This is called *blushing*. Usually the water hasn't soaked all the way through the finish, and in these cases it is easy to remove. Make a small pad by covering a ball of wool or cotton with a piece of close-weave cotton or linen fabric. Wet the pad with denatured alcohol until it is just barely damp. Wipe the pad over the water mark in long, straight strokes with the grain. Keep the pad in constant motion and lift it from the surface after each stroke (**1–56**). The alcohol has an

1-56
When a water mark hasn't penetrated the finish, it can sometimes be removed by wiping over it with a pad that has been moistened with alcohol.

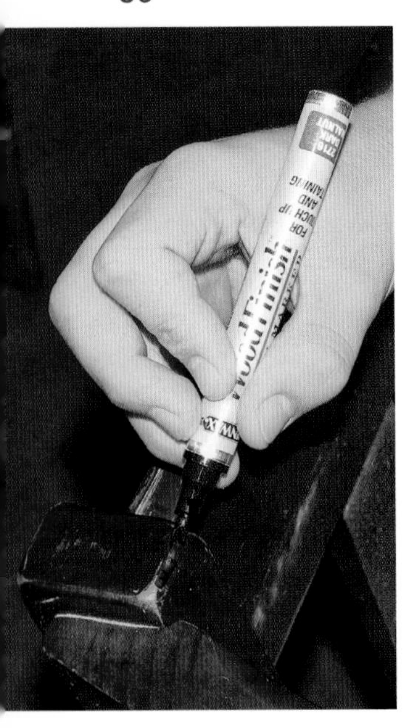

1-57 This type of soft-tip marker is filled with stain and varnish. They are available in a variety of colors that will closely match almost any finish.

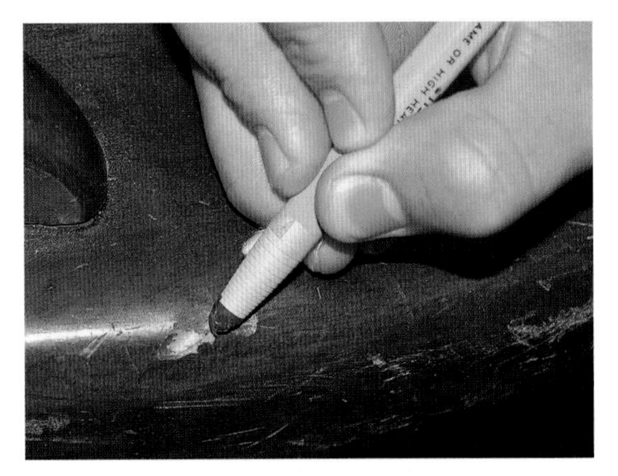

1-58 Scratch hiding pencils will deposit a hard colored wax in a scratch.

attraction for water, and it will draw the water out of the finish. Keep padding over the area until the mark disappears, unless the finish begins to soften; in that case, let it dry for an hour or so and repeat the padding until the mark is gone.

If alcohol won't remove the mark, try rubbing the area with micro-abrasive sandpaper. If the water has been standing on the wood for along time, as happens when a houseplant pot is placed directly on a table, the water will soak all the way through the finish and discolor the wood below or raise the grain. In that case, you will have to sand the finish off of the affected area and start over again. If the area is large, it is best to strip the piece and refinish. If it is not too large, sand down the area until all of the stain is removed; then spot finish the area using the direction given below for worn spots. Sometimes the discoloration will soak so deep into the wood that it is impractical to sand it out; in that case, use oxalic acid bleach as described on *page 65* to bleach out the stain.

SCRATCHES Scratches are probably the most common type of damage that furniture receives. Most are minor and relatively easy to repair. If the scratch hasn't cut through the protective film of the topcoat into the wood below, you can polish out the scratch. Traditionally pumice and rottenstone were used for this operation, but today micro-abrasive sandpaper is a better alternative. Use a small pad of sandpaper to rub out the affected area until the scratch is removed, taking care not to rub all the way through the finish. Then polish the area with finer grit until it matches the surrounding finish. Complete directions for using micro-abrasive sandpaper are given in Chapter 7. You can sometimes fill a minor scratch by rubbing a piece of walnut nutmeat or a block of beeswax over the scratch.

When the scratch is deep, it will cut through the finish and expose the bare wood below. This creates another problem, because the scratch will need to be stained to match the surrounding wood. How you handle a deep scratch depends on the location of the scratch. If it is in a highly visible area like a tabletop, you need to blend the scratch into the surrounding finish perfectly; but it if is in a less visible area like a chair leg, all you need to do is color the scratch approximately the same color as the surrounding finish.

There are several simple ways to color a scratch. One way is to apply colored furniture polish to the scratch; several companies make a scratch hiding polish that is quite effective, especially on dark finishes. There are also specially made soft-tip markers that are filled with stain and varnish available for the purpose of coloring scratches. The markers come in a variety of colors that will closely match almost any finish (**1–57**). Be careful to only color the damaged area; smearing the stain onto the undamaged finish will make the repaired area seem larger and call more attention to it.

The wax filler sticks that were discussed previously are also useful for coloring minor scratches, but because they always remain soft, they should not be used on areas that will receive a lot of wear. You can also get scratch hiding pencils that will deposit a hard colored wax in a scratch (**1–58**).

SPOT FINISHING When a defect must blend into the surrounding finish perfectly, spot finishing is really the only method that will produce satisfactory results. Spot finishing is more art than science. You need a good eye for color and you should practice before using it on an important piece. You will probably not be able to make the repair invisible under close scrutiny, but if you are skillful you can create a repair that will disguise the defect from the casual observer. Always try to confine your repair to the area of the original defect. If you spread the spot finishing material over an area larger than the original defect, you run the risk of making the repair more noticeable than the original problem.

For scratches, you must first stain the wood to match the rest of the finish (**1–59**). Spot-finishing stains come as a powder; they are soluble in alcohol or lacquer. Analyze the existing finish to determine whether a penetrating stain or a surface stain was used. If a penetrating stain was used, dissolve a small amount of the spot-finishing stain in alcohol and apply it with a small artist's brush to the scratch. Try to confine the stain to the scratch; this type of stain will soak through most finishes, so if you get some outside of the scratch, it is difficult to remove. Refer to Chapter 5 for a complete discussion of color mixing.

Next, fill the scratch with spot-finishing lacquer using a small artist's brush (**1–60**). Spot-finishing lacquer is a special type of shellac that is compatible with most finishes. If a toner stain was used in the original finish, dissolve the powdered stain into

1-59 *To repair a scratch, first stain the wood with spot-finishing stain. Apply it with a small artist's brush.*

1-60 *Fill the scratch with spot-finishing lacquer using a small artist's brush.*

some of the spot-finishing lacquer and use a small brush to fill the scratch. When the lacquer has dried, use 600-grit wet-or-dry sandpaper to sand the lacquer level with the surrounding surface; then polish the area to the correct luster with micro-abrasive sandpaper.

WORN SPOTS The finish on corners, edges, and other areas that receive a lot of handling frequently wears off before the rest of the finish (**1–61**). You can spot finish these areas to match the original finish. The most important factor in achieving a good result is your ability to match the original color.

Spot-finishing stains come in a large variety of colors, and you can mix them to achieve any shade desired. Refer to Chapter 5 for directions on mixing colors. Experiment on a piece of scrap wood of the same species until you are satisfied with the color. To begin, make a French polishing pad as described in Chapter 4. Moisten the pad with spot-finishing lacquer (also called *padding lacquer*). Next, dip the pad into the correct color powdered spot-finishing stain (**1–62**). If you need to mix colors, you can dip the pad into more than one color or you can apply the different colors in separate coats. Work the pad over a piece of scrap to evenly distribute the stain in the pad; then pad the stain onto the wood. Rub the pad over the wood in long rapid strokes with the grain. Don't stop the pad while it is touching the wood. Keep padding over the area, adding more stain and lacquer to the pad as necessary until you are satisfied with the color (**1–63**).

1-61 *Edges and corners receive more wear than other areas, so the finish is more likely to wear off them first. This chair frame has a considerable amount of visible wear.*

After the stain is applied, let it dry; then switch to a clean pad. Moisten this pad with clear spot-finishing lacquer and apply several coats to the area to build up a protective coating over the stain. Be careful not to use too wet a pad as you do this or you will remove the stain. After the lacquer is dry, buff it with 4/0 steel wool or polish it with micro abrasive sandpaper to give it the desired luster. The film produced by padding is thin, so take care not to rub through the finish.

DENTS, GOUGES, AND BURNS Dents, gouges, and burns all leave a hole that is lower than the surrounding surface. Before any finishing can be done, the hole must be filled. Sometimes dents can be repaired without filling, because a dent still has the same amount of wood fibers as the surrounding wood—they are just compressed. If you can get the fibers to swell back to

1-62 Moisten a pad with spot-finishing lacquer, and then dip it into some dry powder spot-finishing stain. Work the stain into the pad until it is blended with the lacquer.

1-63 Rub the pad containing the spot-finishing stain over the worn areas in long, even strokes, with the grain. When the color is correct, protect the stain with clear spot-finishing lacquer.

1-64 *Before filling dents, gouges, and burns, clean out the hole with a knife blade or carving gouge to remove any charred wood or loose splinters.*

their original shape, the dent will disappear. The simplest way to make the fibers swell is to apply water to the dent. (*Note: The water may damage the surrounding finish, so take care to apply only a small amount to the dented area.*)

After the dent has swollen back to its original shape, the area will still probably need to be refinished using the spot finishing techniques described above. If the water hasn't removed the dent after several applications, thoroughly wet the area, then heat it. A hair blow-dryer is a good way to heat the wood without damaging it. If the dent still hasn't completely come back to its original shape, try placing an ice cube on it while it is still hot. If all of these methods fail, the area will have to be filled.

There are two ways to fill dents, gouges, and burns: wood putty and burn-in sticks. Before using either type, clean out the hole with a knife blade or carving gouge to remove any charred wood or loose splinters (**1–64**). If you slightly undercut the edges of the hole, the patch will stay in place better.

Wood putty comes tends to shrink as it dries, so you must build it up higher than the surface to allow for shrinkage. Putty is available in several colors, so you can pick one that is close to the correct color.

Use a small putty knife or a screwdriver blade to fill the hole with putty. The blade should be small enough so that you don't smear too much putty on the surrounding finish. For small holes, a screwdriver is better than a putty knife.

Once the putty is dry, use a very small piece of sandpaper to sand it flush with the surrounding surface. Avoid scratching the surrounding finish with the sandpaper.

Use the methods described for repairing worn spots to stain and finish the patch.

1-65 *You can buy a kit that includes everything you will need for using burn-in sticks, including a selection of different color sticks, protective balm, sanding lube, and a burn-in knife.*

When the surrounding wood doesn't have a prominent grain pattern, it is only necessary to match the color of the patch to the wood; but if the wood has a prominent grain that passes through the patch area, you will need to duplicate the grain pattern in the patched area. First, color the patch the same color as the lightest part of the grain. Then dip an artist's brush into a little spot finishing stain mixed with lacquer that is the color of the dark lines of the grain. Use the brush to connect the grain lines that are interrupted by the patch. Artist's oil paints or acrylics can also be used for this operation. You can also use special graining markers to add grain pattern to the finish.

Burn-in sticks are solid sticks of finishing material that can be melted by heat. They come in a wide variety of colors and can be mixed to match any finish (**1–65**). They have several advantages over wood putty. First, they don't shrink; second, they are applied hot and harden as they cool, so you don't have to wait for them to dry. Finally, if they are carefully color matched to the finish, they form a complete repair with no additional finishing necessary. Burn-in sticks are the choice of most professional spot finishers.

Burn-in sticks are applied with a special knife called a *burn-in knife*. The knife must be heated to melt the sticks. Electric burn-in knives are available; they operate like a soldering iron. An ordinary burn-in knife looks like a spatula; it is heated with a propane torch or other heat source. The electric knife is easier to work with because it maintains a constant heat. If the knife is too hot it will cause the finish to bubble, and if it is not hot enough the sticks will not melt properly. I recommend that you spend the extra money to buy an electric knife; it will save

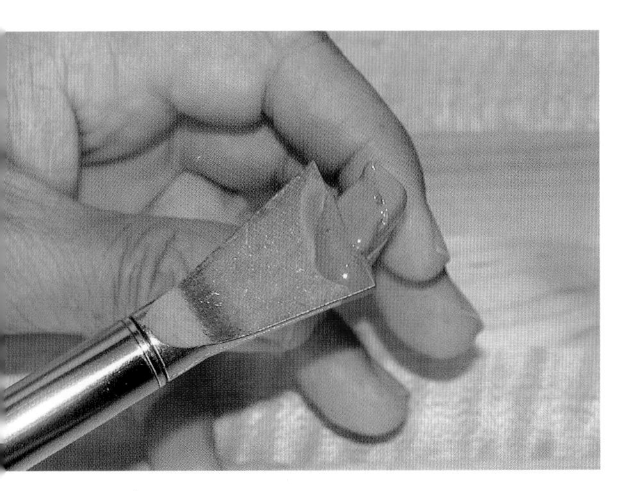

1-66 *Press the end of the burn-in knife against the edge of the stick, and slice off a thin slab of the stick. The heat from the knife will melt the slab into a puddle of liquid filler.*

1-67 *Use the burn-in knife to pour the melted filler into the hole.*

you headaches in the long run. As you work with the hot knife, take care not to burn the surrounding undamaged finish; some suppliers of burn-in sticks also sell a protective balm that is smeared onto the surrounding finish to help prevent damage.

To fill a hole with a burn-in stick, heat the knife, occasionally testing the temperature by pressing a burn-in stick against the blade; the knife is ready when it melts the stick, but it's too hot if the stick burns or bubbles. Press the end of the knife against the edge of the stick, and slice off a thin slab of the stick (**1–66**). Let the slab sit on the knife for a moment until it is completely melted, and then pour it into the hole (**1–67**). Use the tip of the knife to smooth and level the patch, leaving it slightly higher than the surrounding surface. In a few minutes, the patch will cool and harden. Now smear some protective balm on the finish surrounding the repair. This will prevent the hot knife from damaging the finish during the next step (**1–68**).

1-68 *Smear some protective balm on the finish surrounding the repair to prevent the hot knife from damaging the finish.*

1-69 Use the burn-in knife like a chisel to slice off the top of the repair and make it level with the surrounding surface.

Now use the burn-in knife like a chisel to slice off the top of the repair and make it level with the surrounding surface (**1–69**). When the repair hardens, finish the job of smoothing the patch with sandpaper lubricated with special rubbing fluid (**1–70**). Try not to sand the surrounding finish. If you are satisfied with the way the patch looks, use micro-abrasive sandpaper to polish the patch to the proper luster. No additional finish is needed. At this point the patch will be very unobtrusive when viewed from a distance, but you will notice it upon close inspection (**1–71**).

If you want to make the patch even less noticeable, you can add grain lines. Use spot finishing stains and lacquer or graining markers. Graining markers are special fine-

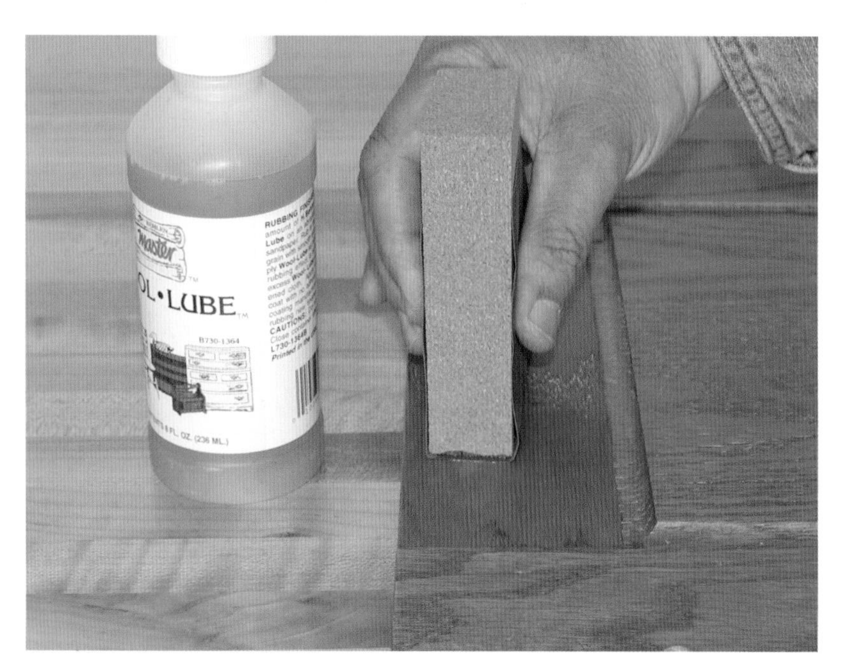

1-70 Smooth the patch using sandpaper lubricated with special rubbing fluid.

1-71 At this point the patch is fairly unobtrusive. If it is not in a conspicuous spot, you can leave it like this.

point markers that use an ink that will bond to the burn-in patch (**1–72**). If you carefully draw in a pattern that matches the surrounding grain, the patch will be hardly noticeable (**1–73**).

You can mix two or more colors of burn-in sticks to make a custom color. To mix the colors, scrape a little of each stick onto the hot knife; then use another hot knife to blend the colors together by mixing them back and forth.

SOLVENT AND STEEL-WOOL REFINISHERS When the existing finish is beyond the help of a finish restorer but not so severely damaged to warrant its complete removal, a solvent and steel-wool refinisher is a good choice. This method removes the top layers of the old finish but leaves the underlying stain and filler intact. It is very useful for removing darkened varnish or for lightening a dark finish to meet modern tastes. There are several brand-name refinishers of this type on the market and all of them produce good results; however, you can save a some money by using lacquer thinner instead of a brand-name refinisher. In most cases, ordinary lacquer thinner will work just as well as the brand-name products. For really tough finishes, you may have to use one of the brand-name products, but lacquer will dissolve most conventional finishes. If the old finish is shellac, denatured alcohol can be used as the solvent. This type of refinishing is not recommended for synthetic finishes like polyurethane, catalyzed lacquer, or conversion varnish. This method also should not be used on painted surfaces.

1-72 *To make the patch even less noticeable, add grain lines using a special fine point marker.*

1-73 *If you carefully draw in a pattern that matches the surrounding grain, the patch is hardly noticeable.*

1-74 *The solvent and steel wool method of removing an old finish leaves the wood ready for the application of a new top coat without any further preparation. Because this old door was finished with a lacquer toner, the stripped surface is considerably lighter than the old finish. If the door had been stained with a penetrating stain and finished with a clear top coat, the stripped surface would have been approximately the same as the old finish.*

Begin by pouring some solvent (lacquer thinner for most finishes, alcohol for shellac) into a shallow dish. Dip a 4/0 steel-wool pad into the solvent and rub it over a small section of the finish to be removed (**1–74**). The solvent will dissolve the old top coat and the particles of finish will lodge into the steel wool; dip the steel wool into the solvent again and rinse out the pad. Work in small sections at a time and replace the solvent when it becomes thick with old finish. When the desired effect is achieved, use a clean steel wool pad and a small amount of clean solvent to clean up the surface by rubbing in long strokes with the grain along the entire length of the board.

Because the fine steel wool won't produce deep scratches in the wood, no further sanding is required. If the finish you are removing is a colored top coat such as a toner lacquer or a varnish stain, the color of the wood after stripping will be much lighter. If the old finish is a clear top coat over stain, the color will remain about the same because only the top coat will be removed. If you're happy with the color left after the top coat has been removed, no staining is required. If you prefer a lighter color, additional rubbing with the solvent will lighten the color. If you want to darken or change the color, you can apply an oil stain. Any type top coat can be applied. Many people prefer to use an oil finish after this type of refinisher is used because it is easy to apply and it uniformly gives good results.

Note: *Wear neoprene or nitrile gloves when using this method, because the solvents will dry out your skin and cause irritation. Lacquer thinner and alcohol are flammable, so work in a well-ventilated area away from pilot lights of other sources of ignition.*

Here are step-by-step directions for the solvent and steel-wool refinishing method:

1. Pour some solvent into a shallow dish. Wear neoprene or nitrile gloves. Dip fine steel-wool pad into solvent. Squeeze pad to remove excess. Rub pad in a circular motion over a small area (approximately 12 inches in diameter).

2. Return the pad to the solvent dish to rinse out the accumulated residue of the old finish. When the area you are working on is cleaned of the old finish, move to another section. You can stop the process at any time to return later without fear of lap marks.

When the solvent becomes thick with residue, replace it. You may need to replace the steel wool also, if the project is large.

3. When the entire surface has been cleaned of the old finish, replace the steel wool with a clean pad and fill the dish with clean solvent. Dip the pad into the solvent and squeeze it fairly dry. Rub the pad with the grain to remove the circular marks left by the previous operation. Finish with long strokes running the entire length of the board to produce the most even effect.

Let the surface dry at least half an hour (much more if the humidity is high) before proceeding with additional finishing steps.

Removing the Finish

When the existing finish has deteriorated to the point that repair and restoration techniques are inadequate, then the finish must be removed. More frequently though, the finish is removed because the existing finish is no longer in line with current taste in color or appearance. In either case, the procedure is the same.

As wood ages, it develops a mellow color and sheen called *patina*. The patina develops only on a thin layer of the wood's surface. When refinishing an old piece, try to preserve as much of the patina as possible. Use a stripping method that gently removes the old top coats and preserves the original color and sheen of the wood. A water-based stripper is more likely to raise the grain and cause some damage to the wood. This means that you will have to sand the wood after using stripper. If heavy sanding is required, some of the patina will be lost. The less sanding that you do after the stripping process the better the project will turn out. After stripping, the wood surface will be uniformly aged and partially sealed. If you sand through this layer in some spots and not others the resulting finish will look splotchy.

There are several methods of removing the old finish, but they can be divided into two major categories: mechanical and chemical.

Removing layers of old paint to reveal the natural beauty of the wood below can be a very satisfying experience; however, if you suspect that the piece has been painted with lead paint, don't strip it yourself. Lead paint is potentially very dangerous. The stripping process frees the lead, which can cause severe health problems. This is particularly dangerous for children and pregnant women.

You can buy a testing kit that will indicate whether the paint contains lead. One type of test kit contains chemically treated swabs. If the swabs change color when they are wiped over the paint, then the paint contains high levels of lead. You can also take a sample to your local health department for testing. If the old paint contains lead, take the project to a professional stripper to have it removed. Professional strippers have the equipment and knowledge to handle the lead.

MECHANICAL METHODS OF REMOVING FINISHES The mechanical methods involve more physical labor than the other methods, but they have two major advantages: they don't leave any residual chemicals on the wood and they won't raise the grain of the wood. All of the mechanical methods are best suited for flat surfaces, because it is very difficult to use them to get into small details.

A *scraper* can be used to mechanically remove some finishes. They work best on brittle finishes. Scraping is best suited for flat areas but there are small scrapers that are shaped to fit moldings and other details. When using a scraper, you need to take care that the scraper doesn't gouge into the wood. Because soft woods are so easily gouged, scraping is better suited for hard woods.

Sanding is another mechanical method of removing the old finish. Use sandpaper with a stearated coating or open coat sandpaper. The process is similar to the technique for new wood, except you need to clean the sandpaper more often. You can use a wire brush to remove accumulations of old finish from the sandpaper.

To remove the finish, start with a very coarse grade of sandpaper such as 50-grit, but switch to a finer grade as soon as you break through to bare wood. Power sanders will speed up the operation. Don't use an orbital sander with 50-grit paper, because the resulting swirl marks will be very difficult to remove. A belt sander is more appropriate, because the sanding action is in line with the grain; but be careful not to damage the wood by holding the sander unevenly or staying in one place too long.

Once the finish has been removed, complete the sanding operation as if you were working with new wood. If the piece you are working on has been veneered or is made of plywood, it may not be possible to completely sand off all of the stain without sanding through the veneer. In that case, you will have to use a chemical bleach if you want to completely remove the stain. However, this is usually only necessary when the new finish will be considerably lighter than the old one.

Heat is another mechanical means of removing the old finish. Most finishes can be softened with heat and easily scraped from the surface, but be careful; heat can loosen glue joints, especially on older furniture, and it may cause veneers to buckle or come loose. A propane torch is sometimes recommended for finish removal, but because it can easily scorch the wood, a it should only be used for exterior surfaces that won't receive a fine finish. *Do not use a torch indoors. This is dangerous because of the possibility of fire. Also, flame should be kept far from glass.*

Usually a special torch tip is used that spreads the flame over a wider area. Aim the tip of the flame at the surface and rapidly move it back and forth over a small area. As soon as the finish begins to wrinkle or takes on a shiny appearance, remove the flame and quickly scrape the area with a scraper. You must work fast, because the finish will reharden as it cools.

Interior work and furniture should not be stripped with a torch. For these applications, use either a heat gun or a heat plate.

The heat plate can be used on clapboard siding and other large, flat surfaces such as large panels and doors. A wire frame makes it possible to put it down without turning the unit off. A shield reflects the heat onto the paint. Some types have small legs to keep the element off the surface; others must be held above the surface being stripped. Because the heat plate uses radiant heat rather than hot air as the heat gun does, it is much easier to scorch the surface, so take care and watch the surface closely. As soon as the finish appears soft, remove the heat plate and scrape the area.

The heat gun works best on thick layers of paint. It can also be used on moldings and turned elements. It looks like a hair dryer, but it produces a much hotter stream of air. *Caution: The air stream from a heat gun will burn your skin. Wear heavy work gloves. Don't use the heat gun near glass. Direct the hot air at a small section of finish until the finish wrinkles or changes appearance. Quickly remove the finish with a putty knife or scraper (**1–75**).*

1-75 *The heat gun softens some types of old finishes and paint so that they can be removed with a putty knife. Wear gloves to protect yourself from the heat.*

CHEMICAL STRIPPERS Chemical strippers involve less physical labor than mechanical methods, but they have several disadvantages. Some types will raise the grain or may loosen veneers or glue joints. Some contain potentially hazardous chemicals and solvents, and they all involve dealing with gooey residue that can be quite messy.

When using chemical strippers, be prepared for the mess and disposal problems involved. Work in a well-ventilated area; protect surrounding surfaces from stray globs of finish and stripper, and protect yourself with protective gloves, goggles and protective clothing. Also make certain that no flames (cigarettes, pilot lights, etc.) are nearby.

Before the advent of modern strippers, caustic solutions such as lye were used extensively to remove old varnish or paint. The problem with caustic removers is that they are difficult to completely neutralize or remove, so they create problems in the new finish, can darken woods high in tannin (such as oak), and they pose safety and health hazards for the user. Modern strippers use a combination of solvents and chemicals to soften the old finish.

When choosing a stripper, it pays to use the best quality. Inexpensive strippers often won't completely lift the finish, so you have

1-76 *After the stripper has loosened the old finish, a putty knife can be used to remove the sludge.*

to do it physically. Better quality strippers will penetrate the finish and loosen its bond to the wood; the finish will wrinkle and blister, making it easy to remove. The blisters become larger as the stripper continues to loosen the bond. Eventually you can use a wide blade putty knife to lift off the old finish sludge (**1–76**).

Unfortunately, one of the most effective stripping compounds, methylene chloride, has been shown to be hazardous and, most strong solvents are also hazardous. Some of the newest types of strippers use chemicals that are much less toxic than older formulas. These new strippers are very effective, so I recommend choosing a low toxicity type. There are several new types of strippers available that use less hazardous materials. They are effective, but they may have to be left on the surface longer to soften the old paint. Follow the directions on the stripper carefully. Even though these new strippers are safer than those that use methylene chloride, you should still wear protective gloves and goggles.

Strippers come in liquid, semi-paste, and paste form. Liquid stripper is most useful for flat surfaces where it won't run off. Semi-paste and paste strippers contain an ingredient to make them gel; they will stick to vertical surfaces better than liquid. *Note: When using a stripper, follow the directions on the container and observe all of the safety warnings.*

Apply a thick coat of stripper with a brush, then let the stripper remain on the project until the old finish is thoroughly softened. You may need to leave it on overnight to soften a thick coat of paint. To increase the effectiveness of the stripper, cover the project with a disposable plastic tarp after applying the stripper. This slows down the evaporation of the stripper so that it will remain active longer. However, be careful because stripper can loosen glue joints and cause veneers to loosen or buckle, so don't leave the striper on any longer than necessary.

After the old paint has softened, use a putty knife to scrap the residue from the surface. Always scrape the paint off with the grain direction. Scraping across the grain may leave scratches that will be difficult to remove. In areas where a putty knife won't fit, rub the residue off with a *stripping pad.*

This is a plastic material that works like steel wool. Don't use steel wool, because it can react with the ingredients in modern strippers and leave dark stains on the wood. Rub the pad in straight strokes with the wood's grain direction. The stripping pad is very coarse and can leave deep scratches if it is rubbed across the wood's grain. The stripping pad can remove most of the paint from moldings, but to get the last remaining traces from inside small details, use a piece of wood dowel sharpened to a point to scrape out the paint residue.

After all of the old finish has been removed, follow the recommendations on the stripper container regarding rinsing. Some strippers contain wax as an evaporation retarder. You must remove all of the wax by rinsing the surface with solvent, or the subsequent finish won't adhere to the wood. Some types should be rinsed off with water; in this case, scrub the surface with a clean, synthetic finishing pad dampened with water. The water will raise the grain of the wood, but rubbing with the finishing pad will usually remove the raised grain. If the surface still seems rough, lightly sand the surface with 320-grit sandpaper. As soon as you remove the raised grain fibers, stop sanding. Don't sand too deep or you will

Table 1-2

Characteristics of Stripping Chemicals

CHEMICAL	WATER CLEANUP	HIGHLY FLAMMABLE	SAFETY	STRENGTH	COMMENTS
Methylene Chloride	yes	no	suspected carcinogen	Strongest, removes most finishes	Because of health hazards, should only be used as a last resort.
Acetone	no	yes	toxic fumes	fairly strong	Usually blended with toluene and methanol.
Toluene	no	yes	toxic fumes	Less strong	Usually blended with acetone and methanol.
Methanol	no	yes	poisonous	weak except on shellac	Usually blended with toluene and acetone.
N-methyl pyrrolidone	yes	no	safer than most	Strong but slow	May be used alone or blended with Di-basic ester.
Di-basic ester	yes	no	safer than most	strong but slow	May be used alone or blended with N-methyl pyrrolidone
Lye	yes	no	poisonous burns skin	strong	May damage or darken wood.

remove much of the patina. Let the wood dry completely before you apply a finish.

Note: *When using a stripper, follow the directions on the container and observe all of the safety warnings. It's important to wear goggles and protective gloves, be certain that there is adequate ventilation, and avoid all heat sources such as lighted cigarettes and pilot lights.*

COMMERCIAL STRIPPING COMPANIES

If you would like to avoid the mess and hazards of stripping, consider having the stripping done professionally. It is especially advisable for intricate pieces such as chairs. The cost of having a commercial stripper remove the old finish is usually quite reasonable, so it's a good idea to call for a quote before stripping something yourself.

Commercial strippers use two different methods of removing the finish; the older method uses a hot dip tank filled with caustic chemicals. This method can loosen glue joints, darken oak, and substantially raise the grain. The other and preferred method is called the *flow over method,* or *cold tank.* This method of commercial stripping won't loosen glue joints and only slightly raises the grain. In the flow over method, the furniture is placed in a dry tank. Solvent-type stripper is pumped by a recirculating pump through a filter and out a hose that flows the stripper over the piece of furniture.

Wood that has been dip-stripped should be air-dried for at least three weeks before refinishing or warping could result.

BLEACHING Bleaching is a process that removes most of the natural color from wood (**1–77**). It is usually used when the desired finish is lighter than the natural color of the wood. It is also used when two pieces of wood to be used in the same project vary a great deal in color. Bleaching the darker board will make it match the lighter one better. Light-colored wood that is left unfinished for a long time will darken and eventually take on a gray look, especially if it is exposed to the weather. Bleach will restore the wood to its original light color.

Note: *Bleaches contain harsh chemicals, so wear protective gloves and goggles.*

Bleaching will raise the grain, so you will have to sand the surface after the bleaching process.

Ordinary household liquid chlorine bleach will work for some bleaching operations. Apply the bleach straight from the bottle. Let the bleach dry and apply another coat if necessary. When the desired effect is achieved, rinse the wood thoroughly with water.

For maximum effect, a commercial wood bleach is recommended. Bleaches made specially for wood are much stronger than household bleach. They usually consist of two parts that must be mixed just before use. Follow directions on the container for rinsing and neutralizing.

Oxalic acid was extensively used as a bleach before the two-part bleaches were developed. Oxalic acid won't remove some types of stains, but it will remove discoloration caused by reaction with the stripper. It is especially good for removing black or gray water marks. It isn't as strong as the new bleaches and it is hard to get an even color when bleaching large areas, but some people still prefer it to the newer bleaches. One reason is that the wood retains more of its original character.

Oxalic acid comes as dry crystals; to use as a bleach the crystals must be mixed with hot water. Oxalic acid is hazardous, so use care; it is especially important not to breathe in dust from oxalic acid. Apply the acid with a nylon brush. When the desired amount of bleaching has taken place, the area must be washed with water. The last step is neutralizing the acid by washing the area with a solution of three ounces of borax mixed with one gallon of water.

After stripping off an old finish, some traces of stain may remain on the wood. Sometimes you can bleach out the stain; it depends on what type of stain was originally used.

There are commercial stain removers that perform very well. The stain removers are formulated to work on specific types of stains. One type removes aniline stains, another type removes oil stains, and a third type removes other miscellaneous types of stains. Most commercially made furniture is stained with aniline stain, so the aniline stain remover is the type to try if you are refinishing a factory-made piece.

1-77 *Bleach can remove most of the natural color from wood. The walnut sample on the left shows the wood's natural color; the sample on the right is the same type of wood that has been bleached. Both samples have been varnished to bring out the color.*

2 Finishing Tools

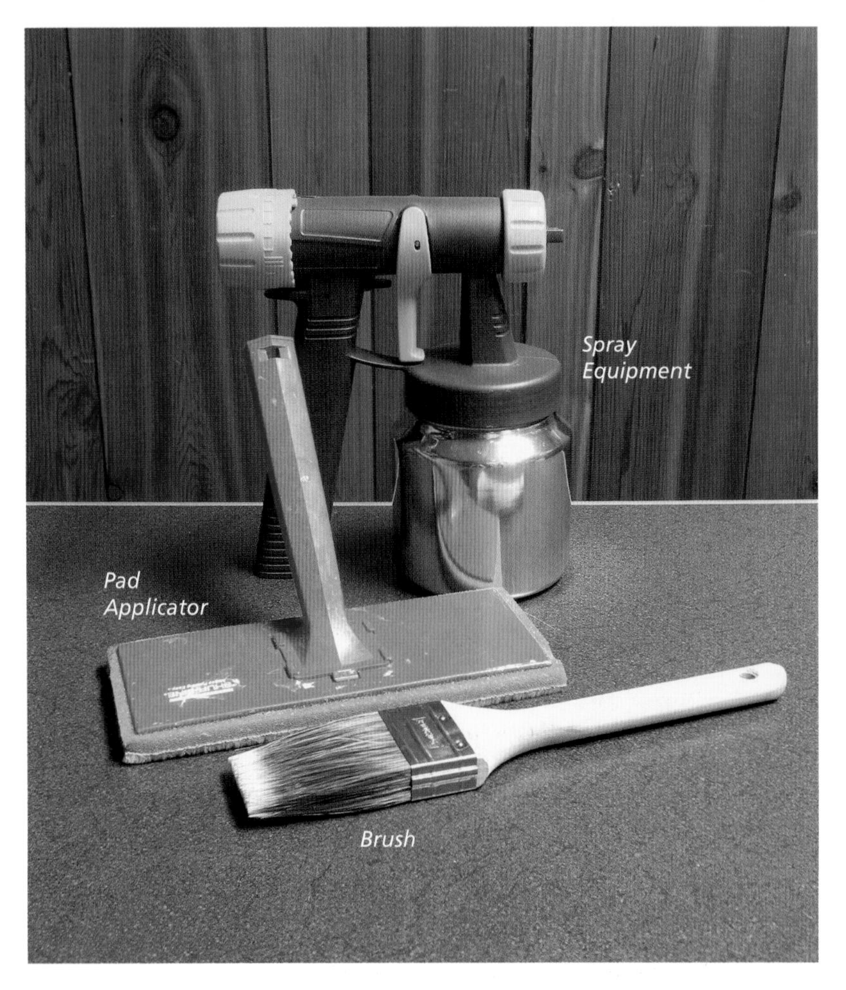

Before applying any finishing material, you need to decide which finishing tools to use. There are several general types of tools for applying a finish. Each has a place in the finishing process. The three most common types of finishing tools are brushes, pad applicators, and spray equipment. The tools you choose will play an important role in how the completed finish looks and the amount of labor involved in applying the finish, so you need to pick the tool that best fits the job at hand.

Brushes

Brushes are the oldest type of finishing tools, dating back to ancient Egypt. Today they're still the tool of choice for many finishing operations, although spraying has taken over as the leader for applying the top coats of a finish.

Brushes consist of a set of filaments attached to a handle by means of a ferrule. The filaments are attached to the ferrule with a setting compound. Vulcanized rubber was once the most popular setting compound, but epoxy and other synthetic resins have now taken the lead. The filaments are separated into groups in the ferrule by tapered plugs called fillers. The ferrule is attached to the handle with nails or rivets (**2–1**).

Brushes are categorized by the type of filament used. Two general categories are *natural* and *synthetic filaments*. Solvent-based products such as lacquer, shellac, and spirit stain can be applied with a brush that contains natural filaments. Water-based products should be applied with a synthetic filament brush. Oil-based products such as varnish, oil stain, or oil paint can be applied with either natural or synthetic filaments.

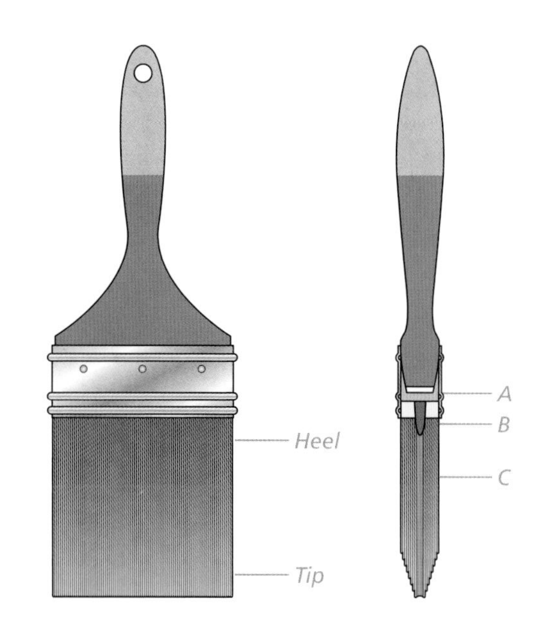

2-1 *Parts of a brush: (A) rivet, (B) setting compound, (C) filler.*

Natural Brushes

The term bristle has acquired several meanings. To most people, it means the filaments in any type of brush. Technically the term bristle can be applied only to the hair of the Chinese hog, but many people refer to any natural filament brush as a bristle brush. Besides bristle, there are many other natural filaments used in brushes. Some are very expensive and are used for specialty brushes such as sign painting, pin striping, and artists' brushes, while others are inexpensive and are used as a substitute for bristle in inexpensive brushes.

Red sable is used for high quality artists' and lettering brushes. It is obtained from the Siberian mink.

Black sable is also used for artists' and lettering brushes as well as striping brushes. It comes from the Central American civet cat.

Camel hair is used mostly for watercolor brushes and striping brushes. It doesn't come from a camel at all; it comes from the tails of Russian and Siberian squirrels.

Ox hair is used alone for striping and sign painters' brushes. It is blended with China bristle to make high quality general-purpose brushes. It is obtained from the ears of cattle.

Horsehair is used when extremely long filaments are needed. It is primarily used in faux finishing and art and calligraphy brushes. Bench brushes used to clean up dust are often made of horsehair.

Palmetto comes from the palmetto tree and is also used as a substitute for bristle.

Tampico is another filament used as a substitute for bristle. It comes from cactus. Because it is resistant to chemicals, it is used in brushes for applying chemical stains and bleaches.

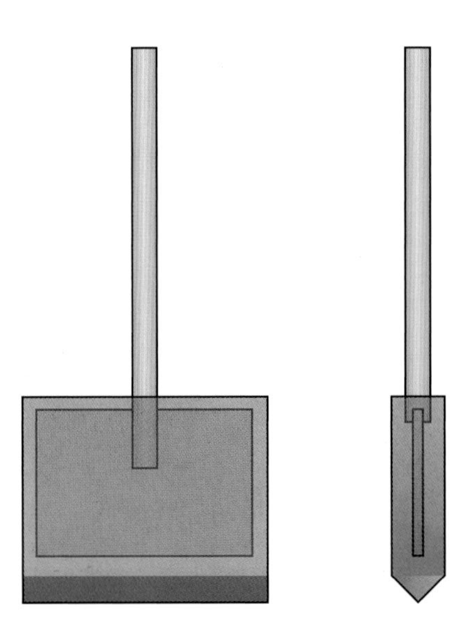

2-2 Foam brush construction. Notice the plastic stiffener that extends through the center of the foam. Without this stiffener, the brush would be too limp to use effectively.

2-3 Foam brushes are very good for applying stain. In this comparison between a foam brush and an inexpensive nylon brush, notice that the foam brush carries more stain and leaves a smooth application of stain without brush marks.

Synthetic Brushes

Since the 1940s, man-made materials have become increasingly popular as a brush material. When it is made properly, a synthetic filament brush can equal or surpass the performance of a natural filament brush. Synthetic filaments are better suited for use with water-based materials than natural filaments. Natural filaments lose their resiliency and become limp in water, while synthetics remain firm and springy. Some synthetics are affected by the solvents found in lacquer or shellac, but the highest quality synthetics are not adversely affected and can be used with virtually any finishing material.

Nylon and polyester are the two most common synthetics used in brush manufacture; both make excellent brushes when the highest grade material is used. Styrene and polypropylene are sometimes used for inexpensive brushes, but their performance is not as good as nylon or polyester.

FOAM BRUSHES Another type of synthetic brush doesn't use filaments at all; instead a plastic foam is used (**2–2**). This type of brush can be very useful for applying stain because it applies a very even coat free of brush marks (**2–3**). Foam brushes can also be used successfully to apply varnish, but they tend to dissolve in lacquer and shellac.

Choosing a Brush

Choosing a brush can sometimes be a very confusing experience because of the wide range of types and prices available. Before attempting to select a brush, analyze what use you will put it to. For example, if you intend to use the brush to apply paint stripper, it would be foolish to purchase a high-quality brush since an inexpensive throwaway brush will do the job. On the other hand, to apply the final coat of varnish to a tabletop requires a very good brush.

The first step in choosing a brush is to decide on the type of filament. If you are using a water-based material, choose a synthetic filament. Nylon or polyester are best. Synthetics also work well with other finishing material besides water-based, so don't rule them out if you aren't using a water-based material. For general work, the best natural brushes use a blend of ox hair and China bristle. The highest quality brushes will contain about 20 percent ox hair and 80 percent bristle by weight. Lower quality brushes will contain fewer ox hairs. The lowest quality natural brushes called chip brushes use inferior shorter bristles that are rejects from the higher quality brush manufacture. They are fine for dust removal and non-critical work, but you shouldn't use them for applying the top coat of a fine finish.

After deciding on the type of filament, examine the individual filaments in the brush. A high-quality filament, whether natural or synthetic should possess the following characteristics (**2–4**):

Taper The filament should be thicker at the end that attaches to the ferrule than it is at the tip.

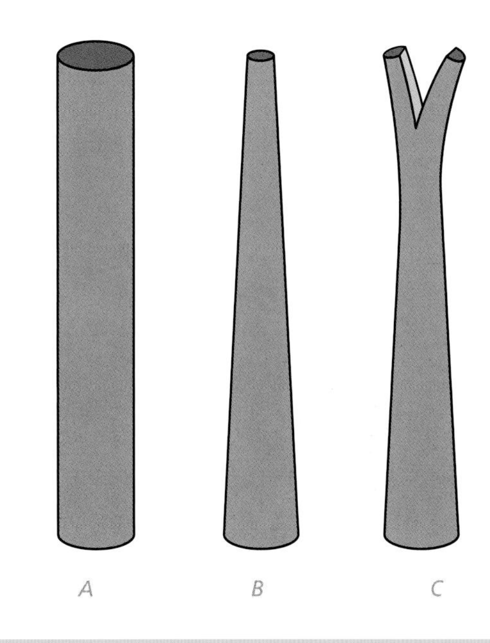

2-4 *Type of filaments: (A) straight, (B) tapered, (C) tapered and flagged.*

Flagging The ends of the filament should be split. This allows the brush to carry more material and contributes to a smooth finish.

Spring The filaments should be resilient without being stiff. Press the brush against the back of your hand to feel the spring of the brush. The brush should bend easily without poking into your skin, and yet it should immediately spring back to its original shape when lifted away from your hand.

Length The filament should be approximately 50 percent longer than the width of the brush. This means that a two-inch brush should have filaments about three inches long.

When you have decided that the filaments are appropriate for the use you will put them to, check out the general construction of the brush. Filler strips in the ferrule divide the filaments into groups; this allows the brush to carry more material, if it is done correctly. Usually one or two filler strips are used. Quality brushes use thin filler strips. Inexpensive brushes sometimes use wide strips to cut down on the amount of filaments needed to fill the ferrule. However, if the filaments used are very inexpensive, there may not be any filler strips at all. Brush the filaments across your hand several times to check for loose filaments. Any new brush will lose a few filaments at first, but excessive filament loss indicates that the setting compound is not adequate.

The shape of the handle is a matter of personal preference. Hold the handle in your hand and see if it fits comfortably and will give you adequate control. A flat or beaver tail handle is generally more comfortable for use on large surfaces, while a round handle is preferable for varnishing because it gives you more control.

Handles can be made of wood or plastic; there is really no difference in the performance, so just because a brush has a wood handle it is not necessarily a better brush. Wood handles come either bare or with a finish applied. Although the finished handles may look nicer, they are a nuisance, if you intend to reuse the brush for a long time. The finish will tend to crack and flake off after exposure to the solvents used in the finishing materials and brush cleaners.

Brush Use and Care

In order to achieve the best possible results from a brush, it must be used and cared for properly. A brush should be held with the handle resting between your thumb and first finger. That flat part of the handle just above the ferrule should be grasped by the thumb on one side and the remaining fingers on the other (**2–5**).

Before using the brush, dip it into some thinner that is compatible with the product you are using. For example, use paint thinner for oil based paint or varnish, lacquer thinner for lacquer, alcohol for shellac, and water for waterborne varnish. This will soften the brush and make it perform better. For best results, dip the brush into the thinner all the way up to the ferrule.

2-5 *Holding the brush in this manner gives you more control.*

Once you have softened the brush with thinner, dip the brush into the finishing material so that about one half of the filament length is submerged in the liquid. Don't dunk the brush in clear up to the ferrule. This is not only messy to work with, it will shorten the life of the brush by deteriorating the setting compound and causing accumulations of the finish to harden inside the ferrule.

As you withdraw the brush from the liquid, gently squeeze the excess from the brush by pressing it against the inside of the container. Don't rub the brush across the lip of the container as this will lead to a condition called *fingering*, where the filaments separate into bunches like several fingers.

The technique of applying the material to the wood depends on what type of finishing product you are using. Stains should be applied in long, even strokes starting at one edge and continuing to the other, always following the grain direction. When applying top coats, start in the center of the board and work the finish towards each edge. This technique prevents the drips that occur if a full brush is used across an edge.

Fast-drying products like shellac or lacquer must be brushed out quickly, and once it has been applied it should not be brushed over again. Slower-drying products like varnish should first be flowed on. This means that a very full brush is used and the material is applied quite heavily. Then as soon as the surface is covered, brush over the surface again without applying any more material. This brushing-out process will smooth and even the coating.

A quality brush can give years of service if it is cared for properly. Always clean the

2-6 *A brush keeper will let you put a brush away with only minimal cleaning. Notice that the brushes are suspended from a rack by the hole in the handle. The end of the brush doesn't touch the bottom of the container.*

brush with the same solvent used to thin the material you applied with the brush. It is generally a good idea to keep a separate brush for each type of material you use, since some materials are not compatible and traces of the old material in the brush may affect the new finish.

When you are working on a project for several day is in a row, you don't need to clean the brush each day. A *brush keeper* is a useful item if you use your brushes frequently. It is a airtight container with a rack to hang the brushes inside (**2–6**). The brushes soak in solvent inside the keeper.

Use a solvent compatible with the finishing material you are using. Keep the solvent level at a point where the solvent will cover the brush filaments but won't immerse the ferrule. With a brush keeper, you can put a brush away after only a quick rinse in solvent. The keeper will prevent the remaining finish from hardening in the brush. Be sure to use the brush only with the same type of material, unless you give it a thorough cleaning. Before you use the brush again, wipe out most of the solvent from the brush.

Instead of using a brush keeper, you can squeeze out most of the remaining finish with a rag and then seal the brush in a plastic sandwich bag. This will prevent the finish from hardening in the brush overnight.

If you will be storing the brush for longer than a few days, you must give it a complete cleaning. First rinse it in the proper solvent to remove as much of the finishing material as possible, then wash it with soap and running water to remove the last traces of finish and solvent (**2–7**). When you wash the brush, don't scrub the filaments back and forth as this will lead to fingering. Instead, work the soap into a lather by rubbing along the length of the brush starting at the ferrule and working towards the tip. When the brush is clean, mold it into its original shape and hang it up to dry. Hanging a brush from its hole in the handle will ensure that the brush will dry in the correct shape. Never store a brush with its weight resting on the filaments, because the filaments will be permanently bent. The common practice of leaving a brush overnight resting on its filaments in a can of thinner is a sure way to ruin a brush.

2-7 *After removing most of the finishing material from the brush, wash it out with soap and water.*

2-8 *You can ensure that a brush will retain its shape as it dries by wrapping it in a piece of paper. Fold the paper to make an envelope that holds the bristles in shape. Place a rubber band around the paper.*

You can ensure that a brush will retain its shape as it dries by wrapping it in a piece of paper. Fold the paper to make an envelope that holds the bristles in shape. And place a rubber band around the paper (**2–8**).

A *brush comb* is a useful tool for cleaning a brush. It has widely spaced metal teeth that separate the filaments of a brush (**2–9**). It can be used to loosen the finish when you are rinsing the brush in solvent. It is also useful when you are trying to recover a brush that was improperly cleaned and has hardened deposits of finish, gluing the filaments into clumps.

A brush that has a large amount of hardened finish can be reclaimed in some cases, depending on what the finish is. Super-hard synthetic finishes like epoxy and polyurethane generally cannot be removed from the brush once they have cured, and the brush must be discarded. Varnish, shellac, and lacquer can usually be successfully removed by suspending the brush in a sealed container of lacquer thinner. Hang the brush by its handle so it won't rest on the bottom of the container. You may have to leave the brush in the thinner for several days to completely soften the hardened finish. There are also commercially made brush cleaners that will soften hardened brushes.

2-9 *A brush comb is a useful tool to help clean all of the finishing material from a brush. The widely spaced metal teeth separate the filaments of the brush to promote more thorough cleaning.*

Pad Applicators

Pad applicators are probably the best method of applying stain evenly. A pad applicator consists of a rectangular section of fabric that has thousands of short filaments attached, making it look like short-napped carpet. The fabric is bonded to a foam backing that is attached to a metal or plastic base. A handle is attached to the back of the base (**2–10**).

Pad applicators have many applications in house painting, but for wood finishing they are most useful as stain applicators (**2–11**).

2-10 *The secret of the pad applicator's ability to hold more material is the foam backing. It acts like a sponge to hold liquid and gradually release it as needed. The carpet-like fabric applies the material to the work like a brush.*

Almost any type of stain can be applied with a pad applicator, but spirit stains may dissolve the foam backing of some types so test a corner of the pad in spirit stain to see if it dissolves.

The foam backing holds a large amount of stain so you can cover a large area without refilling the applicator.

The pad applicator will apply the stain very uniformly; this is especially useful when it is desirable to apply the stain without further wiping to even out the coverage.

To use the applicator, pour a small amount of stain into a paint roller tray. The level of the stain in the tray should be low enough so that you can set the applicator in the tray and not completely submerge it. Fill the applicator by placing it in the tray and pressing it against the bottom of the tray to compress the foam. This will completely soak the foam with stain. Wipe the pad across the slanted part of the tray to remove the excess stain from the filaments.

2-11 *Pad applicators are well-suited for applying stain. Wiping stain can be applied and wiped in one operation. Notice that the applicator is slightly tilted to put more pressure on the back part of the pad.*

Apply the stain to the wood in long, even strokes with the grain. When the pad is full, apply only moderate pressure and increase the pressure gradually as the stain is used up to keep the amount applied uniform. Tilting the applicator slightly so that more pressure is applied to the rear edge will produce the same uniform appearance as wiping the stain after application. This is because the front of the applicator will apply the stain and the rear will wipe it. When using this method, dip only the front half of the pad into the stain.

You can also use a pad applicator to apply varnish to large flat surfaces such as doors or tabletops. Use a good quality pad, preferably one that hasn't previously been used for any other material. When filling the pad with varnish, don't squeeze the pad as this will create air bubbles; just dip the pad into the tray. The pad won't hold as much varnish this way and so you will have to return it to the tray more often, but the resulting finish will be smoother.

Cleaning a pad applicator thoroughly is of prime importance. If any material is allowed to dry in the foam, the pad will be ruined. To clean the pad, pour a small amount of the appropriate thinner into the roller tray and repeatedly squeeze the pad against the bottom of the tray. Change the thinner and repeat until the thinner shows no trace of the stain or varnish. Next, fill the tray with soapy water and again squeeze the pad against the bottom of the tray. Finally, rinse the pad in clear water and squeeze dry. Set the pad on its back to dry. It may take a day or more for all of the water to evaporate from the pad after cleaning, so it cannot be reused for non-water based products again until it is thoroughly dry. If you will be reusing it very soon, omit the water wash.

Spray Equipment

Applying a finish with spray equipment is probably the easiest way to achieve a uniform, even surface free of brush marks. It is possible to spray almost every finishing material available, from stains and sealers to varnish and lacquer. The only real disadvantage to spray equipment is the high initial investment required, but even that disadvantage is becoming smaller all the time as new low-cost machines are introduced.

Safety Precautions for Spraying

The place you set up your spray equipment is as important as the equipment itself. Spraying can produce hazardous fumes that can pose health problems, if adequate ventilation is not provided. In addition, the area you choose should be relatively clean and dust free to avoid contaminating the finished surface.

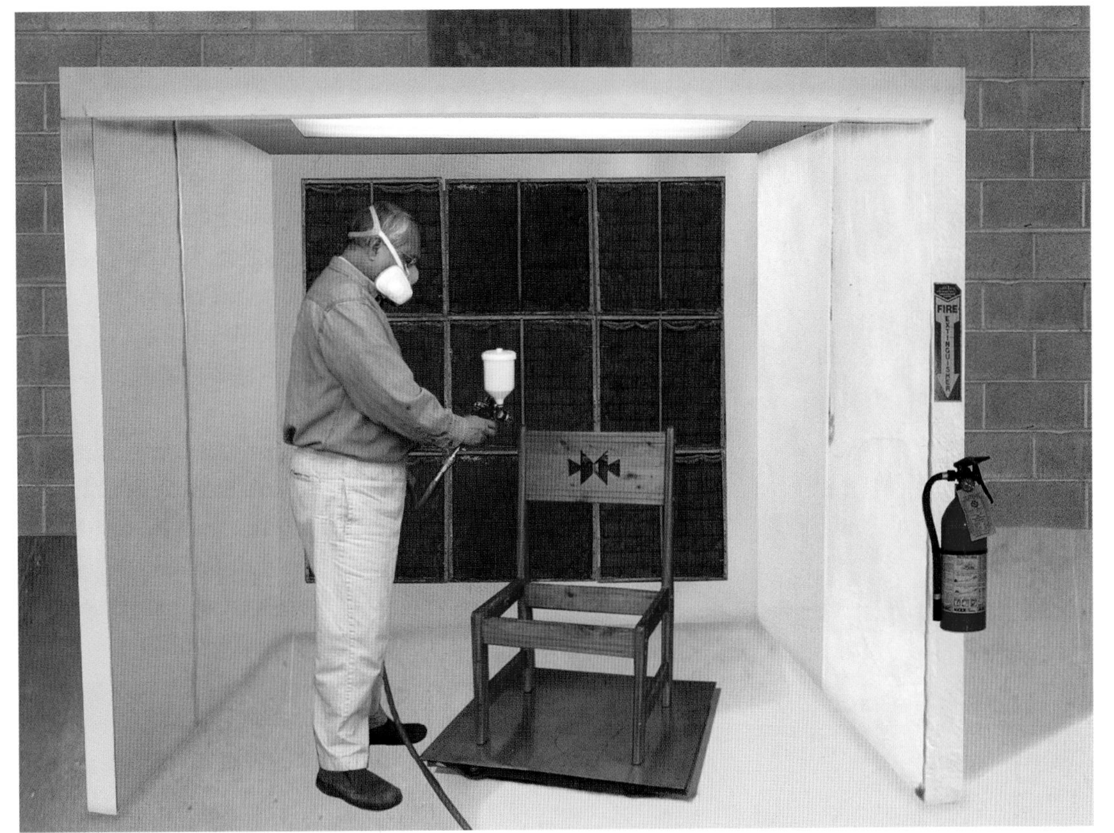

2-12

The ideal place to spray is in a professional spray booth. A spray booth incorporates an exhaust fan with a filter system to ensure adequate ventilation, and a dust-free atmosphere.

2-13 A leg-type booth is suitable for spraying small objects. It doesn't take up a lot of space and it provides a working counter at a convenient height. In this illustration, the red represents the overspray from the spray gun. The blue shows the air flow caused by the exhaust fan. Notice how the air passes through filters at the back of the booth to trap the overspray.

2-14 A full-size spray booth gives you floor-to-ceiling space to spray large pieces of furniture. Filters for the exhaust air minimize air pollution as well. Red indicates overspray from the spray gun. Blue shows the air flow through the filters and out the exhaust stack.

The ideal place to spray is in a professional spray booth (**2–12**). A spray booth incorporates an exhaust fan with a filter system to ensure adequate ventilation, and a dust-free atmosphere. Filters for the exhaust air minimize air pollution as well (**2–13** and **2–14**).

Lacking a spray booth, the next best alternative is to spray outdoors (**2–15**). Unless you have an elaborate exhaust system, it is difficult to provide adequate ventilation indoors. When you spray outside, water down the area before setting up the spray equipment. This will keep down the dust. A slight breeze is good to provide air circulation. Another advantage to spraying outside is there is less chance that overspray will damage anything. When you spray, the air is filled with tiny droplets of the finishing material; this overspray can travel relatively long distances, and if it settles on a piece of furniture, for example, it will create a spot that is hard to remove.

If you are spraying a finish that contains flammable solvents, turn off any pilot lights in the area and don't smoke; the air will be filled with flammable fumes that can explode.

Spraying can produce hazardous fumes that can pose health problems. When you spray, wear a good respirator. A dust mask will filter out the droplets of overspray so they won't get into your nose, mouth and lungs, but a dust mask will not filter out fumes. If the air is filled with fumes, use a respirator that removes fumes. An organic vapor mask uses a chemical filter to remove most common fumes (**2–16**). Keep a supply of extra cartridges on hand and change the cartridge as soon as it begins to loose its effectiveness. Make sure that the mask fits well; if there are gaps between the mask and your face, fumes will leak into the mask. For industrial use, an air-supplied mask provides the wearer with a constant supply of clean, fresh air. A hood or full face mask respirator provides the best protection against toxic fumes, because it protects the eyes, nose, and mouth (**2–17**).

2-15 *Even with HVLP spray equipment there will be a considerable amount of overspray. If you don't have a spray booth, spray out of doors whenever possible.*

Types of Spray Equipment

There is a large variety of spray equipment available, but they all work on the same basic principle. A fluid sprayed from a very small orifice will atomize into small droplets. When these droplets hit a surface, they will form a smooth layer of finish. Most types of spray equipment use air to force the finish through the nozzle and help atomize it, but airless equipment uses a pump to directly pressurize the fluid and force it through the nozzle.

COMPRESSED AIR SPRAY EQUIPMENT

Compressed air spray equipment operates on compressed air supplied by a separate compressor. Air compressors can be powered by either electric or gasoline motors ranging from smaller than 1/4 hp to over 15 hp. The air is compressed by either a reciprocating piston, or by a rubber diaphragm. The air supplied directly from the compressor will be pulsating because of the action of the diaphragm or piston. To smooth out the pulsations and provide some air storage, an air tank is usually attached to the compressor. The tank can be either horizontal or vertical. There is no difference in their operation it is simply a matter of fitting the compressor in to the space available. The

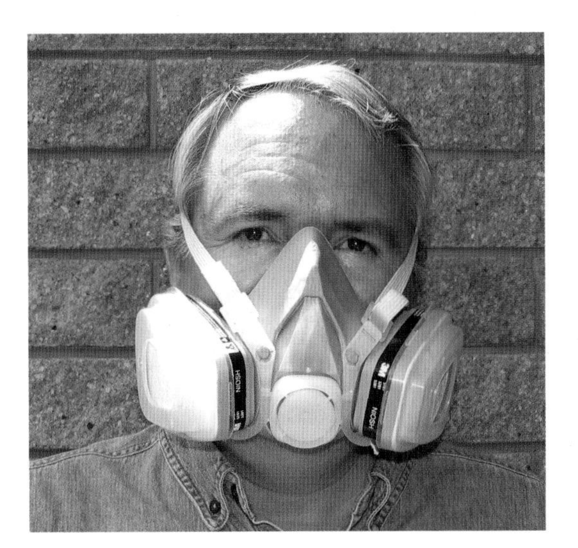

2-16 *The organic vapor mask uses a chemical filter to remove most common fumes from breathing air.*

2-17 *An air-supplied hood respirator provides the best protection against toxic fumes because it protects the eyes, nose, mouth, and entire head. It provides the wearer with a constant supply of clean, fresh air. This type is necessary when ventilation is not adequate.*

2-18 *This large compressor with a vertical tank has plenty of capacity to supply air for any type of spray equipment and operate several air-powered tools at the same time.*

2-19 *This small portable compressor with a vertical tank can supply air for most spray equipment, but you won't be able to use more than one air-powered device at a time.*

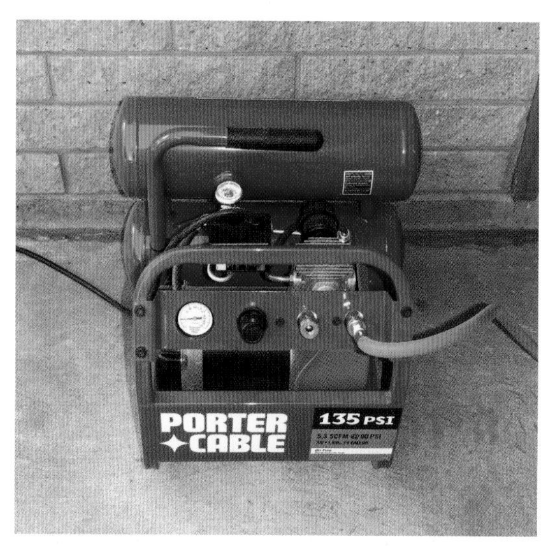

2-20 *This portable compressor with two small horizontal tanks will provide enough air for one air-operated tool or a 4 cfm spray gun.*

important factor is how much air volume (measured in cfm) the compressor can supply.

If you want to be able to run all types of spray equipment and several air-powered tools, you should opt for a larger compressor that supplies over 15 cfm. Smaller compressors will work if you only use one piece of equipment at a time and use spray equipment rated for the lower cfm supply. Most spray guns will require at least 4 cfm. HVLP conversion guns may require 8 cfm or more (**2–18 to 2–20**).

There is usually a pressure switch on the compressor that turns off the motor when the tank is full (**2–21**). A relief valve should be incorporated in every compressor system to bleed off excess pressure. When air is compressed, moisture from the atmosphere is also drawn into the system. This moisture will condense into water; if the water droplets are sprayed with the finish, they can cause defects in a finish. To remove this water along with any oil that may have escaped from the compressor, use an air condenser that combines filters and separators to remove contaminants from the air. The contaminants settle to the bottom of the condenser where they can be drained through a small valve (**2–22**).

The air condenser should be drained at least once a day and thoroughly cleaned once a month. If the equipment is only used occasionally, the air condenser should be cleaned after each use. Some small compressors used for portable spray equipment provide barely enough pressure to operate the spray gun, so no means of reducing or regulating the pressure is provided; however, most compressors provide much more pres-

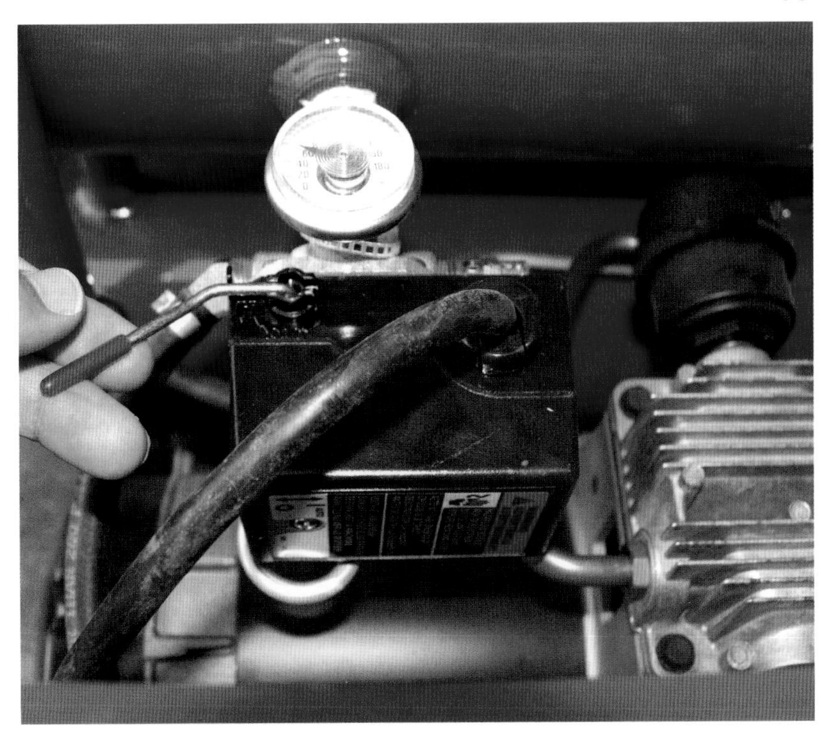

2-21 *When this lever is moved to the ON position, the compressor will run until the tank is full of air at a preset pressure and then shut off. When you use enough air for the pressure to fall below a preset minimum, the compressor will start again.*

2-22 *An air condenser filters the air before it reaches the spray gun. You should drain the accumulated water and oil on a regular basis.*

2-23 *A regulator decreases the air pressure to the proper setting for the material being applied.*

sure than needed to operate the spray gun, so a regulator must be used to reduce the pressure to a usable level (**2–23**).

Professional systems may use an air transformer that combines the function of the regulator with the air condenser and a pressure gauge (**2–24**). The air transformer may have several air outlets that can be individually shut off.

***Note:** In the following diagrams red represents the finishing fluid, Yellow represents compressed air and blue represents atmospheric air.*

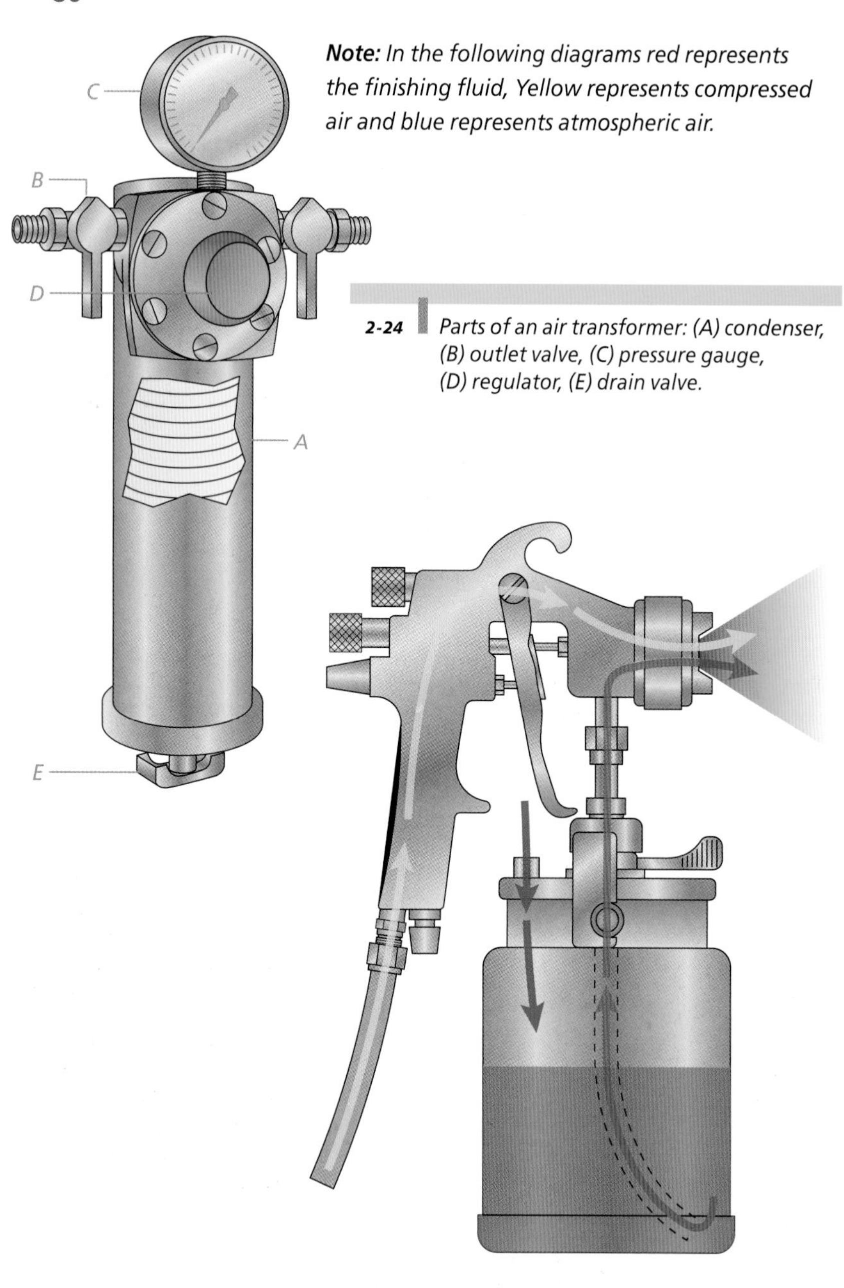

2-24 *Parts of an air transformer: (A) condenser, (B) outlet valve, (C) pressure gauge, (D) regulator, (E) drain valve.*

2-25 *A syphon-feed gun relies on atmospheric pressure entering through a vent hole to force the liquid up the feed tube.*

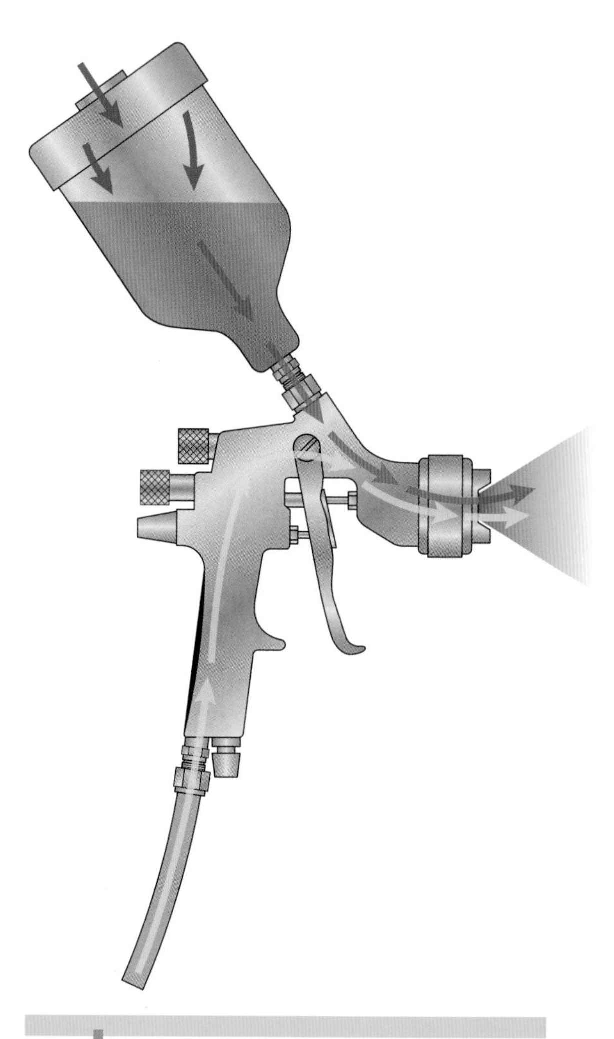

2-26 *In a gravity-feed gun, fluid flows by gravity into the gun where compressed air expels it from the nozzle. An air vent in the top of the fluid cup lid equalizes the pressure as fluid flows out of the cup.*

COMPRESSED AIR SPRAY GUNS There are three main types of spray guns used with compressed air: *syphon feed, gravity feed,* and *pressure feed.*

When rapidly moving air passes a restriction called a *venturi,* a small amount of suction is created. The syphon-feed gun uses this principle to draw thin liquids up a feed tube from a liquid cup (**2–25**). Syphon-feed guns are best suited for applying thin materials like stain or lacquer. Thick liquids, such as varnish, must be thinned considerably before they can be sprayed from a syphon feed gun.

GRAVITY-FEED GUNS The fluid cup of a gravity-feed gun is mounted on top of the gun. The fluid flows by gravity into the gun where compressed air expels it from the nozzle (**2–26**). Gravity-feed guns don't need as much air as a syphon feed gun, making them more efficient. There is usually less overspray with a gravity-feed gun. The fluid cup is usually placed at a 45-degree angle so it can be used with horizontal or vertical surfaces. This arraignment also gives the gun a good balance so there is less wrist strain. Many gravity-feed guns are made almost exclusively of plastic. This makes them well-suited for waterborne finishes.

PRESSURE-FEED GUNS A pressure-feed gun has a sealed liquid cup. Air pressure inside the liquid cup forces the finishing material up the feed tube (**2–27**). This enables the gun to handle much thicker liquids, making the pressure-feed gun more suitable for applying materials like varnish. Pressure-feed guns are available with attached liquid cups or with a detached liquid container (**2–28**). The detached

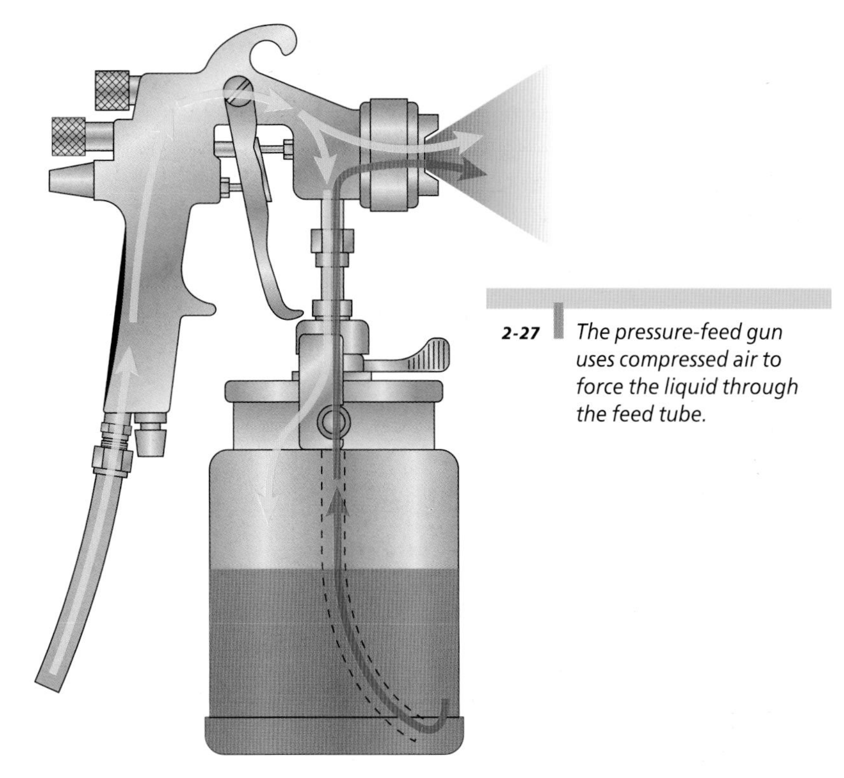

2-27 *The pressure-feed gun uses compressed air to force the liquid through the feed tube.*

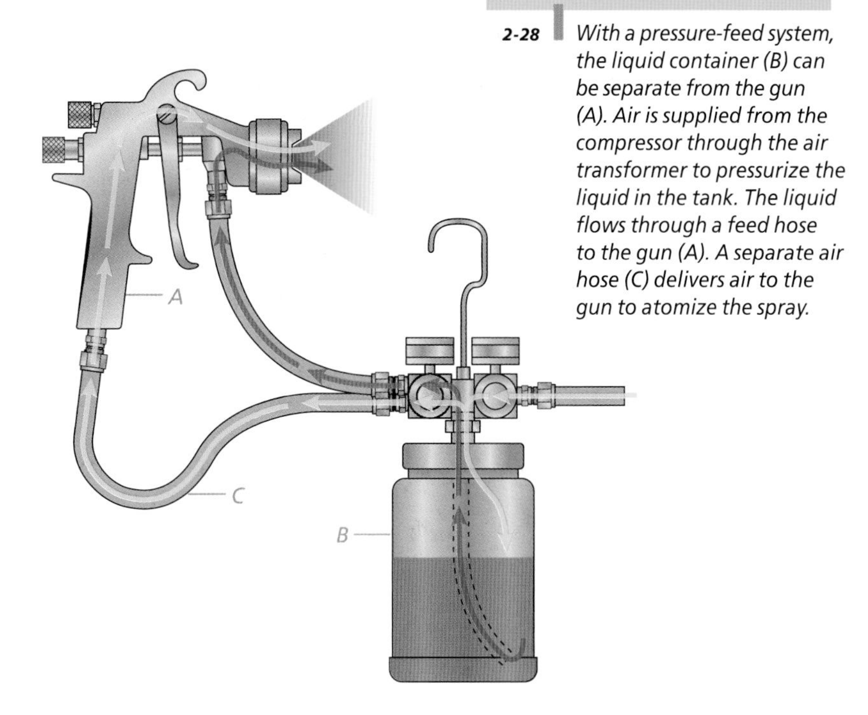

2-28 *With a pressure-feed system, the liquid container (B) can be separate from the gun (A). Air is supplied from the compressor through the air transformer to pressurize the liquid in the tank. The liquid flows through a feed hose to the gun (A). A separate air hose (C) delivers air to the gun to atomize the spray.*

container allows you more freedom of movement and can be larger, so it doesn't need to be filled as often. This can be a big timesaver when you have a large amount of spraying to do. You can get a plastic liner for the pressure pot, making cleanup simple.

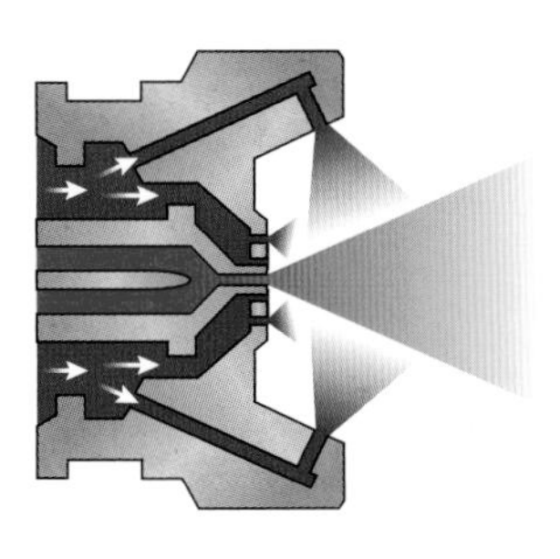

2-29 The external mix cap uses two streams of air to fan out and atomize the liquid stream.

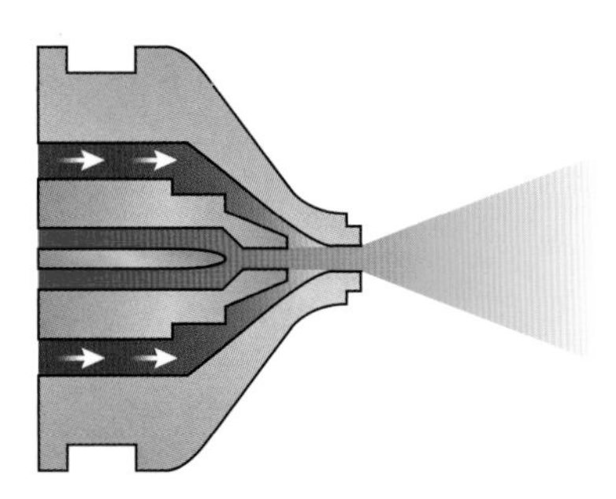

2-30 An internal mix cap atomizes the liquid by forcing it through a very small orifice. The shape of the spray pattern is determined by the shape of the orifice.

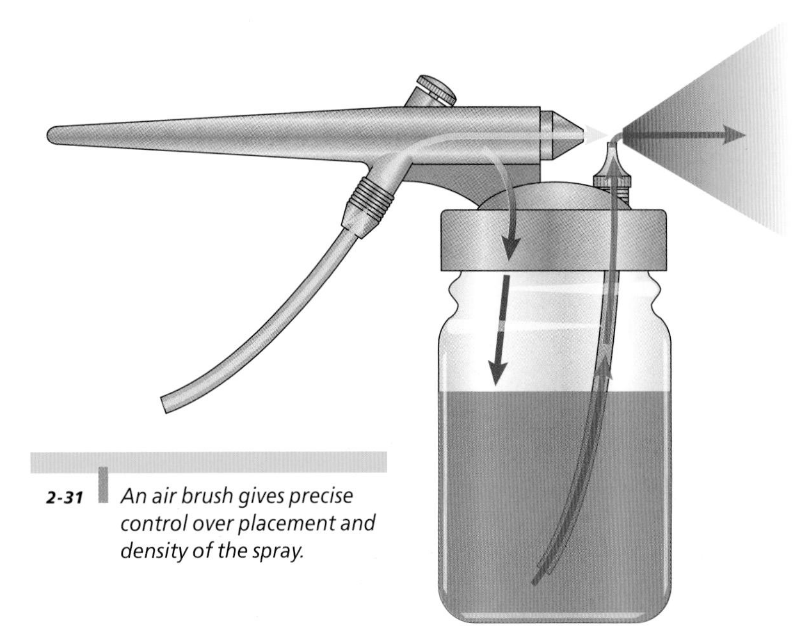

2-31 An air brush gives precise control over placement and density of the spray.

Spray systems that use small compressors without pressure regulation frequently use a type of gun called a *bleeder*; this type allows air to escape from the gun at all times, maintaining a more or less even air pressure in the system. In a bleeder gun, the trigger controls only the flow of liquid, not the flow of air. A bleeder gun is less expensive, but the constant flow of air from the nozzle can be a problem. If you inadvertently aim the gun at the floor or a dusty wall, you can spread dust around the finishing area.

Once the liquid has been fed from the liquid cup to the head of the spray gun, it must be atomized into small droplets. This is accomplished by mixing the liquid with the compressed air. There are two ways to do this: the external mix cap and the internal mix cap (**2–29** and **2–30**). With the external mix cap, the liquid is forced out of a small orifice in the center of the cap as a small stream; jets of air from the sides of the cap are aimed at the stream of liquid. When the air jets hit the liquid, the stream is broken up into tiny droplets and fanned out into the proper pattern for efficient spraying.

The external mix cap is especially well suited for spraying fast drying materials like lacquer, because there is less chance of accumulating a buildup of material around the nozzle. The external mix cap also gives you accurate control of the spray pattern, because you can vary the force of the air jets that fan out the liquid stream. Most professional equipment uses an external mix cap.

The internal mix cap mixes the air with the liquid inside the cap; the spray pattern is determined by the size and shape of the orifice that the air-liquid mixture is forced through. The internal mix cap is less expensive, but it gets clogged more easily and it doesn't provide as accurate a spray pattern.

An *air brush* is a small type of spray gun that gives you precise control over placement and density of the spray (**2–31**). They are useful for applying decorative details or for spraying small objects. Because the density of the spray can be varied by finger-tip control, an air brush can be used to apply stain to wood that varies widely in color. You can apply a heaver coat of stain to the lighter areas of the wood and blend them together by adjusting the spray density.

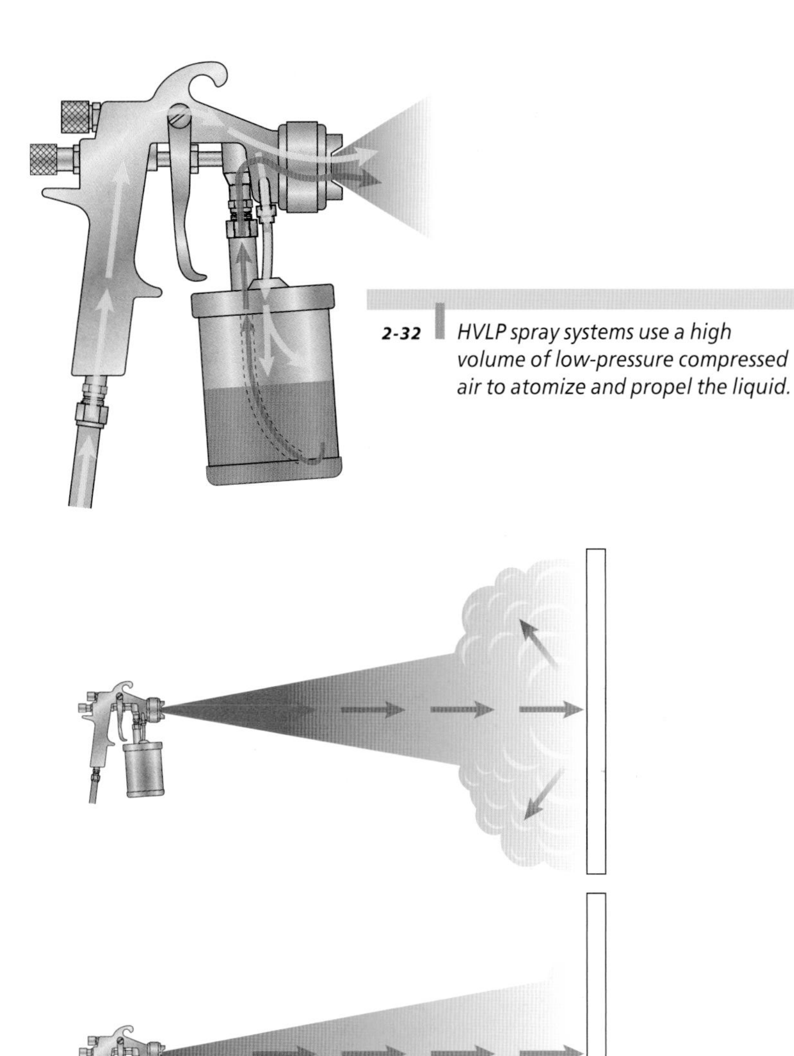

2-32 HVLP spray systems use a high volume of low-pressure compressed air to atomize and propel the liquid.

2-33 When the fast-moving finishing material from a conventional spray gun hits a surface, much of it bounces off, creating overspray. With an HVLP system, more of it stays on the surface because the liquid is traveling at a slower speed. However, even with HVLP there will be some overspray, so be sure to provide adequate ventilation.

HIGH-VOLUME, LOW-PRESSURE (HVLP) GUNS Conventional compressed air spray guns use a small volume of high pressure air to atomize the liquid. This expels the fluid at a high velocity toward the surface. Because the droplets are traveling at such a high speed, a large amount of the liquid bounces off the surface and is wasted as overspray. The measurement of how much finish actually stays on the surface is called *transfer efficiency*. A traditional compressed air spray gun may have a transfer efficiency between 20 and 40 percent. That means that over half of the finish is wasted and it's floating around the room where it can settle in unwanted areas.

HVLP spray systems use a high volume of low-pressure compressed air to atomize and propel the liquid (**2–32**). Because the liquid is traveling at a slower speed, more of it stays on the surface. The transfer efficiency of a HVLP system can range from 65 to 90 percent (**2–33**).

Because of the high transfer efficiency, HVLP systems use less finishing material to achieve the same finish thickness, and they are easier to control. Less overspray keeps the finishing area cleaner and the air more breathable.

HVLP guns can be operated from conventional air compressors or special turbines. To operate a HVLP gun from a conventional air compressor, you will need a large compressor to provide enough air volume. Most guns will require at least a 3 hp compressor. You will also need a gun designed to convert the high pressure compressed air to a lower pressure. Some guns called *conversion guns* use an external regulator to convert the high pressure air. Other guns use internal baffles and valves to lower the pressure inside the gun. Compressed air HVLP guns are well-suited to industrial applications; they deposit the material quickly and efficiently, and they provide a very accurate spray pattern; however, you must have a large compressor.

2-34 A small turbine-driven HVLP system.

For small shops and home use, a turbine-driven HVLP gun is an attractive alternative. You can buy a complete system for less than the cost of a conventional compressor (**2–34**). The turbine works on the same principle as a shop vacuum. It's like attaching a sprayer to the exhaust of a shop vacuum, except the turbine is more powerful.

Turbines can have several stages; each stage is essentially a fan. The more stages in the turbine, the more pressure it can produce. A two-stage turbine is powerful enough to spray very thin finishing materials, but you won't be able to spray heavy-bodied or high-solids materials. A three-stage turbine is probably the best size for a small shop. It is powerful enough to spray thicker materials and yet is still fairly inexpensive. For larger shops, choose a five- or six-stage turbine. These can spray heavy-bodied or high-solids materials efficiently with less thinning.

High-quality turbines should also incorporate two other features: tangential flow and bypass cooling. Tangential flow aims the air from the turbine directly into the hose, while the peripheral flow system used in low end turbines uses an exhaust collar to collect the air from the turbine. Bypass cooling allows you to use the unit for longer periods of time without overheating the motor.

AIRLESS SPRAY EQUIPMENT Airless spray equipment uses a hydraulic pump to pressurize the liquid to be sprayed. This pump may be a large external unit, in the case of industrial airless sprayers; or, in the case of small home units, it can be contained inside the spray gun itself (**2–35**). The liquid

2-35 *A small airless sprayer.*

is atomized by forcing it through a small orifice at high pressure. No air is mixed with the liquid.

The small home variety of airless sprayer is comparable to a syphon-feed gun in capabilities. The liquid to be sprayed must be thinned to allow the sprayer to handle it. Most units of this type require that the liquid be thinned to a very close tolerance for them to operate correctly. To achieve this, they come with a viscosity cup to gauge the viscosity of the liquid. The small type of airless spray equipment performs about as well as an inexpensive syphon-feed gun with an internal mix cap. Because there is no compressed air to help atomize the liquid, the droplets are larger, so the spray is coarser than you would get with a compressed air gun. This isn't a problem for general painting and staining, but it makes it difficult to achieve a furniture-grade finish with some materials.

Larger airless equipment has some advantages that make them desirable for production spraying. The large pump can handle most finishing products unthinned or with very little thinning. This type of airless equipment is best suited for spraying large objects and long production runs. The finishing material can be drawn directly from its original container (**2–36**). The liquid is fed to the spray gun through a hose, so you only have to carry the weight of the spray gun and you can spray in any direction, even straight up. There is also less time lost refilling the liquid container.

Industrial-type airless sprayers do a better job of atomizing the liquid than the small home variety, but they still don't provide as fine a spray as compressed air equipment. To get the best of both types, choose a air-assisted airless spray gun. This type uses a pump to feed the liquid to the gun, but a supplemental supply of compressed air, fed to an external mix cap, helps to atomize the finish. The only disadvantage of this type is the expense; the equipment itself is more

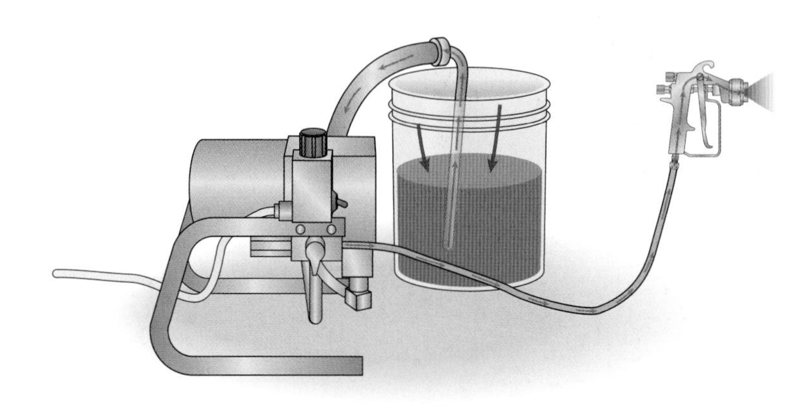

2-36 *A large airless sprayer is similar to a pressure-feed gun. The liquid container is separate from the gun and usually can hold five gallons at a time. Some models make provisions for drawing the liquid directly from the container it comes in. The pump can be driven by an electric motor, a gasoline engine or an air motor.*

expensive, and you will also need an air compressor to supply the supplemental air.

Industrial airless equipment is not well-suited for jobs that only require a small amount of material to be sprayed before changing to another type of material, because it is fairly difficult to clean and requires a large amount of liquid to fill the lines. It is best used in situations where one type of liquid will be sprayed repeatedly. If the system will be used on a daily basis, most industrial airless sprayers can be left charged overnight so there is not a lot of time lost in cleanup. In one shop I worked at, we kept an airless sprayer charged with lacquer all the time. Of course you couldn't do this with the newer conversion finishes because the finish would harden in the hoses.

Spraying Technique

No matter what type of equipment you use, the basic technique of spraying is the same, and technique plays a larger role in achieving a quality finish than equipment. I have seen an experienced operator get acceptable results with the most humble equipment, while an inexperienced operator using poor technique can make a mess even using the best equipment.

The first step is to adjust the gun so it is delivering the proper amount of liquid in the correct spray pattern. The viscosity of the finishing material plays a role in this. Follow the manufacturer's recommendations for thinning the material. A *viscosity cup* is useful for determining the proper thing of the finishing liquid. It is a small cup that contains a measured amount of liquid. There is a small hole in the bottom of the cup; the liquid's viscosity or thickness can be gauged by timing how long it takes for the liquid to run out through the hole. (**2–37**). Submerge the cup in the liquid and draw it out. Start timing when the top of the cup is past the surface of the liquid in the container. Stop timing when the stream coming out of the hole starts to dibble instead of forming a steady stream. The manufacturer will recommend a specific time for the cup to empty. If it empties too slowly, the liquid must be thinned; if it empties too rapidly, the liquid has been thinned too much and additional unthinned liquid must be added.

2-37 *A liquid's viscosity can be gauged by timing how long it takes for the liquid to run out through the hole in the bottom of the viscosity cup.*

Once you have determined that the liquid is the correct viscosity, fill the spray gun cup and point the gun at a large scrap board to test the spray pattern. There are several controls on the spray gun that you

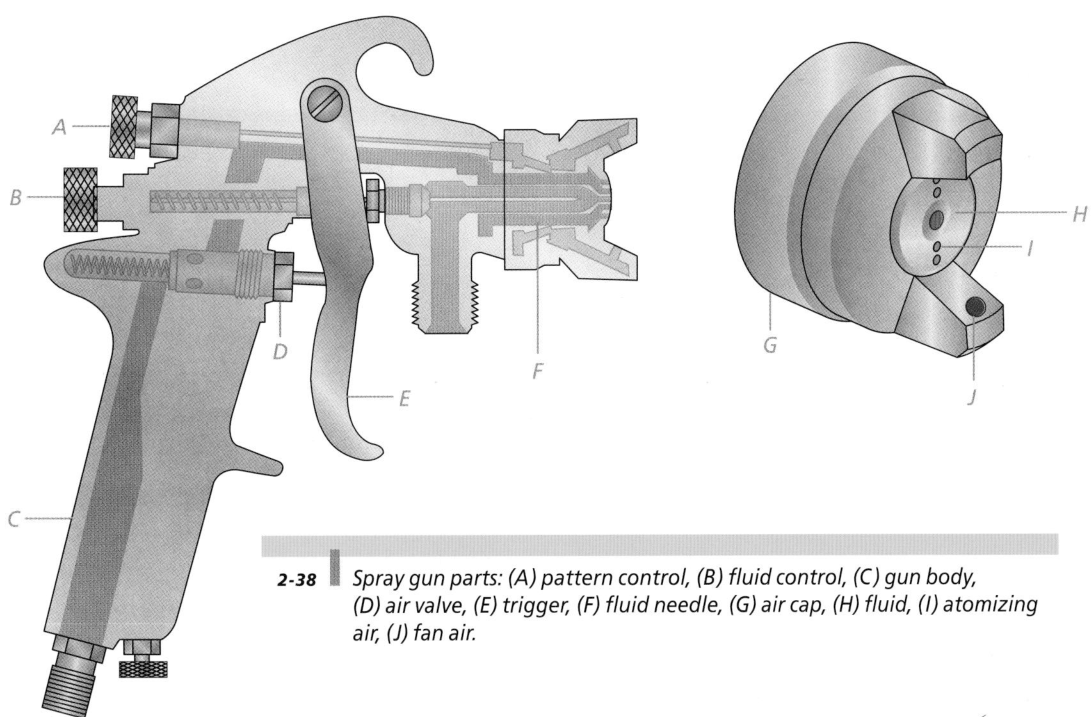

2-38 *Spray gun parts: (A) pattern control, (B) fluid control, (C) gun body, (D) air valve, (E) trigger, (F) fluid needle, (G) air cap, (H) fluid, (I) atomizing air, (J) fan air.*

will need to adjust to achieve the proper spray pattern (**2–38**). Set the air pressure regulator to the setting recommended for the material you are using. Most wood-finishing materials should be applied at pressures under 50 pounds per square inch (PSI). Some guns will have a "cheater" valve that allows you to make small pressure adjustments at the gun. Start with this valve wide open and use it if you need to slightly lower the pressure. Adjust the fluid control until you can get an even wet coat with the minimum amount of liquid. Opening the fluid control too much will result in runs and sags, especially for the beginning operator.

Next, adjust the spreader or pattern control; the spray pattern should be oval in shape and have a slightly heavier coating in the center to allow for overlapping of strokes at the edges of the pattern (**2–39**). The fluid control may need some readjustment after the pattern has been set. Finally, set the pattern for the direction of travel. The length of the oval pattern should be at a 90-degree angle to the direction of travel.

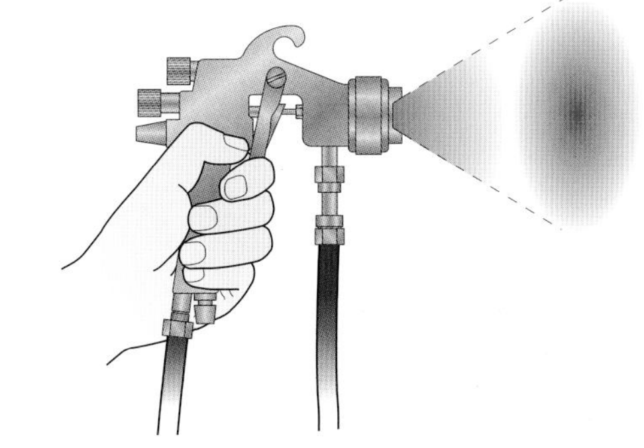

2-39 *A normal spray pattern is oval in shape and gives a slightly heavier coating in the center to allow for overlapping of strokes at the edges of the pattern.*

To apply the finish, hold the gun at a right angle to the surface at a distance of six to ten inches. It is important that you hold the gun at a constant distance from the sur-

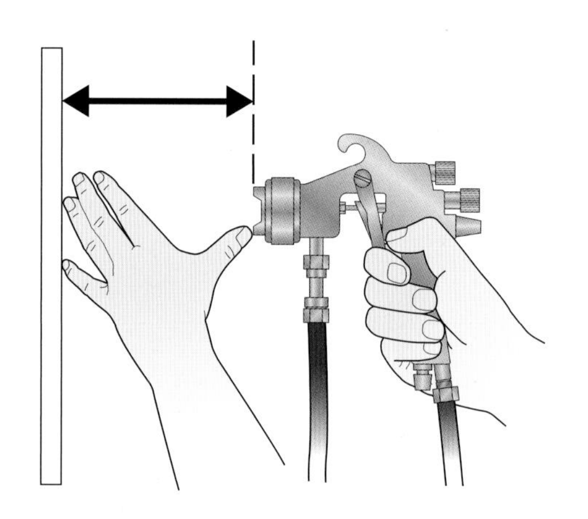

2-40 *You can estimate the correct distance to hold the gun from the surface for most work by spreading your hand in this manner.*

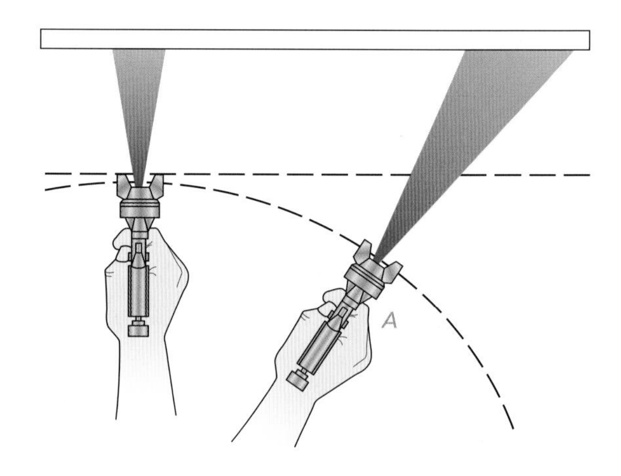

2-41 *The gun must remain parallel to the surface through the entire stroke. If the gun is arched as shown at (A), the film thickness of the finish will be thick in the middle and thinner at the edges.*

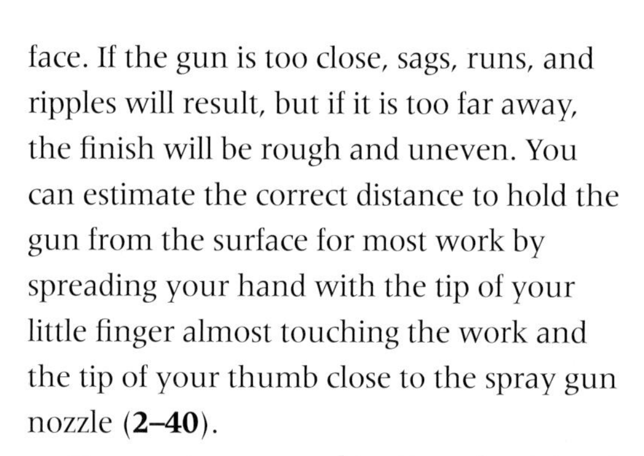

face. If the gun is too close, sags, runs, and ripples will result, but if it is too far away, the finish will be rough and uneven. You can estimate the correct distance to hold the gun from the surface for most work by spreading your hand with the tip of your little finger almost touching the work and the tip of your thumb close to the spray gun nozzle (**2–40**).

You must use a combination of wrist and shoulder movement to achieve a proper stroke with the gun. The gun must remain parallel to the surface through the entire stroke. If you only pivot your arm at the shoulder, the resulting motion will be an arc, causing the gun to be farther away from the surface at the beginning and end of each stroke. This causes the finish will be too thick in the middle and too thin at the edges Instead, you must hold the gun at a uniform distance from the surface throughout the stroke (**2–41**).

Pull the trigger at the beginning of each stroke, starting slightly before the edge of the work. Release the trigger at the end of the stroke a little after the edge of the work. After releasing the trigger at the end of the stroke, follow through on the stroke by continuing the motion of the gun slightly past the edge of the work. This follow-through will help you maintain a constant speed across the surface, so there won't be a buildup at the edge where you slowed down to change directions. At the beginning of the next stroke, position the gun so that the pattern will overlap about one third of the previous stroke. The overlap will ensure an even coating, because the fan pattern deposits more material in the center than at the edges.

Start the first stroke along the edge closest to you and aim the gun so that the overspray will land on the unfinished surface. Spray corners first with the gun pointing directly at the point of the corner.

Vertical surfaces should be sprayed from the top down. Angle the gun so that you don't overspray on previously sprayed surfaces.

When spraying a horizontal surface with an airless or pressure-feed gun that is supplied by a hose, the gun should be held at a right angle to the work. This is not possible with air or airless guns that carry the finish in a cup attached to the gun, because the liquid will spill out and the feed tube won't draw the liquid properly. So with this type of gun, hold it at approximately a 45-degree angle to the surface.

How you position the work for spraying can play a role in achieving a quality finish. Whenever possible, position the work so that its largest area will be flat. This reduces the possibility of runs or sags. Support the work with small blocks or nails driven partly into the bottom of the work or into the surface of a board to keep the work off the floor or spray table. This allows any finish that may accumulate at the bottom edge to drip off. Otherwise, the excess finish may ooze under the object and glue it to the surface below. When all surfaces of an object must be sprayed, it is sometimes possible to hang the object from a wire.

Projects such as bookcases or shelf units that have many small openings are easier to spray if the finish is applied before they are assembled. That way, all of the parts can be laid out flat, and the chance of overspray marring the completed finish of an adjacent surface is eliminated. If you can't completely disassemble a cabinet, at least try to remove the back. This will make it easier to get into all of the corners and prevent a lot of overspray bouncing around inside the cabinet.

2-42 *A run is a large drip of finish that runs down a vertical surface.*

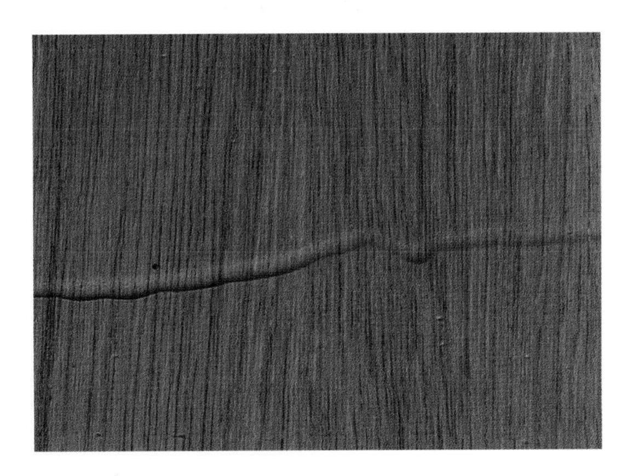

2-43 *A sag is similar to a run, only it covers a wider area.*

When you first begin to use a spray gun, you will more than likely have a few problems. Here is a list of the most common ones along with their probable causes:

Runs and sags: A run is a large drip of finish that runs down a vertical surface (**2–42**).

A sag is similar to a run, only it covers a wider area (**2–43**). Both are caused by too much finish being deposited in one spot. Several errors in technique can cause runs and sags. The gun may have been moved too slowly or at an uneven speed. The feed may be set too heavy. The material may have been thinned too much, or the gun may have been held at an improper angle.

Sandpaper finish or orange peel: A sandpaper finish is rough like sandpaper, rather than being smooth and glossy (**2–44**). An orange peel finish may have some gloss, but it is textured like an orange. Both can be caused by holding the gun too far away from the surface, using too little thinner or the wrong thinner, using too little air pressure with varnish or too much air pressure with lacquer. Allowing overspray to land on the surface of the work will also create a rough finish, especially with lacquer. Don't panic if it looks like a freshly applied waterborne finish has orange peel problems. Waterborne finishes flow out more slowly than solvent-based finishes. At first a waterborne finish may look like it will have a rough orange peel surface, but it will flow out slowly as it dries, leaving a smooth surface.

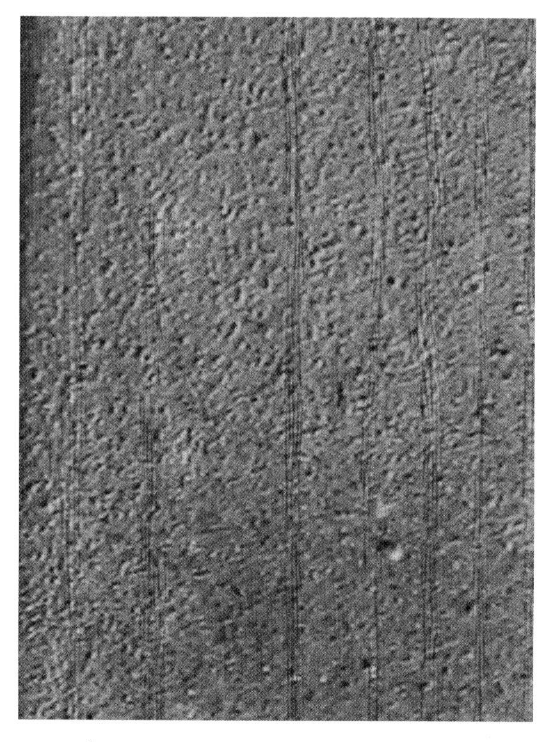

2-44 *A sandpaper finish is rough like sandpaper rather than being smooth and glossy.*

Ripples: A wavy or rippled surface is caused by holding the gun too close to the work or by setting the air pressure a bit too high.

Sputtering: If the gun sputters or spits blobs of finish, the liquid may not have been thinned enough. The vent in a syphon-feed gun may be clogged. The mixing cap may be loose, or its seal damaged, or one of the packing nuts on the control needles may be loose or damaged. If you failed to clean the gun completely after the last use, you will probably have sputtering problems. The solution is to completely disassemble the gun and clean it thoroughly.

Cleaning Spray Equipment

Cleaning spray equipment is not difficult, but if it is not done thoroughly, the equipment will become clogged and require disassembly and very vigorous cleaning. After each use, empty the cup of all remaining finish and fill the cup with thinner.

Install the cup on the gun and shake it around to clean the cup lid and the top of the feed tube. Now spray the contents of the cup through the gun to clean the internal parts. If a lot of overspray has accumulated on the outside of the gun, wet a rag with thinner and wipe off the gun. Use a rag to clean the threads on the cup and the gun and wipe off the cup rubber gasket. On syphon-feed guns, make sure that the vent hole is clear. Remove the mixing cap and soak it in thinner for a few minutes, then wipe it dry. If a rubber O-ring is used to seal the mixing cap, remove it and wipe it off; also clean the seat for the O-ring and the threads to which the mixing cap attaches. If you follow this cleaning procedure, you should not need to disassemble the gun further; if, however, the gun is put away without a thorough cleaning, you will probably have to completely disassemble it to get it working again.

Remove all gaskets and packing rings and wipe them off with a rag dipped in solvent. Don't soak rubber parts in solvent, because the solvent will cause the rubber to swell and deteriorate. Place the metal parts except the gun body in a shallow pan and cover them with lacquer thinner. Let the parts soak for about half an hour. Next, put on some protective gloves and use a small brush to clean all of the parts. Use a pipe cleaner soaked in lacquer thinner to clean out the passage ways in the gun body; orifices can be cleaned out with a wooden toothpick. Don't use wire or other metal objects to clean orifices, because they may enlarge them or create burrs.

As you reassemble the gun, apply a very small amount of lubricant to the parts listed below in **2–45**. Never use any lubricant that contains silicones, because this can lead to a condition known as fish eyes, small round depressions appear in the top coat caused by a tiny amount of silicone, contaminating the finish. The fluid needle packing should be given a few drops of light oil occasionally to keep it soft. The air valve packing also requires light oil. Light machine oil will keep the trigger operating smoothly. The fluid needle spring gets a light coat of petroleum jelly.

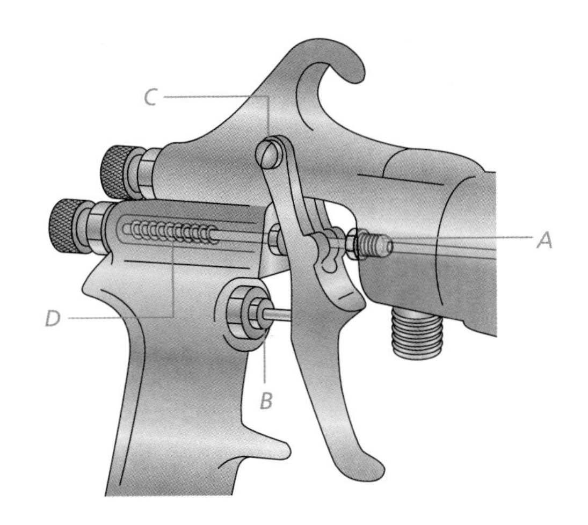

2-45 *Spray-gun lubrication. (A) The fluid needle packing should be given a few drops of light oil occasionally to keep it soft. (B) The air valve packing also required light oil. (C) Light machine oil will keep the trigger operating smoothly. (D) The fluid needle spring gets a light coat of petroleum jelly.*

Aerosol Finishing Products

For small projects, aerosol finishing products may be more efficient than preparing and cleaning a spray gun. You can use spray cans to get professional results, if you use quality products and good technique.

Choose aerosol products carefully; inferior types will produce very poor results, while a quality product will give results that are comparable to those achieved with a spray gun. The spray head or valve is one major determiner in producing good results. About the only way to be sure if a particular product uses a good valve is to buy one can and experiment with it. A good valve will be easy to press; it will produce a fine evenly

2-46 *An ordinary aerosol spray head (right) produces a round pattern, while an adjustable fan spray head (left) gives results comparable to a spray gun. A pair of tweezers makes adjusting the valve easier.*

distributed spray, and it won't sputter or spit out blobs of finish. The best type has a fan pattern (**2–46**). The fan pattern covers a larger area in one sweep and generally produces a more even finish. The standard type head produces a circular spray pattern. You can achieve good results even with a circular spray pattern, if you carefully follow the techniques described below.

A nozzle may become clogged if you have used some of the finish and then let the can sit for several days before you use it again. Don't try to clean a clogged nozzle with a pin. This usually doesn't work and, even it if does, the hole made is usually too big and a poor spray pattern is produced. Never poke anything into the valve on the can! This can cause a serious injury. The most common place for the nozzle to clog is in a small slit on the stem. Remove the nozzle from the can and run your fingernail through the slit (**2–47**). This will unclog most nozzles. One of the best solutions is to replace the clogged nozzle with a nozzle from an empty can. Make sure that the nozzles are of the same type. Whenever I empty a spray can, I save the nozzle for this purpose.

Once you have found a quality product, you must use proper technique to achieve good results. Always follow the directions on the can. Most products recommend that you shake the can before use. Some cans will have an agitator ball. When you first start shaking the can, the ball will usually be stuck in the sediment at the bottom. Once it shakes loose, you will hear it rattle against the side of the can. The agitator ball helps to stir up the pigments that settle to the bottom of the can. Clear finishes that don't have any solids to settle out don't need an agitator ball. Shake the can for the length of time recommended on the label, usually about one minute. Also shake the can occasionally between strokes as you use the product.

To spray finish on vertical surfaces, hold the spray can straight up. For horizontal surfaces, tip the can to about a 45-degree angle. The feed tube inside the can is bent so that it will pick up the fluid even when the can is tilted; but to take advantage of this feature, you must orient the spray nozzle correctly. The lip of the can usually has a small inked dot. Turn the nozzle so that it points to this dot. This lines up the nozzle with the bend in the feed tube (**2–48**).

As you apply the finish, hold the can about 6 inches from the surface. If you hold the can too close, the finish may drip or run. If you hold it too far away, the finish will start to dry before it hits the wood, producing a rough surface.

2-47 *The most common place for the nozzle to clog is in a small slit on the stem. Remove the nozzle from the can and run your fingernail through the slit.*

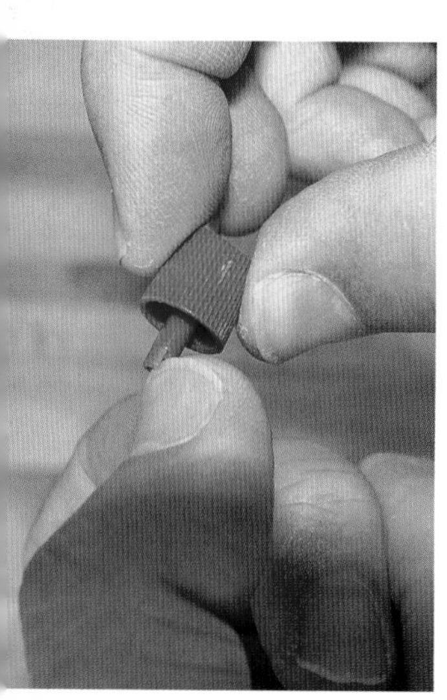

Start to spray just before you reach the edge of the project, and move the can in a straight line to the other side. Stop spraying just after the can is past the other edge. Try to keep the can the same distance from the surface all the time. Move the can at a steady pace. The objective is to spray a light coat that will cover the surface. If you move too slowly, the coat will be too thick and drips and runs will develop. If you move too fast, the coat will be too thin. It is better to be slightly fast, because you can go back over the surface again to build a thicker coat. Drips and runs caused by going too slowly are more difficult to deal with.

If drips and runs do develop, wipe them off while they are still wet. Use a clean rag, then spray a little more in the same area.

2-48 *The feed tube inside of an aerosol can is bent to allow it to pick up the liquid even when the can is almost empty and tilted 45 degrees. Notice the agitator ball. It helps mix pigmented material. Clear finishes may not have an agitator ball.*

After the coat is dry, you will probably need to sand the area with 220-grit sandpaper before applying another coat.

You can buy a handle that will fit onto most aerosol cans. This makes the product behave more like a spray gun. If you will be doing a lot of work with spray cans, this accessory will make it less tiring on your fingers and give you more control (**2–49**).

If you can't find the finishing product you need in an aerosol can, you can use the sprayer shown in **2–50**. This aerosol sprayer has a removable glass jar that can be filled with any liquid. Thin the liquid to the same viscosity that you would use with a siphon-feed spray gun.

2-49 *This handle makes a spray can behave more like a spray gun.*

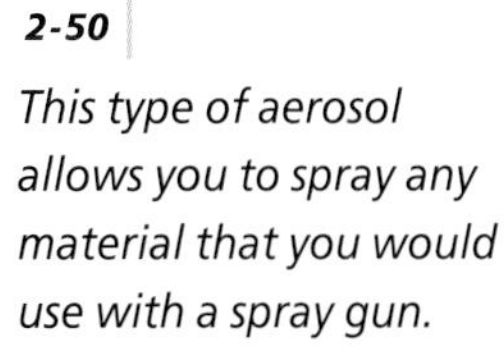

2-50 *This type of aerosol allows you to spray any material that you would use with a spray gun.*

Staining and Filling Wood

Each species of wood has a natural color that is enhanced by the application of a clear finish. Individual boards will have slight color variations. Also, the effects of time can change the color of a board. As the wood that has been left unfinished or given a clear finish ages, a natural darkening occurs; this acquired color is called *patina*. As time went on, people became accustomed to the patina achieved over hundreds of years and wanted to duplicate it on new work without waiting for it to occur naturally, so the process of staining was born.

Today stains are used to color almost all wood that receives a clear finish. However, there are some woods such as walnut, cherry, rosewood, mahogany, and oak that are so beautifully colored naturally that they

3-1 *A pastel stain includes white pigments to give the wood a light color.*

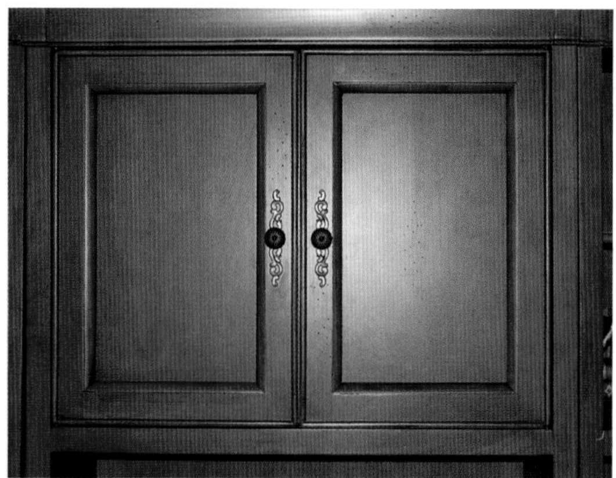

3-2 *Dark stains are often used on light woods to imitate the look of walnut, cherry, rosewood, or mahogany. Dark woods are also often stained to enhance the grain and even the color from board to board.*

3-3 *Birch is an example of close-grained (fine-textured) wood.*

3-4 *Ash is an example of open-grained (coarse-grained) wood.*

are often left in their natural state and given only a clear finish. In fact, most other varieties of wood are stained to imitate the natural color of these naturally beautiful woods. Even these woods are often stained, not so much to change the color, but to enhance the grain and even the color from board to board.

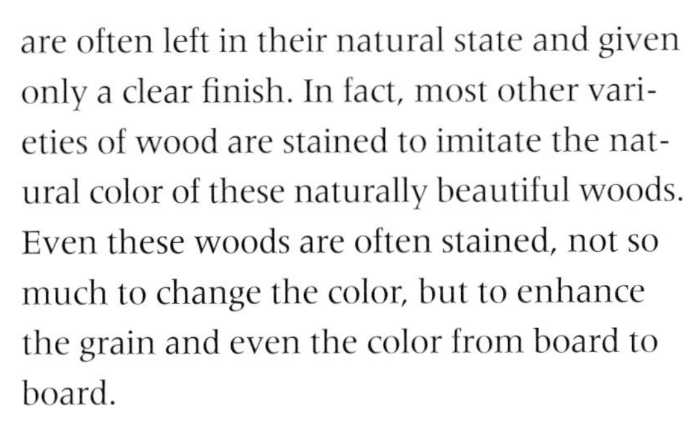

Of course taste in furniture and woodwork is partly a matter of what is in fashion; at times light-colored wood is in fashion and dark woods are bleached and the light woods like birch and maple are left unstained and or given a pastel finish (**3–1**). At other times, dark woods are in fashion and everything is stained dark (**3–2**).

Filling is another process that can change the natural characteristics of a piece of wood. Some woods are closed grained, which means they have pores so small that they are virtually undetectable. Cherry, birch, and maple are closed-grained woods (**3–3**). These woods will take a finish that is extremely smooth and glossy. On the other hand, open-grained woods such as ash, oak, and mahogany have large pores that are a prominent feature of the grain (**3–4**). These woods lend themselves well to satin finishes that allow the texture of the wood to show through. But if a smooth gloss finish is desired, the pores must be filled level with the surface.

Wood can also be classified as either *ring-porous* or *diffuse-porous*. This quality also affects the way the wood accepts stain and filler. Ring-porous woods like oak and ash have larger pores concentrated in the earlywood part of the growth ring of the tree. This means that the grain pattern is defined by the large pores. Diffuse-porous woods like birch and mahogany have uniformly sized pores throughout the growth ring. In these woods, the grain pattern is defined by variations in color, while the pore pattern is uniform. Some woods fall between these two categories, walnut is an example of a semi-ring porous wood that has a fairly even distribution of pores but the pores in the earlywood are slightly larger than the pores in the latewood.

Types of Stain

Stains are dyes or pigments used to color wood. Stains are classified by the type of colorant and vehicle used. (The *vehicle* is the liquid part of the stain.) Colorants can be either pigments or dyes. Pigments are opaque substances such as minerals that are ground to a fine powder. To impart color, they form a thin layer on the surface of the wood. Because they are opaque and lie on the surface of the wood, they tend to hide some of the details of the grain. Dyes are transparent and color the wood by soaking into the individual fibers. Because of this characteristic, they let all of the grain detail show through. Each has certain advantages.

Pigmented stains enhance the pattern of the pores, because the pigments build up in the pores. Dye stains enhance other grain features and do not highlight the pore patterns. You can tell what kind of colorant a stain uses by looking at the stain after it has had a chance to settle. Pigmented stains will have a thick layer of solid matter at the bottom of the container. A *dye stain* remains dissolved, so there isn't much settling. Some stains contain both pigments and dyes. When they settle, there will be a layer of pigment at the bottom but the vehicle will still contain the dissolved dyes.

The liquid (technically called the *vehicle*) used in making the stain also affects how the stain will perform. Water, alcohol, and oil are commonly used. Pigments and dyes are also mixed with lacquer or varnish to make special-purpose stains.

The vehicle must be compatible with the top coat that will be used. You can usually apply an oil or solvent-based top coat over any type of stain, but you need to be careful what type of stain you use under a water-borne top coat. Usually it is best to use a stain and topcoat from the same manufacturer, so that you can ensure that they will be compatible. If the stain is incompatible with the top coat, the top coat may not adhere to the surface. This can be a severe problem that will require you to strip the finish and start over, so it pays to check for compatibility before you apply the finish. If you have any doubts, finish a test sample first.

3-5 *Pigmented stain uses pigments that will settle to the bottom of the container after a period of time. The stirring stick in this photo has been put into the can all the way to the bottom. Notice that only the tip is covered with pigment while a larger section is wet with the clear vehicle. You must thoroughly stir the contents before use and occasionally during use to distribute the pigments throughout the liquid.*

Oil-Based Wiping Stains

Pigmented stains are sometimes called *wiping stains*, because wiping is an important part of the application. Wiping stains contains finely ground pigments. Because it is more of a surface coating than a penetrating one, a wiping stain can be smoothed out by wiping, This type of stain is extremely forgiving. It is slow drying, giving you plenty of time to work, and lap marks and uneven areas can be smoothed out by wiping. Because there is no water in the vehicle, you don't need to worry about grain raising.

Oil stains are most compatible with oil-based varnish. Usually you should let the stain dry for 24 hours before applying any further finish; however, if there is some reason that you must hurry, you can sometimes apply an oil varnish coat after several hours. Check the container label to make sure.

The pigments in this type of stain will settle to the bottom of the container after a period of time, so you must thoroughly stir the contents before use and occasionally during use (**3–5**). Wiping stain can be applied with a brush, by spraying, or with a cloth. No matter how it is applied, you should wipe it with a cloth after application to produce the best effect. Use a clean, lint-free cloth folded into a pad. Wipe in long, even strokes in the direction of the grain. Occasionally refold the pad so that a clean surface is exposed. Try for a uniform appearance that gives you the color desired without hiding the natural beauty of the wood. The color intensity can be varied by how hard you wipe the stain or how long you let the stain sit on the wood before you wipe it. Leaving the stain on the wood for only a short time and wiping it off very hard will produce a light color, while wiping lightly after the stain has been on the wood for several minutes will produce a darker color.

Wiping stains are very useful when there are variations in the color of the lumber used in the project. You can even out the colors by wiping harder in the dark areas and using less pressure in the light areas. In some cases, you can wipe the entire surface evenly at first, let the stain dry for about half an hour, then wipe over the dark areas again to bring them closer in shade to the rest of the wood. Sometimes it may be necessary to wet the rag with a little paint thinner.

Gel Stains

Some stains use a gel vehicle. This is a type of wiping stain that has a thick jelly-like consistency (**3–6**). Gel stain is especially good for beginners, because it is more forgiving. Gel stains don't soak into the wood very much, and so you can even out the color by wiping to a greater degree than you can with stains that penetrate deeper; this can be a big advantage when staining softwoods. After applying the stain and letting it sit on the wood for a while, you wipe it off with a clean rag. You can control the color intensity of the stain by the amount you wipe off. You can also even out the color and eliminate lap marks while wiping the stain.

3-6 *Gel satins have a thick jelly-like consistency.*

3-7 *You can use a varnish stain when you want to darken the finish of something that is already finished in a light color.*

Varnish Stains

A varnish stain combines colored pigments with varnish. It is typically marketed as a one-step finish. Even though you can theoretically let a varnish stain stand as a complete finish, it will be more durable if you apply a clear top coat of varnish over the stain. The problem with applying the stain and the varnish in one step is you can't control the stain as well because you must apply a uniform coat. However, on some projects this isn't a problem. Ring-porous woods like oak take this type of finish well.

Factory-made furniture and radio cabinets from the 1930s through the 1950s used a finish that looks like modern varnish stain. If you want to replicate this look, varnish stain will fill the bill.

You can apply varnish stain with a brush, pad applicator, a spray gun or from an aerosol can. The method of application is more like a varnish than a stain. Refer to Chapter 4 for instructions on applying varnish. When you want to darken the finish of something that is already finished in a light color, you can apply darker varnish stain over the exiting finish (**3–7**). This eliminates the need for stripping, but you must apply the finish uniformly to avoid noticeable streaks. Before applying a varnish stain over an existing finish, clean the surface with a wax remover and dull the gloss with 220-grit sandpaper.

Pigmented Waterborne Stains

Pigmented waterborne stains are very popular because they are nonflammable, release fewer harmful fumes, and water can be used

Wood Conditioners

Some light-colored woods—pine and birch in particular—will sometimes look muddy when a very dark stain is applied. The best way to get the stain to be absorbed more uniformly is to seal the wood before you apply the stain. Most manufacturers make a wood conditioner for this purpose. You apply the clear wood conditioner before applying the stain; it will prevent the stain from penetrating as deeply into the soft parts of the wood, so the overall color is more uniform.

Be sure to use a wood conditioner that is compatible with the type of stain you are using and follow the instructions. Some types must be applied just before staining; if they are allowed to dry for more than a few hours, they will become ineffective. Other types must be allowed to dry before the stain is applied. Wood conditioners designed for waterborne stains also help to minimize raised grain.

3-8 Pigmented waterborne stain looks slightly milky in the can, but it dries to a transparent color.

for cleanup. They look slightly milky in the can, but dry to a transparent color (**3–8**). They perform almost exactly like pigmented oil stain, except that they dry faster. Some types recommend that you first apply a wood conditioner before using waterborne stain. Be sure to follow the manufacturer's recommendations. Even though they are waterborne, they may actually contain some oils and solvents. Some are formulated so they won't raise the grain of the wood as many water stains do. To preserve this property, apply the stain straight from the can without any thinning.

If the directions on the can don't tell you whether the stain will raise the grain or not, test the stain on a piece of scrap wood to make sure. If it does raise the grain, you should raise the grain with a damp rag and sand off the raised grain fibers as described in the section on wood preparation before you apply the stain. Pigmented waterborne stain dries rapidly, so it should be wiped immediately after application. If the color is too dark, you can lighten it by wiping with a cloth dampened with water. However, this method will tend to raise the grain.

Penetrating Oil Stains

When dyes rather than pigments are mixed in oil, the resulting stain is called a *penetrating oil stain* (**3–9**). The stain penetrates into the fibers of the wood rather than coating the surface. Because the dyes are transparent, the stain does not obscure the grain as much as a pigmented stain will. Penetrating oil stains can be applied with a brush or rag and wiped just like a pigmented oil stain. Penetrating oil stain can also be applied with spray equipment. When it is sprayed on, no wiping is necessary if the color is uniform.

One of the most popular types of penetrating oil stain combines the stain with a tung oil or Danish oil finish. This system allows for staining and finishing in one operation. Like all oil-based products, they are flammable and the vapors can be harmful.

Water-Soluble Dye Stains

Water-soluble dye stains are considered the ultimate when clarity of grain and permanence are desired. Commonly called *water stains*, they come as a dry powder that must be mixed by the user with water. The dyes used in water stains are the most transparent and most fade-resistant type. Water stains soak deep into the wood, deeper than any other type of stain. Additional coats of stain can be used to deepen the color without fear of obscuring the grain.

Although they have many advantages, water stains are not appropriate for all applications. Because water is used in the formula, the stain will raise the grain, so before you apply the stain you should dampen the wood with a sponge that has a little water in

3-9 Penetrating oil stain use dyes that dissolve in the vehicle. The dye doesn't settle out. If you dip a stick into a can of this type of stain before it has been mixed, the stick will be dyed a uniform color.

it. Then sand the wood to remove the raised grain as described in Chapter One. Water stain can be difficult to apply and lap marks can be a problem if you let one section dry before you apply stain to an adjoining section. Water stains may cause thin veneers to swell and buckle.

Water stain must be mixed with warm water before use. A small bottle of the dry stain usually makes two quarts of liquid. To prepare the stain, heat the water to boiling and let it cool slightly. Add the contents of the bottle to the water and stir. You can mix smaller or larger quantities as long as you observe the same proportions. Finishing suppliers sell disposable mixing containers and gradated measuring cups that make it easy to measure and mix the ingredients (**3–10**). Let the mixture cool and store the mixed stain in a glass or plastic container. Don't store it in metal. The stain tends to oxidize metal, and the resulting compounds in the stain will create unintended colors to appear when the stain is applied to the wood.

Applying water stain takes more skill than wiping stains because of a tendency to show lap marks. The best way to apply a water stain is with a spray gun. You can also use a brush, rag, or sponge to apply the stain, but it will take practice before you will be able to apply the stain evenly. Apply a full wet coat and quickly wipe it with a rag to even out the application.

3-10 *Water stain must be mixed with warm water before use. A bottle of the dried stain usually makes two quarts of liquid.*

Tap water is normally all right to use in wood finishing, but if your water is high in minerals, especially iron, it's best to use distilled water. The minerals can interact with chemicals in the wood to produce unwanted stains on the wood.

Spirit Stains

Spirit stains use alcohol-soluble dyes. They are similar to water stains in appearance, but won't raise the grain as water stains do. Spirit stains dry rapidly, allowing you to apply other finishing coats the same day, but because of the rapid drying time, they won't soak into the wood as deeply as water stains and are more difficult to apply.

Generally, spirit stains are not used for complete pieces of furniture. Spirit stains are most useful as touchup stains; the stain will penetrate through some top coats, particularly shellac, so it can be used to touch up an area that has already been sealed. Spirit stains come as a dry powder. To prepare them for use, mix the powder with alcohol. The type of alcohol sold as shellac thinner works well.

Non-Grain-Raising Stains

Non-grain-raising stains have the advantages of a water stain without the disadvantage of raising the grain. However, non-grain-raising stains, commonly referred to as NGR stains, are flammable and toxic. NGR stains use dyes that are similar to the dyes used in water stains, but they are dissolved in a mixture of solvents like glycol, acetone, toluene, and alcohol. NGR stains dry almost as fast as spirit stains, so they are rather difficult to apply evenly with a brush.

The preferred method of applying NGR stains is with a spray gun. For this reason, they are not commonly sold as a do-it-yourself product, but they are widely used in the furniture industry. You can buy small quantities of NGR stain from several mail-order woodworking firms that cater to advanced home craftsmen. If you must apply a NGR stain with a brush, add some retarder that is sold specifically for that purpose to slow down the drying time.

Toners

Toners (also called *shading stains*) are actually a surface coating mixed with dyes or pigments. They are widely used in the furniture industry because they can produce uniform results on a variety of woods. Much of the furniture sold today has been stained with a toner. This enables the manufacturer to use several of the less expensive hardwoods in the same piece of furniture and finish it to a uniform color. Toners can only be applied by spraying. You can apply toners to bare wood or wood that has already had another type of stain applied. Toners are very useful if you are trying to match a piece of factory built furniture. Aerosol cans of the product are available for those who lack spray equipment.

You can make your own toner by adding a compatible dye or pigment to the finish coat you are using—for example, alcohol-soluble spirit stain added to shellac or water-soluble pigments added to waterborne varnish. If you are using conversion products, consult the customer rep that supplies the products for compatible colorants. The type of concentrated dye shown in **3–11** is compatible with most finishes, including shellac, lacquer, and water-based and conversion finishes. Toners will partially hide the grain of the wood, especially if applied in a heavy coat. This can sometimes be an advantage if you are trying to match two pieces of wood with very different grain patterns.

3-11 *You can make a toner by adding a compatible dye or pigment to the finish coat you are using. The type of concentrated dye shown here is compatible with most finishing materials.*

Toners are frequently used to achieve an effect called *shading*. This is most often used on cabinet doors or drawer fronts. The entire surface is stained to a uniform color, and then a toner of a slightly darker color is sprayed around the edges. The spray gun is pointed at an angle towards the center of the work, so that the edges receive the heaviest coat of spray and the coating tapers off so that it gradually blends with the base color at the center of the panel.

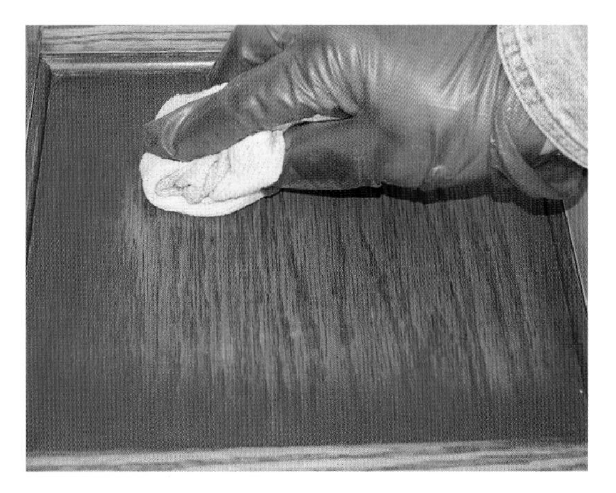

3-12 *You can use a glaze to achieve various effects depending on how you wipe the glaze. If you want to create an antique effect, you can leave more glaze in the corners and recesses.*

Glazes

Glazes are heavy-bodied stains that are applied on top of a sealer coat. Usually you first stain the wood with another type of stain, and then apply a sealer. After the sealer is dry, sand it with 320-grit sandpaper. You can buy specially made glazes or use a thick wiping stain for the purpose. Be sure to use a product that is compatible with the sealer and top coat you will be using.

The glaze is wiped over the sealer. You can achieve various effects depending on how you wipe the glaze. You can wipe it uniformly to alter the color or add depth to the underlying stain. If you want to create an antique effect, you can leave more glaze in the corners and recesses (**3–12**). The glaze will also build up in distressing marks adding to the antique effect. You can also create the shading effect described in the section above by wiping more thoroughly in the center of a panel and leaving more glaze around the edges.

Staining Technique

The stain you choose to use and the way you apply it play a major role in how the completed finish will look. Illus. **3–13** and **3–14** show examples of two different staining techniques. The piece shown in **3–13** has been glazed to heighten the rustic antique appearance. It would lose much of its charm if the color variations were covered up. The piece shown in **3–14** relies on a uniformity of color to give it a traditional and unified appearance. In both cases, the final finish would not have been as well done if a different stain or method of application had been used.

One of the most important techniques in staining is experimentation. Always try a stain on a scrap of wood of the same type as the piece you are finishing to see if the effect produced is what you wanted. Also experiment with different methods of application on scrap wood. The effect that a stain will have on a given piece of wood is difficult to predict without experimenting first. The color samples that the stain manufacturers provide are only a guide, because each species of wood takes a stain differently, and even individual boards of the same species will vary in how they stain.

When you begin to stain the actual project, start on an inconspicuous area first, so if you are unhappy with the result there is still time to change the stain.

Always apply and wipe stains with the grain. This makes any lap marks less conspicuous (**3–15**). Pigmented stains should be applied heavily at first to allow for wiping. Work with one area of the project at a time;

3-13 This finish uses a glaze to heighten the rustic antique appearance.

3-14 The uniformity of color in this chest gives it a traditional, unified appearance.

for example, apply the stain to one door of a cabinet and wipe it before applying the stain to the next door. If you applied the stain to the entire project at once, there would be a variation in color between the parts you wiped first and those that were wiped last. This is because it takes longer to wipe the stain properly than it does to apply it, so the last part to be wiped has had the stain on it for a longer period of time. If you have to let the stain set on the wood a long time before wiping, you can apply the stain to another section while you are waiting for the first to set if you time your work carefully so that all sections receive an equal amount of setting time.

A pad applicator will make the job of applying almost any type of stain easier. Pad applicators work very well with wiping stains; and the application and wiping can even be done in one step in some cases, as was described in Chapter 2. Pad applicators also simplify the task of obtaining an even lap free coat of water stain, if you can't apply it with a spray gun.

Sanding in the stain is an effective way to deal with grain raising in waterborne stains.

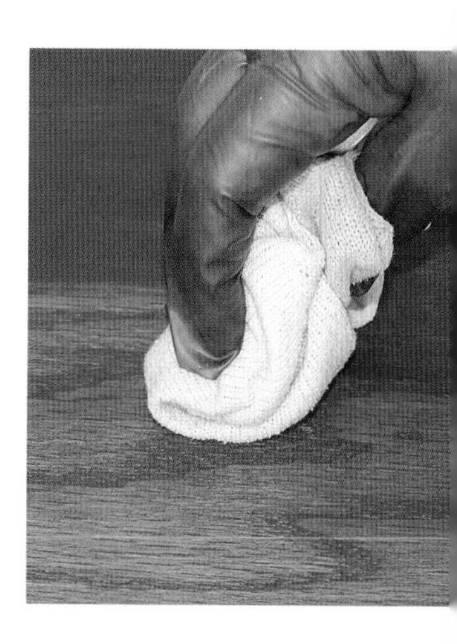

3-15 Wiping is an important part of applying many stains. Always wipe stains with the grain. This makes any lap marks less conspicuous.

However, don't use this technique with stains that require a pre-application of wood conditioner. Use 320-grit wet-or-dry sandpaper folded into a small pad. Put on protective gloves and sand the surface of the board while it is wet with the stain. If the stain starts to dry as you are sanding, add a little more stain. When the sandpaper glides smoothly over the surface, you can stop sanding.

A finishing pad can also be used to sand in the finish; and since the pad acts like a sponge, you can use it to wipe on the stain and sand it in a single step.

If you didn't get a glue spot thoroughly cleaned off before now, you will notice it in the staining process. The area with the glue will not stain well and will show up as a light spot. You can sometimes eliminate the spot by sanding in the stain over the glue spot (**3–16**).

Water stains can be applied with a damp sponge, a rag, or a brush. Use a nylon or polyester brush for applying water stains, or you can use a foam brush.

3-16 *If a glue spot shows up during the staining process, sanding in the stain will sometimes hide it.*

If you are familiar with using pigmented wiping stains, you will have to completely change your staining technique to apply water stains. A wiping stain can be applied slowly, and any lap marks or unevenness can be corrected when wiping off the stain with a rag. When you apply water stains, apply them evenly. Water stains soak into the wood quickly, and lap marks or uneven application will show up in the final finish, if you are not careful when applying the stain. Work quickly and don't let the stain from one stroke dry before you apply the next stroke; if you do, dark lap marks may occur. You will get a more even color if you use diluted stain and apply several coats. Wiping the stain on with a rag usually will result in fewer lap marks that brushing.

Multi-Step Staining

If you've ever tried to match the finish on a piece of factory-made furniture you probably have had a difficult time getting an exact match. That is because many professional finishers use a multi-step staining technique (**3–17**). To apply a multi-step stain, you begin by staining the bare wood with a stain that is usually a brighter and lighter color than the finished look you want. This stain can be either a dye stain or a pigmented wiping stain.

After the stain has dried, apply a coat of sealer. Use a sealer that is compatible with the other finishing materials you are using. Dewaxed, shellac, vinyl sealer or lacquer sanding sealer are often used. Let the sealer dry then sand with 320-grit sandpaper. Next, apply a glaze as described in the section above. If you're happy with the look,

3-17 *The multistep staining technique gives the finish a more uniform color and adds to the visual depth of the finish. A sample of bare wood is shown on the left. Next, a light-colored dye stain has been applied. On the next sample, the dye has been sealed and a dark glaze has been wiped on. The sample on the right has a dark toner applied directly over the glaze.*

you can apply a top coat over the glaze. If you want to modify the color or depth further, you can apply another coat of sealer and apply more glaze or you can apply a toner directly over the glaze. A coat of toner gives the finish a more uniform color and adds to the visual depth of the finish. After the toner is dry, apply the clear top coats.

Filling Pores

Woods such as oak, walnut, ash, and mahogany have large pores in their surface. Because of this, they are called *open-grained woods*. If you want to produce a smooth-as-glass finish on an open-grained wood, you will have to fill the pores. Of course, it is not always desirable to have a filled surface; sometimes the style of the furniture requires that the texture of the wood shows through. For example, oak is commonly left unfilled when a textured satin finish is desired. Contemporary walnut furniture is also usually left unfilled. Whether you fill the pores or not is purely a matter of personal taste and the style of the furniture being finished. Unfilled wood is usually given a satin finish, while filled wood looks good with either a high gloss or a satin finish.

Filler is best suited for projects with flat surfaces. If the project has many intricate carvings, turnings, or cutouts, don't fill the grain. It can be very difficult to remove the excess filler from these areas, and the accumulated filler will ruin the appearance of the project.

Paste wood filler is a product specifically designed to fill the small pores on the wood surface. Make sure that the paste wood filler is compatible with the other finishing products you are using. Read the label of the paste filler before buying the other products, and use the stain and varnish recommended on the label. Some water-based varnish is not compatible with oil-based paste wood filler. If you apply an incompatible top coat over paste wood filler, the finish may peel, blister, or discolor. These effects may take several weeks to show up; so even if the finish looks good in a test sample, problems could arise later.

The traditional type of paste wood filler is oil-based, but the newer water-based fillers are superior and easier to use. The best type is transparent when dry, so it doesn't obscure the grain. For dark woods like walnut, there is a tinted filler available that matches the color of the wood. Since the introduction of superior water-based fillers, I recommend them over the oil-based fillers for most uses.

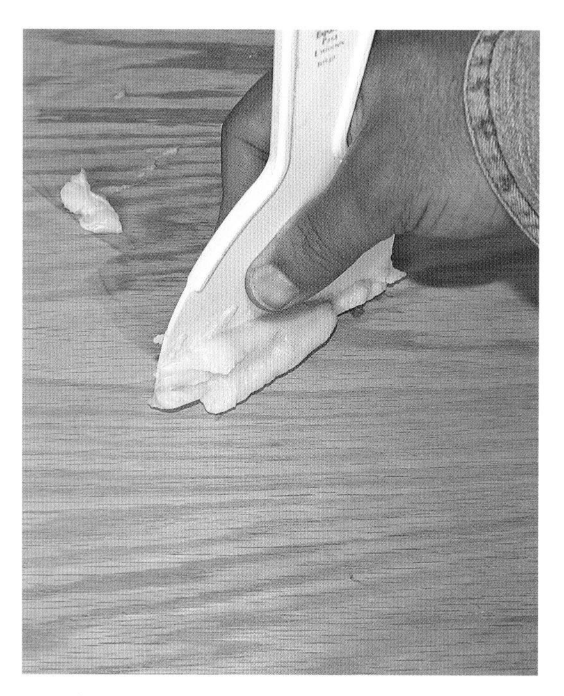

3-18 *To apply water-based filler, spread the filler over the wood using a plastic spreader.*

Water-based filler is usually applied before staining the wood. To apply water-based filler, you spread the filler like butter over the wood using a plastic spreader (**3–18**). Work it into the grain and then scrape most of it off, using the spreader. Let the filler dry for half an hour, and then sand the surface smooth. The filler will sand to a powder without clogging the sandpaper. This step not only fills the grain, but since it is a water-based product, it raises the grain. When you sand away the excess filler, you also sand off the raised grain, so there won't be any raised grain problems in later finishing steps. You can apply a stain as soon as you have sanded the surface.

The older oil-based product is a mixture of linseed oil, dryers, and silex. *Silex* is a mineral that has been ground to a fine powder. Oil-based paste filler is available in several colors as well as natural. Usually the filler is applied after the wood has been stained, but it is possible to apply natural filler first and then stain the wood; this will only work if an oil stain is used.

When applying filler over a stained surface, choose a color that is slightly darker than the color of the stain. This is not a hard-and-fast rule. You can use a lighter filler, but a darker one usually looks better. Sometimes a white filler is used to produce a limed effect (**3–19**). If you can't find a colored filler that suits your needs, you can tint natural filler with Japan colors or universal tinting colors.

You can achieve dramatic and unusual effects by using contrasting fillers to emphasize the pore patterns. Master wood finisher George Frank elevated this technique to an art form. He developed the technique of using bright colored dyes like red or green to color the wood and then using a filler tinted to a contrasting color (**3–20**). You can see more examples in George Frank's book *Classic Wood Finishing* that I was privileged to revise a few years ago.

Paste filler as it comes from the can is in a concentrated form; before it can be used, it must be thinned with turpentine or paint thinner. Thin the filler to the consistency of very thick paint. You should be able to brush it easily, but don't thin it too much or it won't fill the pores correctly.

Applying filler may slightly change the color of the wood. Before applying the filler, test it on a scrap of wood that has been stained with the same stain as the wood you intend to fill. If the filler changes the color of the stain in a way that you don't like, seal the surface of the wood with a thin coat of shellac before applying the filler.

Apply the filler with a brush, working it into the pores by brushing cross grain. Stir the container of filler occasionally, because the solids will tend to settle to the bottom. Don't fill a large area all at once; work with small sections so all of the excess filler can be removed before it dries. Let the filler dry 5 to 20 minutes until it becomes dull.

When the surface of the filler looks dull, use a piece of cheesecloth to wipe the excess from the wood. Wipe across the grain to pack the filler into the pores. Then use a clean cloth and wipe with the grain until there isn't any filler left on the surface, but try not to remove the filler from the pores.

Very intricate pieces are hard to fill, because it's so difficult to get all of the excess filler out of all of the small nooks and crannies. In most cases, it's best not to fill intricately shaped or carved pieces, but if you must, be sure to remove every trace of filler from the surface. You can use a stiff brush to get a lot of it, but finally you will have to resort to a small dowel that has been sharpened to a point to remove the last traces from the small recesses.

Let the filler dry at least 24 hours before proceeding with any other finishing steps. If a top coat is applied too soon, the filler won't dry properly; it may turn gray or it may lift the top coat.

3-19 *A white filler can be used to emphasize the grain and produce a limed effect.*

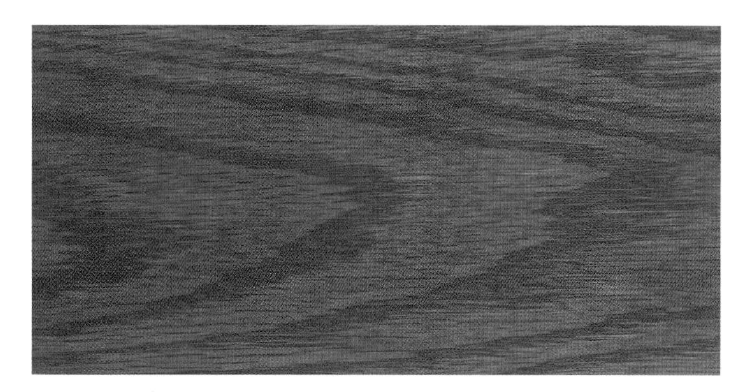

3-20 *You can use contrasting filler for dramatic effects. In this case, the oak sample was stained green, and red filler was used to fill the pores.*

4 Protective Coatings

A wood surface that is not protected by a coating is susceptible to damage from water, natural aging, abrasion, and dirt. To protect the wood from these elements, some type of protective coating is usually applied.

There are a wide range of protective coatings available. Each has uses for which it is best suited. Some are more durable than others, some enhance the beauty of the wood better than others, and some possess qualities that adapt them for special purposes. The protective coating is usually applied over a coat of stain, but sometimes a clear coating is all that is necessary to bring out the natural beauty of the wood.

Protective coatings can be classified as one of three general types: clear finishes, paint, or protective stains.

4-1

Penetrating finishes are one of the easiest for the novice to apply. They produce a smooth satin finish that looks good on contemporary furniture and antique designs.

Clear Finishes

In this book I have grouped clear finishes into three categories. *Do-it-yourself finishes* are easy to apply and provide consistently good results for less experienced finishers. *Classic finishes* are older products that take more skill to apply but, are still within the capability of advanced do-it-yourself finishers. They are typically used to duplicate an antique finish. *Professional finishes* are newer synthetic coatings that are very durable, but they may require special equipment or advanced techniques to apply.

Do-It-Yourself Finishes

If you're new to wood finishing the products in this section are a good way to start, but these products are not limited to beginners. They are often the choice of advanced finishers, because they produce consistently good results.

PENETRATING FINISHES Penetrating finishes are one of the easiest for the novice to apply, and yet they produce such good results that they are the choice of many professionals (**4–1**). Penetrating finishes are marketed under several names: Danish oil, penetrating oil, or tung oil finish are commonly used terms.

Penetrating finishes soak into the wood and harden and seal the top surface of the wood to form the protective barrier. This ability to penetrate the wood surface gives these finishes three inherent advantages. A penetrating finish will not chip or flake off the surface, and scratches and dents are not as visible because the finish extends under the top surface of the wood. The finish also hardens the wood, making it less susceptible to damage. Some penetrating finishes are non-toxic when dry, making them safe to use on food-related items or children's furniture.

Surface preparation is of extreme importance when using a penetrating finish, because the surface of the wood will become the top surface of the finish. For this reason, you should use a finer grit sandpaper for the final sanding than is necessary with surface coatings. This property is a definite advantage for the inexperienced wood finisher, because it makes it easy to achieve a highly professional-looking smooth surface without worrying about brush marks, laps, sags, runs, or dust. The surface of the completed finish will be just as smooth as the surface of the wood.

Tung Oil Tung oil is one of the major ingredients in most penetrating finishes. It is also called *China nut oil*, *China wood oil*, or *nut oil*. It is a natural oil obtained from the nut of the tung tree. It is capable of being polymerized into a natural plastic. It is frequently used as an ingredient in paint and varnish. It produces a finish that is waterproof and is not affected by alcohol, fruit acids, carbonated drinks, or acetone.

Tung oil is one of the more expensive ingredients in a finish, so it is used in varying concentrations in different products. Products containing high amounts of tung oil will produce a very good finish, and they possess the ability to build to a high gloss with successive coats, but the novice will find that products that contain less tung oil

4-2 *The amount of cooked oil in a penetrating oil finish determines the luster. In this photo, the oil used on the sample in front has a high percentage of cooked oil. You can see the light reflected by the sheen. The rear sample's finish has a low percentage of cooked oil, resulting in a flat finish.*

may be easier to use because they contain other ingredients that make the application easier.

Natural tung oil can be modified by a process called *cooking* (**4–2**). Cooked oil is faster drying because its molecules have been polymerized. By combining natural tung oil with cooked tung oil and other ingredients, several types of tung oil finish can be produced.

Tung oil sealer is a deep penetrating product that contains about 20 percent cooked oil. It is used to seal and fill the pores of the wood deep below the surface. It is not used alone but provides a base for other tung oil products. All penetrating oils can be used as their own sealer; some recommend thinning the first coat; others don't. A separate sealer coat is only necessary when very deep penetration is needed.

Low-luster finish is used to produce a finish that is practically flat, with very little gloss. It allows all of the wood's texture to show. These types of finishes contain about 25 percent cooked oil. They dry rapidly and are very easy to apply. They produce the type of finish that is associated with Danish modern furniture. They penetrate the surface deeply and will wear well in applications that receive a lot of traffic, such as floors and countertops, because as the surface is worn away the wood below still contains finish. Additional coats will increase the durability and patina of the finish, but they do not build to a high gloss.

Medium-luster finish contains approximately 35 percent cooked oil. It produces more gloss with fewer coats than the low-luster finishes and creates a harder surface; however, it doesn't penetrate as deeply. Additional coats will build to produce a glossy surface and hide some surface texture. It is about the same as low-luster finish in ease of application.

High-gloss finish, sometimes called *gun stock oil*, contains over 50 percent cooked oil. It will build to a high gloss. It doesn't penetrate the wood as deeply as the others, and it requires more skill to apply. The material must be worked while it is still completely fluid; it begins to gel soon after application and can get very tacky. If the oil has not been completely applied before it begins to gel, it will show lap marks and unevenness in the finish.

Pure tung oil finish is the name usually used to designate an oil that contains almost exclusively natural tung oil with only a small amount of thinners added. It doesn't have any cooked oil in the formula. This type is preferred by many experienced finishers. It is more difficult to apply than finishes with additional ingredients, and it dries slower than those with cooked oils. But the quality of the finish produced is very high.

Other Penetrating Oils Soybean oil, perilla oil, oiticica oil, linseed oil, safflower oil, sunflower oil, and synthetics like polyurethane are also used in the manufacture of penetrating oil finishes. Each manufacturer uses a different formula for its penetrating finish. If a finish is not advertised as high in tung oil, it likely contains some of these other oils, although at least a small amount of tung oil is used in virtually all penetrating finishes. Tung oil is considered the best overall oil for penetrating finishes, but other oils each possess individual qualities that, when properly blended, can provide desirable characteristics to a penetrating finish. Don't rule out a product just because it isn't entirely made from tung oil; try different brands and formulas. You may prefer one that blends several oils.

Penetrating oils are often mixed with dyes and pigments to create a product that colors the wood and finishes it all in one step. Unlike some other so-called one-step finishes, this type really produces quality results. The oil is applied in exactly the same manner as natural colored oils; you can apply as many coats as you like without fear of obscuring the grain of the wood. When you have achieved the desired shade, you can stop or you can apply additional coats of clear oil.

Salad bowl oil is used to protect wood that will be used in food handling and preparation. Although practically all modern wood finishes are nontoxic when dry, many finishers prefer to use a finish specifically designed for food contact. Salad bowl oil uses ingredients that are on an FDA list of matrials approved for use in contact with food (**4–3**). Some finishers use ordinary salad oil for this purpose, but this is not usually a satisfactory finish because the oil can turn rancid; so it is best to use an oil made specifically for this purpose.

Applying Penetrating Finishes Penetrating finishes are usually applied with a rag, but they can be brushed or sprayed. Cover the wood with a generous amount of the oil and let it soak into the wood for about ten minutes. Reapply oil to any areas that have soaked in all of the oil applied.

If you desire a very smooth finish and want to fill the grain of open-grained woods, flood the surface with oil and use 600-grit wet-or-dry sandpaper to wet-sand the surface. The sanding dust combined with the oil will produce a filler that will fill the pores.

4-3 *When applying an oil finish to projects like butcher-block counters that will be used for food preparation, use an oil that is FDA-approved for use in contact with food.*

Steel wool is sometimes recommended for this purpose, but small particles of the steel will accumulate in the pores as well as the filler, so sandpaper or synthetic finishing pads are preferred. Before the oil begins to dry and become tacky, wipe all of the excess from the wood with a clean lint-free cloth. This method works well on woods like walnut or cherry that have relatively small pores.

Woods like oak or mahogany that have larger pores may need an additional filler. You can use oil-based paste filler with a penetrating oil. Apply one coat of the finish and let it dry; then thin some paste filler with the penetrating finish and apply it according to the directions given in Chapter 3. Pumice can also be used to fill the pores. Apply a coat of oil to the wood, and then sprinkle a little pumice onto it. Sand the wet surface with 600-grit wet-or-dry sandpaper. The sanding will make a paste of wood dust mixed with pumice that will blend with the color of the wood and fill the pores. Continue sanding until the pores are full, adding pumice if necessary. When you are finished sanding, wipe off any remaining filler with a rag.

You can apply as many additional coats of the oil as you desire to achieve the look

4-4 *After the final coat of oil is dry, burnish the surface by rubbing vigorously with a clean soft cloth to bring out a soft luster.*

4-5 *Aerosol cans make it easy to apply penetrating oil to intricate carvings.*

you want. Let each coat dry between coats. Drying times differ from brand to brand, so check the label for exact instructions.

After the final coat is dry, burnish the surface by rubbing vigorously with a clean soft cloth or a piece of lamb's wool (**4–4**). You can leave the surface as is or apply a coat of wax.

After a penetrating finish has dried, you can apply a coat of wax to bring out more luster. For the first coat, use paste wax or a liquid wax made specifically for use with penetrating finishes. If you apply a light-colored wax to a dark finish, the wax that builds up in the pores of the wood will turn white and have an undesirable appearance. To avoid this, manufacturers of penetrating oil products usually sell a wax that is tinted dark brown. Use a soft cloth to apply the wax, rubbing it in with a circular motion. Let it dry as specified on the container, and then wipe it off with a clean soft cloth. Repeat this step until you are satisfied with luster.

Penetrating finishes are particularly well suited for carvings because they won't build up in the carving details and they let the natural sheen left by sharp cutting tools show in the final finish. Penetrating oil finishes are available in aerosol cans that make it even easier to apply the finish to intricately carved surfaces (**4–5**).

Storing Penetrating Oil Because these oils dry by combining with oxygen rather than by evaporation, you should keep the amount of oxygen in the container to a minimum. A full container of oil allows little room for oxygen, but a partially empty one may allow enough oxygen to remain inside to gel the contents.

There are several ways to expel the oxygen from the container. If the container is flexible plastic, squeeze the sides together until the oil comes up to the top and then put on the lid. Metal and glass containers require different techniques. Some people add glass marbles to the container to fill up the space. An easier method is to spray in some anti-skinning gas from an aerosol can (**4–6**). This product contains a nonreactive gas that displaces the oxygen. If you will be reusing the oil in only a few days, it is not

4-6 *One way to expel the oxygen from a container of oil is to spray in some anti-skinning gas. This is an aerosol mixture of nitrogen, argon, and carbon dioxide. It is heavier than oxygen, so it will displace the oxygen in the container.*

Important Safety Considerations

Penetrating finishes are easy to apply, but like any product that contains solvents and oils, there are certain precautions that you should observe. First, work in a well-ventilated area. The fumes from a penetrating finish are usually not as strong as those from other products containing solvents, but you still need to protect yourself against concentrated fumes. Use an organic vapor mask to filter out solvent fumes. Wear gloves to protect your hands from the solvents. Repeated exposure to solvents can cause chapping, skin rashes, and cracks to develop.

Dispose of rags used to apply an oil finish in a water-filled metal container with a lid. Oily rags are a fire hazard. Don't leave rags in a pile in the work area; always dispose of them after each work session. Penetrating oils dry by a process called *oxidation*. This means that the oils combine with oxygen from the air to harden. The oxidation process can create enough heat to cause the rags to burst into flames, if they are left in a pile after use. This is called *spontaneous combustion*. You should be careful of spontaneous combustion whenever disposing of rags that have been used with any finishing material that contains oil.

necessary to worry about leaving oxygen in the container, but if you will be storing a penetrating oil finish for a long time in a partially empty container, removing the oxygen will ensure that the product will still be usable when you need it again.

Waterborne Danish Oil Finishes If you want the advantages of a penetrating finish without the toxic fumes and fire hazards, try a waterborne Danish oil finish. They perform well and dry quickly. You can usually recoat in two hours. They are really more of a wipe-on varnish so they don't penetrate as deeply, but they give the same smooth satin look as a penetrating oil finish. Apply the finish with a rag. If you follow the instructions, there usually won't be raised grain, but if you encounter some raised grain, rub the surface with a synthetic finishing pad to remove it.

Maintaining and Repairing Oil Finishes One of the main advantages of an oil finish is that it is very easy to keep the finish looking brand new. An additional coat of finish can be applied at any time to bring the luster back. After cleaning the surface, apply the oil the same way you would apply furniture polish. Wipe it on with a rag and buff it out. Damaged areas can be repaired by applying more oil to the area. If the wood is solid rather than veneered, dents, scratches and burn marks can be sanded out and additional finish applied. Small defects are removed best by applying oil to the area and wet-sanding the defect with 600-grit wet-or-dry paper. Larger defects may require that a coarser paper be used first to remove the damaged wood, and then the 600-grit paper be used to achieve the final finish (**4–7 to 4–9**).

GEL FINISHES Gel finishes combine some properties of an oil finish with some properties of a varnish. You apply them with a rag like an oil finish, but they will build up a surface film like varnish (**4–10**). You can get a high gloss with some gel finishes.

Use 320-grit sandpaper for the final sanding before applying the finish. Don't sand the bare wood with finer sandpaper. Finer sandpaper will polish the surface, making it more difficult for the finish to

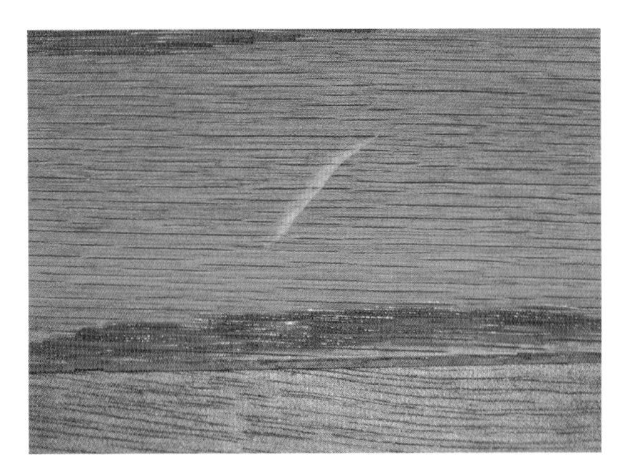

4-7 *A scratch in the surface of a penetrating oil finish can be repaired easily.*

4-8 *Apply penetrating oil finish to the scratch and use wet-or-dry sandpaper to sand out the defect.*

soak into the wood. This type of finish will pick up lint from rags with loose fibers, so choose a lint-free cloth. The type sold at paint stores as a staining cloth is effective, but a household rag will also work as long as it doesn't leave lint in the finish.

Apply the finish to the wood by wiping it on with long, straight strokes. This finish builds a surface coat, so you need to be more careful as you apply it than you would with a penetrating oil. Swirl marks may be visible if you wipe in a circular motion.

Add more finish to the cloth as needed; it's best to keep the cloth wet with gel to lubricate it as you wipe it on. If you let the cloth get tacky, it may leave marks in the finish.

When you have applied the finish to a small section, wipe it in the direction of the grain to even it out. To create a low-luster finish, wipe off most of the finish that remains on the surface with a clean cloth. For more luster, leave the finish on the surface and let it dry. Additional coats will add to the luster. You can get a high gloss with about three coats.

4-9 *After the finish is dry, no trace of the scratch is left.*

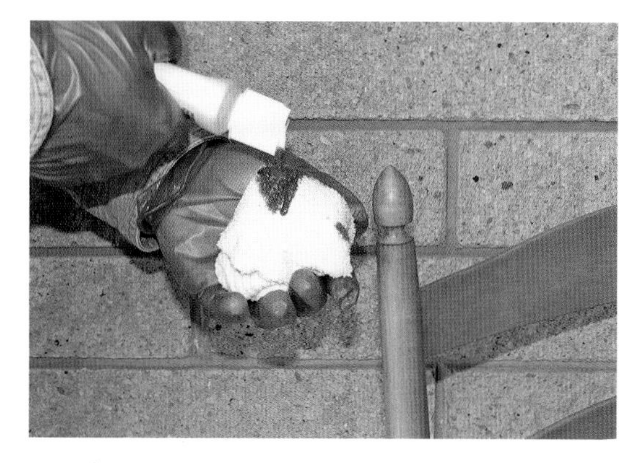

4-10 *Gel finishes can be applied with a rag like an oil finish, but they will build up a surface film like varnish.*

It isn't necessary to sand between coats, but if there are rough areas, sand them with 400-grit wet-or-dry sandpaper or a synthetic finishing pad. To prevent the sandpaper from clogging, apply a small amount of the gel finish to the sandpaper to act as a lubricant. Wipe off the excess finish immediately after sanding. You can use the finishing pad without any lubricant.

WATERBORNE FINISHES Many new finishes use water to replace most of the toxic VOC (volatile organic compound) solvents used in older finishes. These finishes are called *waterborne finishes* because the water carries the finishing material but it doesn't actual dissolve it like VOC solvents. Usually waterborne finishes are an emulsion. In an emulsion, oil can be suspended in water, but they don't actually mix. Waterborne finishes usually still contain a small amount of VOC solvents to dissolve the resin.

Some waterborne finishes are called *varnishes*, because they contain resins and solvents similar to traditional varnish; while those with resins and solvents similar to lacquers are called *waterborne lacquer*. A chemical emulsifier allows microscopically small globules of resin dissolved in solvent to be suspended in water. This gives the finish a milky appearance while it is still wet. The water thins the material to the appropriate working consistency. Once you have applied the finish, the water evaporates, leaving the globules of resin and solvent on the surface. At this point, the milky appearance will disappear, but the surface my look slightly bumpy, like an orange peel. As the globules flow together, the surface will become smooth. After the water has evaporated, the material left on the surface is essentially the same as a solvent-based finish. The small amount of VOC solvent that keeps the resin soft slowly evaporates and the resin hardens.

Waterborne finishes are easy to work with, but they require some different techniques. Use compatible fillers and stains to avoid problems in the finish coat. Do not use oil-based paste wood filler with waterborne finishes, unless the manufacturer specifically states in the directions that the finish is compatible with oil-based paste wood filler. Some companies make a water-based filler that is compatible with their waterborne finish.

Before applying the finish, make sure that all of the wood preparation is done. If you stain the wood, use a water-based stain that is compatible with the brand of finish being used. When the wood fibers on the surface of a board absorb water, they stand up. Even after they dry, they still are raised above the surface. This raised grain can produce a rough texture in the finish.

If you sand in the stain as recommended in Chapter 3, you won't need any further wood preparation. If you are applying finish to unstained wood, you may need to raise the wood's grain and sand the wood again before applying the finish; however, the newest types of waterborne finishes don't raise the grain very much. You may be able to simply sand the bare wood with 220-grit sandpaper, and then apply a coat of finish. After the first coat is dry, a light sanding with 220-grit sandpaper will remove the slight amount of raised grain.

Test the finish on a scrap of similar wood to see how much grain raising takes place (**4–11**). If there is a lot of raised grain, then you should raise the grain and sand it smooth before applying the varnish. You will need a sponge, a container of water, and 320-grit wet-or-dry sandpaper. Work on one small section at a time. Wet the sponge, and then wring out most of the water. Don't soak the wood surface; just dampen it. Wipe the wet sponge over the wood; then fold the 320-grit wet-or-dry sandpaper into a small pad. Dip it in the water to wet it. Sand the surface of the wood, working with the grain direction. If the sandpaper starts to dry out, dip it into the water again. When the surface feels smooth, wipe it dry with a rag. Let the wood dry overnight, and then sand it again lightly with 320-grit sandpaper. By raising the grain of the wood and sanding off the raised fibers before applying the finish, you ensure that the fibers that would have risen are gone, so the finish is smoother.

Synthetic finishing pads can also be used to remove raised grain. Dip the pad into water and ring it out until it is just damp. Rub the pad over the wood, adding more water as necessary to wet the surface of the wood. When the wood is still wet, rub the pad over the surface several times until all of the rough raised grain has been removed. Let the wood dry, and then wipe the surface again with a dry finishing pad.

Use a wet rag or a tack cloth to remove dust from the surface and between coats of waterborne finishes. Although earlier waterborne finishes had compatibility problems with the resins used in tack cloths, today's finishes and tack cloths that have been designed for waterborne finishes won't interact adversely.

Waterborne finishes usually shouldn't be thinned before use. They are a precise mixture of water, anti-foaming agents, resin, and solvent. Adding water can upset the balance and result in excess foaming or poor flowing. If the finish isn't flowing well, add a compatible flowing agent recommended by the manufacturer rather than adding water.

Waterborne finishes are more sensitive to incompatibility with other products than VOC solvent-based products. For best results, use compatible products all made by the same manufacturer. If you must use an incompatible type of stain below a waterborne finish, seal it with a coat of dewaxed shellac or a sealer recommended by the product's manufacturer before applying the waterborne finish. You'll save yourself a lot of grief by testing for compatibility on a scrap before applying the finish to the work. If the products are not compatible, the topcoat may blister and peel.

4-11 *Before you use a waterborne finish, test it on a sample of wood similar to the wood in the project. If the wood is rough after the finish is dry, you should follow the procedure given for raising the grain before you apply the finish to the project.*

Note: Even though waterborne finishes produce less fumes, they still contain some VOC solvents, so wear an organic vapor mask and provide adequate ventilation.

Weather conditions can affect waterborne finishes. They work best around 70°F and 30 to 50 percent humidity. If you must work in a cold room, warm the container of finish in a pan of hot water; don't use a stove or any type of open flame. If the humidity is too high, the finish won't dry well. You can help it dry by placing fans in the room to keep the air moving.

Waterborne finishes react with iron and steel to produce dark stains on wood, so don't use steel wool if you will be using a waterborne finish. Use a synthetic finishing pad instead. Most metal spray equipment is plated with anti-corrosive coatings, so you can use waterborne materials. Some new spray equipment is made almost entirely of plastic to eliminate any corrosion problems.

Natural bristle brushes will go limp in water, so use a synthetic brush instead. Foam brushes work well, but be careful not to squeeze the brush excessively or you will create a lot of foam. Waterborne finishes tend to get a lot more bubbles than VOC solvent-based products. This can be disconcerting at first, if you're not used to it; but most of the bubbles will disappear all by themselves as the water evaporates. Bubbles are usually only a problem if you allow a lot of foam to remain on the surface.

WATERBORNE VARNISHES If you tried a waterborne varnish several years ago and were disappointed with the results, don't let that prevent you from trying the new waterborne varnishes. Many of the new varnishes perform as well or better than VOC-based varnishes. Once a waterborne varnish is dry, it is resistant to water, detergents, and alcohol. Waterborne varnishes are much more pleasant to work with than VOC-based varnishes. There are less fumes, and the varnish can be cleaned up with water while wet. Even though these products are very safe, you should still wear plastic gloves and an organic vapor mask when using them.

When applying varnish, work in a clean, dust-free area. Waterborne varnish will dry more quickly than solvent-based varnish so dust isn't as big a problem, but each particle of dust that lands on the project during that time will create a small bump (called a *dust nib*) on the surface. Remove all dust from the project before applying the varnish. Use a vacuum with a brush attachment or a bristle brush to remove most of the dust, and then wipe the surface with a wet rag to remove the last remaining dust. Read and follow the directions on the varnish container carefully. Each product has some different characteristics.

4-12 *The waterborne varnish on this brush appears milky white, but it will dry crystal-clear.*

When you open the can of varnish, it may look milky white, but don't worry: waterborne varnish dries crystal-clear (**4–12**). In fact, it is so clear that some manufacturers offer an amber additive to give the finish the look of traditional varnish, which has an amber tint. Unless you want to give the wood an amber tint, this additive is not necessary.

Before using the varnish, gently stir it with a paint-stirring stick. Don't shake the can or use a drill-mounted paint stirrer, because this creates too many bubbles. Apply the varnish to one section of the project at a time. Apply a thin coat of varnish with a synthetic bristle brush (**4–13**). A foam brush may cause bubbles in some types of waterborne varnish. Dip the brush into the var-

4-13 *Apply waterborne varnish quickly and work on one small section at a time. Brush in long, straight strokes in the direction of the grain of the wood. Once you cover the section, quickly brush over it again lightly without adding any more varnish.*

nish until the bristles are about half way into the varnish. Gently wipe the excess varnish off on the lip of the can, trying not to create any bubbles. You usually can't eliminate all of the bubbles in waterborne varnish; even if you don't make any in the can, air escaping from the wood will create a few bubbles. Don't worry if there are a few bubbles in the varnish; usually they will pop and flow out before the varnish dries.

Apply the varnish quickly and work on one small section at a time. Brush in long, straight strokes in the direction of the grain of the wood. Once you cover the section, quickly brush over it again lightly without adding any more varnish. This will even out the application. Since most waterborne varnishes begin to dry soon after application, try to get a smooth coat with the initial application. If you go back to try to smooth out irregularities later, the varnish may have begun to dry. Brushing over it a second time will roughen it instead of smoothing it out.

Most waterborne varnishes should be sanded between coats. Because varnish doesn't burn-in to previous coats, the finish won't adhere to the surface well if you don't remove the gloss by sanding.

Sanding also removes any raised grain, brush marks, or dust nibs. Use 320-grit sandpaper or a synthetic finishing pad for sanding between coats. Do not use steel wool. Steel wool can leave behind small steel fibers that will react with the next coat of varnish to leave a discolored spot. Sanding waterborne finishes with stearated antiloading sand paper used to cause fish eye problems, but today most manufacturers have changed the way they make antiloading sandpaper to make it compatible with waterborne finishes. Make sure that the finish is completely dry before you begin to sand. If it is still wet, sanding it will cause it to ball up and leave large streaks on the surface.

A synthetic finishing pad is the easiest way to prepare the surface for the next coat. Rub the pad over the varnish in long, straight strokes with the direction of the grain. Stop when the surface is uniformly dull (**4–14**).

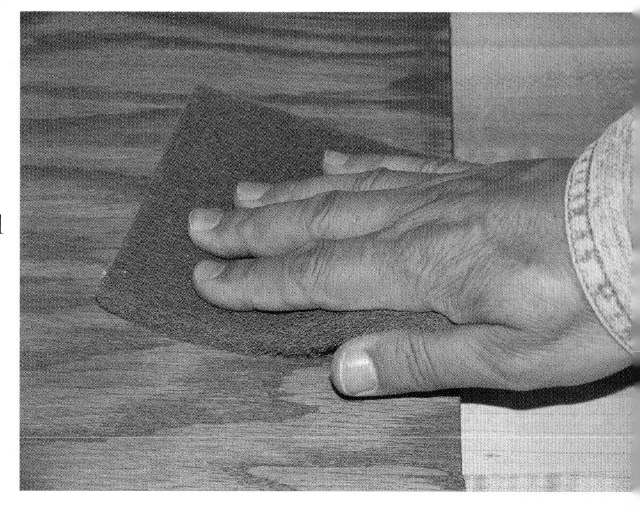

4-14 *Use a synthetic finishing pad to prepare the surface for the next coat. Rub the pad over the varnish in long, straight strokes with the direction of the grain. Stop when the surface is uniformly dull.*

Don't rub too hard or you may cut completely through the varnish.

If you use sandpaper, use a sanding block with a soft backing to prevent the sandpaper from cutting into the finish and allow the sandpaper to follow small irregularities in the surface so that the entire surface gets sanded evenly. The reason for sanding between coats is to create a uniformly dull surface and to level off any raised grain or dust nibs; there is no need to remove a lot of material. Sand with the grain using light pressure on the sanding block. When you are done sanding, wipe away the dust with a damp cloth.

You can apply waterborne varnish to flat areas such as floors with a lamb's wool pad applicator. This is a finishing tool that resembles a sponge mop wrapped with lamb's wool. To use a pad applicator, pour some of the varnish into a roller tray. Dip the applicator into the varnish, and then squeeze it against the sloped part of the tray to remove the excess. Place the pad on the work and move it in a steady stroke from one end to the other. Apply moderate downward pressure to the pad, and tilt it slightly so that it is more compressed at the back. This will spread out the varnish in a very thin, smooth coat.

The pad applicator will hold a lot of varnish, so you may be able to make a complete pass before you add more varnish. This produces a very smooth coat of varnish. Dip the pad into the varnish again for the next stroke. Overlap the strokes about 1/2 inch.

SOLVENT-BASED VARNISHES Varnishes that use large quantities of VOC solvents instead of water are called solvent-based varnishes. They emit toxic fumes and can pose a fire hazard, but they are still popular, because they don't raise the grain at all, and they don't have as many compatibility issues as waterborne varnish.

Most solvent-based varnishes used today are made with synthetic resin. They are easier to use, more durable, and more versatile than the older natural oil varnishes. They are also faster drying than natural oil varnish, so there is less chance of dust accumulating on the wet surface. The most popular synthetics are *acrylic, polyurethane, alkyd,* and *phenolic.* Polyurethane is probably the most universal of the synthetics; it is used for interior as well as exterior work and produces a hard and durable finish. Phenolics are used in some exterior- and marine-grade finishes.

You can apply the varnish with a brush or spray equipment. The varnish usually must be thinned with solvent before spraying. Some varnishes will react with paste filler, turning the filler gray; and some stains will bleed through varnish. To solve either problem, you may want to consider using a sanding sealer made specifically for the purpose before varnishing.

Always varnish in a well-ventilated area that is relatively dust-free. Because varnish dries so slowly, dust is a major problem. Damp mopping the floor just before varnishing will help to keep the dust down. Wipe the surface to be varnished with a tack rag to remove as much dust as possible. Stir satin varnish, because it contains a flattening agent that will settle to the bottom of the can. Stir it slowly and try to avoid whipping air into the varnish.

Varnishing Problems

Modern varnishes are quire foolproof and will produce acceptable results even when they are applied improperly, but there are still problems that occur:

Fish eyes and crawling: When the surface that the varnish is applied to has a greasy or oily substance on it, the varnish won't adhere well. When the area is small, a round depression, called a *fish eye*, is formed. If the area is large, the problem is referred to as *crawling*. The best solution to this problem is to prevent its occurrence. Keep anything that contains grease, oil or silicones away from the surface to be finished. This problem is most prevalent when varnishing previously finished surfaces. Furniture wax and many household products contain silicones and other substances that will cause this problem. Some strippers contain wax that can also affect the adhesion of the final finish if they are not removed. When you suspect that the work may be contaminated by one of these substances, wash the surface with lacquer thinner or with a special silicone remover sold for this purpose.

Fish eyes and crawls are very hard to repair once they occur; if they cover a large area, the best bet is to remove the varnish with a rag soaked with thinner before the varnish is completely dry and start over. Small fish eyes can be sanded out but large ones will leave a noticeable depression if they are sanded out.

Rough texture: A rough surface texture can result if dust is allowed to settle on the varnish before it is dry. Dust in the surface is very easy to recognize; the rest of the surface will be smooth and glossy, but where the dust has landed there will be a small pointed bump. Sometimes the dust fiber will extend out of the top of the bump like a small hair. These dust nibs can be sanded out and will not affect the next coat, if they are sanded completely level with the surrounding surface. As you sand a dust nib, you will notice that they are usually surrounded by a circular area that is depressed below the surrounding area. This is because the dust acts as a wick conducting material from around the dust fiber up to a point. This makes thoroughly sanding out a dust nib a little more difficult, because the entire area must be sanded down to the low point of the depression.

A rough surface can also result when the wood was not thoroughly sanded beforehand. Varnishing causes preexisting defects to become more apparent.

Using old varnish that has skinned over or has a lot of material that has settled to the bottom can also create a rough surface.

If the varnish is applied too sparingly and brushed excessively, the surface will show brush marks and lap marks that didn't level themselves.

Runs and sags are caused by applying the varnish too heavily to a vertical surface. The surface tension of the varnish cannot hold it against the force of gravity. If you notice a run or sag while the varnish is still wet or after the varnish has become tacky, you may be able to remove it with a rag damp with thinner; and then brush a little fresh varnish over the area. Runs that have dried must be sanded out.

Wrinkling is another problem that is caused by applying too much varnish in one coat. It is mostly likely to occur in corners and joints where the varnish from two adjoining surfaces run together. The varnish is so thick in these areas that the top skins over before the varnish has a chance to dry. As the varnish below does eventually dry, it contracts, causing wrinkles in the skin that formed first. To prevent wrinkling, brush out any area that may accumulate an excess of varnish. Once wrinkling occurs, let the varnish thoroughly dry and sand out the wrinkles. The wrinkled area will take much longer to dry than normal because the varnish is so thick. If it is not completely dry when it is sanded, the varnish will roll up into gummy balls and pull away from the surface, creating a depression.

Classic Finishes

When you want to duplicate the look of an older finish, you may choose to use one of the classic finishes described in this section. They have been in use for many years and they can often provide a subtle beauty that is difficult to achieve with more modern finishes. However, they generally are not as durable as modern finishes.

Traditional Linseed-Oil Finish

Modern penetrating finishes have mostly replaced the traditional linseed-oil finish. Linseed oil is not as water resistant as the modern oils, and it will darken with age. However, if you are trying to duplicate an antique finish, you may want to use traditional linseed-oil finish (**4–15**).

4-15 *A traditional linseed oil finish on mahogany.*

If you are used to working with modern penetrating oils, you will have to change your procedure when using linseed oil. Modern penetrating oils can be applied in a heavy, wet coat, because they are formulated to dry rapidly and harden even if a lot of oil has soaked into the wood. If you use this technique with linseed oil, the oil that has soaked into the wood will take a very long time to dry. The undried oil in the wood can bleed onto the surface at a later date, causing small spots of oil that will leave the surface glossier in some areas than the surrounding finish. The best procedure for applying linseed oil is to apply it in very thin coats and allow each coat to dry overnight.

You can use either raw or boiled linseed oil for this finish. Raw linseed oil does eventually dry; it just dries more slowly than the boiled oil and its drying time is unpredictable; sometimes it will remain tacky for weeks. If you use raw oil, allow at least three days between coats to make sure that the oil has had plenty of time to dry. The drying times given in the directions below are for boiled linseed oil.

The first coat of oil will rapidly soak into the wood. When this coat dries, it will partially seal the wood so that additional coats will not soak in as rapidly. Wipe the oil on with a rag and buff it using a lot of hand pressure. Wipe the oil off the surface before it starts to get gummy. Wipe it hard so that all of the oil left on the surface is removed. The only oil you want to remain is the oil that has soaked into the wood. Oil left on the surface will get tacky and attract dust.

Let the first coat of oil dry two days, to ensure that the oil has had a chance to polymerize. If you apply additional coats too soon, the first coat of oil may bleed through onto the surface. For the second coat of oil and all subsequent coats, wipe on a thin coat with a rag and buff it hard to make sure that you have wiped off all of the excess oil. Don't allow any wet oil to remain on the wood surface, or it can get gummy and attract dust. You can apply as many additional coats of oil as you feel is necessary to achieve the finish you want. Each additional coat of oil should be wiped on in a thin coat and then buffed off completely. Let each coat dry overnight, to give it a chance to absorb oxygen from the air before you apply another coat.

After the final coat has dried overnight, burnish the surface by rubbing it hard with a soft cloth. This will bring out the luster of the finish. Using this procedure, you can get a soft satin gloss.

Wax

Wax can be used as a stand-alone finish or as a final protective coating on top of another finishing product. Wax gives the wood a very mellow look, but as a stand-alone finish, it doesn't offer much protection. Don't use wax on surfaces that may get wet or receive a lot of wear. Wax finishes date to the earliest beginnings of woodworking. Beeswax is the type of wax that has been used most commonly through most of the history of woodworking, but today there are many types to choose from.

Wax is a fatty substance that may be animal, vegetable, or mineral in its origin. The most common waxes are beeswax, obtained from honeycombs; paraffin wax, a petroleum product; and carnauba wax, from the Brazilian wax palm. There are many other waxes that can be used in woodworking; usually they are not sold alone but as ingredients in commercially blended waxes.

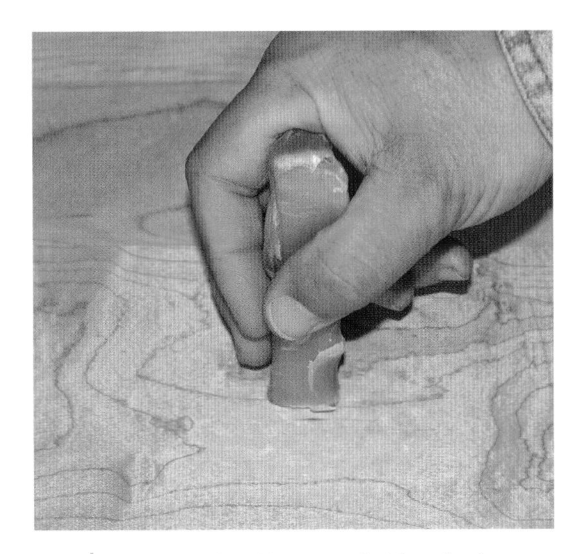

4-16 *To apply a hard beeswax finish, rub a lump of hard wax over the wood vigorously to generate enough heat to slightly melt the wax.*

BEESWAX FINISH Beeswax can be applied either as hard wax (straight beeswax with no additives) or soft wax (a mixture of beeswax and spirits of turpentine). The hard wax produces a better shine, but it is more difficult to apply. The soft wax is easier to apply, but it doesn't polish to as high a gloss.

To apply a hard beeswax finish, rub a lump of hard wax over the wood vigorously to generate enough heat to slightly melt the wax (**4–16**). Working in the warm sun or near a heat source makes the process easier. Once the wax has been applied, it must be smoothed and polished. The hard wax is difficult to remove, so you can't simply wipe it off as you would a modern wax. A cork block rubbed hard over the wax generates heat from friction as it is rubbed. This melts the wax and forces it into the pores of the wood. After the wax has been smoothed with the cork block, you can buff it with a soft cloth.

Soft wax is easier to apply. The wax is applied as a soft paste that hardens after the solvents evaporate. Soft wax can be used to produce a satin gloss. Commercially prepared soft beeswax is available from woodworking supply stores. It comes in a tin like other paste waxes. The techniques of application are the same as for modern paste wax.

Soft beeswax is simple to make. Begin by cutting some beeswax into small pieces. Put the wax in a glass container and pour in an equal amount of spirits of turpentine. You can use naptha instead of spirits of turpentine, if you want. Seal the container and let it sit in a warm area such as a sunny windowsill for several days, stirring it occasionally. When the wax is completely dissolved, it is ready to use.

PASTE WAX FINISH Modern paste waxes are a blend of several waxes and usually incorporate the harder waxes such as carnuaba. They will be more durable than straight beeswax.

Wax can be applied to bare wood. Applying the wax to bare wood is the oldest method, but it is also traditional to apply a sealer coat of very thin shellac to the wood before applying the wax. Brush on a coat of one-or two-pound-cut shellac. The shellac will be completely absorbed by the wood. Lightly sand the surface with fine sandpaper after the shellac is dry. Now apply the wax with a brush or a cloth. A cloth works better on closed-grained woods, and a brush is good for open-grained woods.

To apply the wax with a cloth, dip a clean cloth into the wax, and then rub it over the wood surface in a circular motion. Rub it into the wood vigorously; then immediately use a second cloth to wipe off most of the excess wax. Let the wax harden for about ten minutes; then, using a third cloth, buff the surface. Let the wax harden for an hour or two and then repeat the process. You can keep adding coats of wax until you are satisfied with the finish. If the wax is applied to bare wood, the first few coats will soak into the wood.

When you are applying wax to an open-grained wood and you want to preserve the natural texture of the wood and give it a satin sheen, you can use a brush to apply the wax and buff it. You will need two soft brushes. The best brushes are soft horsehair brushes used to shine shoes or brushes made for use on leather tack (saddles, etc.). Dip the first brush into the wax and brush it over the wood using short, straight strokes with the grain. Work the wax into the pores. After the surface has been covered with wax, use the same brush to remove the excess. Don't add any more wax to the brush. Rub the brush over the surface in long, straight strokes with the grain. This will remove most of the wax from the pores and distribute the wax evenly on the surface. Let the wax harden for about ten minutes before buffing.

Use a separate brush to buff the wax. Go over the surface with the buffing brush in short strokes to remove the remaining wax from the pores; then make long, straight strokes with the grain the full length of the wood. This will leave the wood with a soft satin gloss, and the texture of the grain will be visible.

USING WAX TO PROTECT OTHER FINISHES Wax can be used to protect any other type of finish. It can be applied over shellac, oil, varnish, and all of the modern finishes. Wax will restore the gloss and, regular waxing will protect the underlying finish from wear. Paste wax is the traditional choice for furniture polishing. Apply the wax in a circular motion. Use another cloth to wipe off most of the wax left on the surface; then let the wax harden for about ten minutes and buff it to a gloss with a third clean cloth.

TINTED WAX When you apply wax to a dark, open-gained wood, the wax that builds up in the pores can show up as a lighter color; you can prevent this by using a tinted wax. Tinted wax has a dye or pigment added to darken the color of the wax, so that it will blend in with the color of the wood. Tinted wax doesn't stain the wood; it just colors the pores. If you to want to color the wood, you should apply a stain before you wax it. Black tinted wax is often used on oak. The black wax accentuates the open-grain pattern of oak and is very characteristic of old oak finishes (**4–17**). Black wax can be applied to the bare wood or over a shellac or varnish finish.

You can buy commercially made tinted wax or make your own. To make tinted wax, add a small amount of universal tinting color to paste wax. Tinted wax left on the surface of the wood can rub off on clothing, so buff the wax until you can wipe a white cloth over the surface without picking up any color.

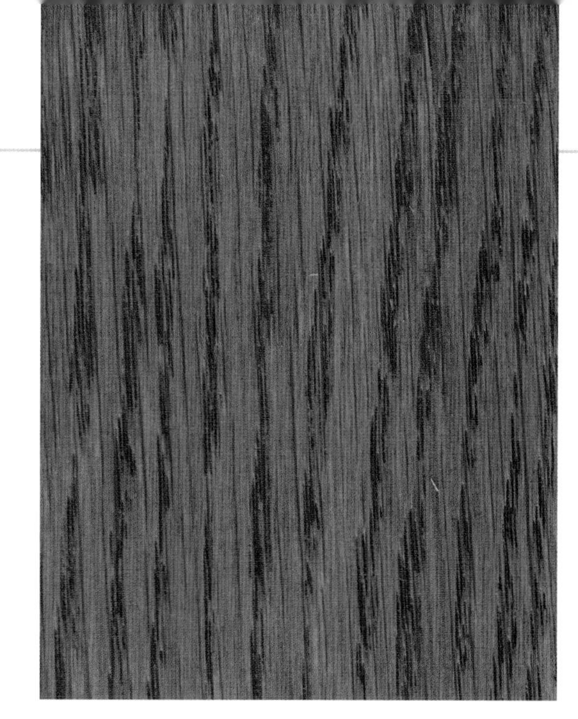

4-17 *Black wax accentuates the open-grain pattern of oak and is very characteristic of old oak finishes.*

WAX POLISHING ON THE LATHE Wax is a good finish to apply to turnings while they are still on the lathe. Applying the wax to a rotating turning will generate enough friction to melt the wax, and it can be polished to a high gloss. Before applying the wax, sand the turning as smooth as you can.

The simplest type of wax finish is the hard wax finish. Hold a lump of hard wax against the work as it rotates on the lathe. The wax will soften and rub off onto the wood. When the wood is completely covered with wax, buff the wax by holding a rag against the rotating work. Hold the rag in one spot long enough to melt the wax, and then slowly move the rag from one end of the turning to the other.

You can buy special lathe waxes. They usually come as a stick of hard wax. The wax may contain dyes, pigments and fillers to optimize the characteristics for lathe finishing. Simply hold the stick against the rotating work to apply the wax. Buff the wax as described above.

You can also apply paste wax to a turning on the lathe. Dip a rag into the wax, then apply it to the wood as it spins on the lathe. Let it harden for a few minutes, and then buff it with a soft cloth as the lathe spins. Several coats will be necessary to build up a good film of wax.

Natural-Oil Varnishes

Traditional varnish is made from natural oils and resins (**4–18**). It is a surface coating that builds up a layer on top of the wood instead of penetrating deeply. Varnish is highly regarded for its durability and ease of application. It uses slow-evaporating solvents that enable it to be brushed on with more success than faster-drying products. Varnish can also be applied with spray equipment.

Varnishes are blended for many different applications; there is not one universal varnish. The one you should choose depends on the application you intend it for.

Natural-oil varnishes are classified by the amount of oil they contain; those with a lot of oil are called *long-oil varnishes* and those with less oil are called *short-oil varnishes.*

LONG-OIL VARNISHES The large amount of oil used in long-oil varnishes makes them very tough and elastic. Exterior, spar and marine spar varnishes are all long-oil varnishes. They dry slowly and produce only a moderate gloss. Long-oil varnishes should be used whenever weather resistance is the prime consideration. Long-oil varnishes are not well-suited for fine furniture because they can't be rubbed or polished and their long drying time makes it more likely that dust will be trapped in the finish.

MEDIUM-OIL VARNISHES When a durable interior finish is needed that has more gloss than a long-oil finish, a medium-oil varnish is used. Sometimes called *cabinet varnish,* medium-oil varnish is probably the most versatile type because it can be used on a variety of projects. Varnishes of this type can be rubbed with pumice and rottenstone; however, the finish achieved by rubbing won't be as fine as a short-oil varnish would produce.

SHORT-OIL VARNISHES When a rubbed finish is desired, the best results are achieved when a short-oil varnish is used. Short-oil varnishes are strictly for interior use and are primarily used on fine furniture that won't receive rough handling. The finish produced by a short-oil varnish is hard and somewhat brittle. The extreme hardness is the property that allows this type to take such a fine

4-18 *Natural oil varnishes dry very slowly. This gives you more control over a brushed finish. After covering the surface with varnish, brush over the area again without adding more varnish. This will smooth out the surface and flatten out any ridges left by the previous brushing.*

rubbed finish. Short-oil varnishes are commonly called *rubbing varnish, polishing varnish,* or *piano varnish.*

APPLYING NATURAL-OIL VARNISHES

Brushing is the usual method of application for varnish. You can spray varnish; usually it must be thinned with turpentine or paint thinner before spraying. A thin coat of dewaxed shellac will act as a good sealer for interior use under natural varnish. Shellac should not be used for exterior applications because the moisture will affect the finish. For many varnishes, the recommended sealer is the varnish itself thinned 50 percent. This type of sealer will seal the wood's pores, but it won't prevent reactions between filler or stain and the varnish.

Always varnish in a well-ventilated area that is relatively dust-free. Wipe the surface to be varnished with a tack rag to remove as much dust as possible.

Gloss varnish should not be stirred, as this only introduces air bubbles. *Satin varnish* contains a flattening agent that will settle to the bottom of the can, so you must stir satin varnish; but do it slowly and try to avoid whipping air into the varnish. Whether you intend to use satin or gloss as the final coat, you should apply gloss varnish as the first coat. The flattening agent in satin varnish will produce a cloudy finish that obscures the grain, if too many coats of it are applied; so satin varnish should be used for the last coat only.

Use a good varnish brush that is large enough to cover the surface with the minimum of brush strokes. Dip the brush into the varnish about half way. Press the brush against the inside of the can to remove the excess without creating air bubbles. Flow on the varnish by using the brush fairly full of varnish and refilling it before it becomes dry. After you have covered the surface with varnish in this manner, go over the same area with the brush without filling the brush with varnish. This brushing out will smooth and even out the varnish.

Sometimes it is recommended that the varnish be flowed on with the grain, then brushed out across the grain followed by brushing out with the grain. It is said that this will force the varnish deeper into the pores of the wood; however, if this method is not done carefully, the resulting finish may have a checkerboard look. Usually it is better to do all brushing with the grain. Any resulting brush marks are much less noticeable.

The technique of applying varnish differs from that of many other finishes in that a heavy coat is desirable. A heavy coat of varnish will level itself, creating a smooth surface. If the coat is too thin brush marks and laps will show more readily. However, too thick a coat will produce runs and drips, and it will dry too slowly; so try to apply just the right amount to get the varnish to level.

Whenever possible, position the work so that the surface being varnished will be horizontal. This allows you to apply a heavier coat that will level itself better without fear of runs or drips. Work with only one surface at a time, completely brushing out the area before moving to the next surface.

Follow the directions closely regarding the time between coats. Natural varnishes usually require 24 hours or more between coats, depending on the humidity.

After the varnish is dry, sand out dust nibs brush marks. Use 180-grit or finer sandpaper to sand between coats. Wet-or-dry sandpaper can be used with water as a lubricant to prevent the varnish from gumming up the sandpaper. Apply the water sparingly to avoid having it run into joints and swelling the wood. The best way is to use a damp sponge or rag; wipe it across the surface and then sand the area. Occasionally dip the sandpaper into a pan of water to wash it off. Wipe the accumulated paste from the work with a sponge or rag.

When sanding is complete, wipe all of the remaining sanding residue from the surface and let it dry. Wipe the dry surface with a tack cloth to remove the last traces of dust and then apply the next coat. Two coats are sufficient for most ordinary work, but more coats can be used when you wish.

Lacquer

For many years lacquer was the professional's first choice as a finishing coat. Practically all factory-built furniture made in the mid-twentieth century received a lacquer finish (**4–19**). Lacquer is hard and abrasion-resistant; it wears well and doesn't break down with age; it is resistant to water, alcohol, carbonated drinks, heat, and mild alkalis and acids. Unlike almost all other classic finishes, it is almost completely clear with only a slight amber color of its own, so it won't alter the color of the wood or stain very much.

The word lacquer has been used for many years to describe a variety of finishes, but in this book I will use it to mean the synthetic nitrocellulose lacquer that was developed soon after World War I as a by-product of the explosives industry. This type of lacquer is an entirely synthetic product that contains none of the natural substance "lac" that is found in shellac.

4-19 *Practically all factory-built furniture made in the mid-twentieth century received a lacquer finish.*

Lacquer dries rapidly and several coats can be applied in one day. The surface hardness of lacquer makes it ideal for rubbing with pumice and rottenstone or steel wool.

The only major disadvantage of lacquer is that it usually must be applied with spray equipment. There are some brushing lacquers available that contain a retarder to slow down the drying, but they really don't level as well as varnish. If you need to use lacquer and absolutely can't spray it, then use a brushing lacquer; but if at all possible, apply lacquer by spraying.

The solvents used in lacquer will dissolve almost any other finish; for this reason lacquer is said to be "hotter" than other finishes. A "hot" finish like lacquer should not be applied over a "colder" finish such as varnish. If you apply a "hot" finish over a "cold" finish, the "hot" finish will dissolve the "cold" finish and the project will be ruined. On the other hand a "cold" finish can be successfully applied over a "hot" one. That is why shellac or lacquer can be used as a sealer under varnish.

APPLYING LACQUER Lacquer produces a very thin layer per coat, so many coats are needed to finish the surface. Since lacquer dries rapidly, several coats can be applied on one day, so even though many coats are necessary, the finishing process is usually completed in less time than is needed for other finishes.

Sealers

Most of the time it is best to apply the same finish for the first coat that you are using for the rest of the finish. But in some special situations a sealer is necessary. A sealer is a special product that is applied under a top coat. There are several reasons for using a sealer.

One of the most common types of sealer is a *sanding sealer.* This is often used with finishes that are difficult to sand. For example, some varnishes get gummy when you sand them and the varnish quickly clogs the sandpaper. In this case, you can use a sanding sealer as the first coat. It has additives that make it easy to sand. If you use sanding sealer as the first coat, you can sand out all the roughness that typically appears in the first coat easily. When you apply the rest of the coats using the top coat varnish, you only need to give them a light sanding to ensure proper adhesion.

Some woods tend to absorb finishing materials more than others. These thirsty woods may soak up some tops coats in patches, leaving dull areas in the coat. Sanding sealers have the ability to seal the surface so that subsequent coats won't soak into the wood. This property is called *holdout*. A sealer with good holdout properties will allow the top coats to flow out evenly and produce a smooth, even surface.

Another reason to use a sealer is to prevent adverse interaction between a previous coat of stain, glaze or filler, and the top coat. For best results you should use compatible products that won't require a sealer, but sometimes you can only get the look you want from a product that may cause problems with the desired top coat. In this case, use a sealer that is compatible with both products. Two of the most useful sealers of this type are *dewaxed shellac* and *vinyl sealer.*

Dewaxed shellac has had the natural wax found in most shellac filtered out. It is compatible with practically all finishes and it effectively seals the underlying layers so that stains won't bleed and there won't be adhesion problems. Vinyl sealer is a professional product that performs the same function, but it is compatible with most conversion finishes.

Isolante sealer is a catalyzed polyurethane product that provides a barrier coat between oily woods and stains when applying a polyester top coat.

Although sealers can solve some problems they can also introduce other problems to the finish. Sealers are typically softer and less water resistant than the top coats. This means that when you want the highest degree of durability, you should avoid using a sealer.

Because many coats are needed, it is sometimes advantageous to use a lacquer sanding sealer as the first coat. Sanding sealer has solids added to the formula that help to fill the wood and build finish thickness. After the sealer has dried, it is sanded to provide a smooth surface for subsequent coats of lacquer. The addition of solids to sanding sealer makes them less transparent than lacquer and alters the color a little. The effect is only slight and usually of no consequence, but if optimum clarity is desired, use lacquer without a sanding sealer.

Before spraying lacquer, it should be thinned about 25 percent with a quality thinner designed specifically for the purpose. The exact amount of thinner should be determined by experimentation and will vary depending on the application. If the air humidity exceeds 50 percent, about one-third of the thinner should be replaced by retarder; otherwise, the lacquer may absorb moisture from the air and become slightly cloudy. This condition is called *blushing*.

4-20 *These samples illustrate the color difference between grades of shellac. Left to right: button, orange, blond, and white shellac on oak.*

When spraying lacquer with air-operated equipment, begin by setting the air pressure at 40 PSI and vary it up or down from that setting until optimum performance is achieved. Refer to Chapter 2 for specific instructions on how to use spray equipment.

Unlike varnish, each coat of lacquer will slightly dissolve the preceding coat, providing an excellent bond between coats; so sanding to provide a mechanical bond between coats is not necessary. However, you can sand between coats to remove dust and imperfections in the surface. Unless you are working in an extremely dusty location, dust won't be a problem with lacquer; it dries so fast the dust doesn't have time to settle.

Don't try for a heavy coat of lacquer; build the finish with many thin coats.

Shellac

Shellac is one of the oldest wood finishes. Most of the beautiful antiques you see in museums use some form of shellac to produce the classic finish that is so admired. Shellac is a resinous substance that is made from the secretions of a small insect called the *lac bug (tachardia lacca)*. Most shellac comes from India, where it is gathered by hand from deposits left by the lac bug in plum trees. It is processed and refined into several grades of buttons or flakes that produce liquid shellac when dissolved in alcohol.

Shellac is a very desirable finishing material because it is easy to apply, dries quickly, and forms a flexible and elastic top coat that is very durable and able to withstand the rigors of time, as shown by the condition of finishes on antiques several hundred years old. However, shellac does have some disadvantages. Two major drawbacks are the fact that it is not very water resistant (water left on the surface will cause a white milky spot) and alcohol will dissolve it, so shellac should not be used for tabletops or bar tops where spilled drinks are likely. Another disadvantage is a limited shelf life compared to other finishing materials.

Shellac is available in several types representing different degrees of refinement (**4–20**). *Raw shellac* is a dark orangish brown color; refining the shellac removes this color. But the refining process also decreases the shelf life of the shellac, so the more refined the shellac, the shorter its shelf life. The highly refined forms of shellac also seem to be less durable than the less refined grades.

Button shellac is the least refined grade of shellac available today. It gets its name from the fact that the first step in refining produces a disc called a *button*. The button is broken into pieces and sold as button shellac. This grade has a very long shelf life; the buttons can be stored for years without deteriorating. The dark brown color of button shellac makes is suitable for use only when a very dark color is desired for the final finish. It is mainly used to duplicate antique finishes.

Orange shellac is a more refined grade of shellac, but it still retains some of the orangish brown color of the raw shellac. In this book I use the traditional name for this product, but some companies now refer to this as amber shellac in their consumer line of products. It also has a relatively long shelf life. Orange shellac is used for dark-colored finishes, as is button shellac; but because it is a light shade, more of the underlying color of the wood shows through.

Blonde shellac is light amber in color. It can be used for all but the lightest finishes without imparting any noticeable change in the color of the finish.

White shellac is almost completely clear. It is produced by bleaching all of the color out of the shellac. To avoid confusion, many companies now label this product clear shellac, but I will continue to use the traditional name in this book. When a very light-colored finish is desired, white shellac must be used; but if it is not necessary to use white shellac, blonde shellac will probably give better results. The bleaching process makes white shellac less durable, and white shellac has the shortest shelf life of any type of shellac.

When purchasing white shellac, always check the expiration date stamped on the container. Only purchase the amount of white shellac that you need for the job at hand and use the product promptly. Dry white shellac comes in a powder form and only has a shelf life of two to three months after which it won't dissolve properly, so white shellac is almost exclusively sold in liquid form. The liquid has a shelf life of about one year, but because some of that time has expired before you buy the product, you should use the shellac within a few months of purchase.

White shellac that has gone out of date won't dry properly. It will remain gummy and never harden. If you want to use shellac that has gone past its expiration date, always test it on a scrap to make sure it will dry; if it does, it is safe to use. The expiration dates printed on the container are usually conservative, so it is often all right to use the product for several months past the date.

4-21

This photo shows what shellac looks like in its dry form. Left to right: button, orange, and blond.

There are two other grades of shellac that aren't as commonly available but are still made by some manufacturers. *Garnet shellac* is more refined than button shellac, but retains more of the brown color than orange shellac does. *Beta shellac* is lighter than orange shellac, but not as light as blonde.

MIXING SHELLAC Except for white shellac, the shellac flakes or buttons have longer shelf life than the liquid shellac, so it is best to buy the flakes and then mix a fresh batch of liquid shellac just before use (**4–21**). To make liquid shellac, the flakes or buttons are dissolved in alcohol. The best type of alcohol to use is *ethyl alcohol*; this is the same type of alcohol found in liquor. However, water mixed with the alcohol will harm the shellac, so only alcohol designated as a solvent should be used. Methanol, or wood alcohol, tends to make the shellac brittle or gummy and should not be used to dissolve the flakes. By law, ethyl alcohol has to be made undrinkable to be sold as a solvent; to do this, small amounts of poisonous substances such as wood alcohol or other solvents must be added to the alcohol. Ethyl alcohol that has been treated in this manner is called *denatured alcohol* or *proprietary solvent*. It's best to stick with a high-quality solvent for shellac, because too much wood alcohol in the mix will degrade the quality of the shellac.

Liquid shellac is categorized by the amount of dry flakes used in relation to the amount of solvent. This is referred to as the *cut*. If one pound of flakes is dissolved into one gallon of solvent, a one-pound cut is produced. Typically, shellac is mixed as a four-pound cut (four pounds of flakes to one gallon of solvent) and then thinned at the time of application to a two- or three-pound cut. Usually only a pint or quart of liquid is mixed at one time.

To make one quart of four-pound cut shellac, put 12 ounces of shellac flakes in a glass container and pour three cups of alcohol over the flakes. Put the lid on the container and let the flakes dissolve. You can speed up the process by occasionally shaking the container. When the flakes are thoroughly dissolved, strain the shellac through several layers of cheesecloth or a commercial paint strainer (**4–22**).

Before using the shellac, you will need to add additional alcohol to thin the required cut. The first coat of shellac should be thinned to a one-pound cut; subsequent coats can be a one- or two-pound cut. Sometimes a three-pound cut is used for the final coat. To dilute four-pound cut shellac to three-pound cut, add one-half pint of alcohol to a quart of four-pound cut shellac. To make a two-pound cut shellac, add three-fourths quart of alcohol to a quart of four-

4-22 *When the shellac flakes are thoroughly dissolved, strain the shellac. A disposable paint strainer like the one shown here works well.*

pound cut shellac. One-pound-cut shellac requires two quarts of alcohol added to one quart of four-pound cut shellac.

You can see that if you follow these proportions exactly, you may end up with a lot more shellac than you need. For example, you will end up with three quarts of one-pound cut shellac. Most finishers dilute shellac in smaller quantities and add the alcohol until the shellac seems the right consistency. Once you become familiar with the various cuts, this is easy to do and allows you to slightly vary the consistency to fit the job at hand. Some finishers rub the shellac between their thumb and forefinger to judge the cut. It takes judgment and experience to accurately thin shellac by feel, so at first measure the amount of alcohol you add. You can scale down the amounts as long as you keep the proportions the same as shown above.

APPLYING SHELLAC Shellac can be applied with a brush, a sprayer, or with a pad. When shellac is applied with a pad, the technique is called *French polishing*.

The alcohol used to dissolve the shellac has an affinity for water and will absorb the water from a damp surface or from humid air. So, shellac should never be applied to a damp surface or when the air humidity is especially high. If water is allowed to combine with the shellac, the resulting finish will have a milky white appearance. Shellac cannot be applied over fresh stain; the stain should be allowed to dry for 24 hours before shellac is applied.

BRUSHING ON SHELLAC To brush on shellac, thin it to a one-pound cut for the first coat. Use a good-quality natural filament brush. Because shellac dries so quickly, the material must be applied and brushed out in one operation. Apply the shellac to the wood in one long uniform stroke, then immediately brush over the area again to smooth out the coating. Apply more shellac to the next area, slightly overlapping the first stroke. Don't try to make a brushful go too far; refill the brush as soon as it shows signs of becoming dry.

Once you have covered an area, don't go back to brush it out again; the shellac will already be partially set, and prominent brush marks will be left. The secret to successfully brushing shellac is to work quickly. The shellac remains liquid on the surface of the wood for only a short time; once it has begun to gel, any further brushing will degrade the finish.

After the first coat has dried thoroughly (at least four hours), sand the surface with

320-grit sandpaper to remove any dust nibs. Shellac has a tendency to gum up sandpaper, so use open coat or non-clog paper. As soon as a spot of gummed-up shellac begins to appear on the sandpaper, remove it with your fingernail or pocketknife.

Only a light sanding is necessary to remove dust nibs; each coat of shellac will weld itself to the previous one, so it is not necessary to rough up the surface to ensure good adhesion. If you want to build up the coating fast, switch to a two-pound cut for the next coat and finish with a three-pound cut for the final coat. But for the best finish, stay with a one-pound cut and apply five or more coats. Allow at least four hours between coats, and sand between coats if the surface appears rough.

SPRAYING ON SHELLAC For spraying, thin shellac to at least a two-pound cut. A small syphon-feed gun, gravity-feed gun or HVLP gun can easily handle shellac. Keep air pressure low, 30 PSI maximum. The distance from the work is more critical with shellac than when spraying other finishes; if it is too close, runs and sags develop quickly. Holding the gun too far away will result in a rough sandpaper texture. The proper distance is approximately six inches, but this will vary some depending on the air pressure used and the cut of the shellac.

French Polishing

French polishing is a traditional method of applying shellac that uses a cloth pad to apply the finish. French polishing produces the best possible finish from shellac, but it requires a lot of skill, labor, and patience to apply a French polish. Before the advent of lacquers and spray equipment, French polishing was widely used for fine furniture, but the time and skilled labor needed to produce a French polish finish have virtually eliminated it as a method of commercial finishing. However, do-it-yourselfers and custom craftsmen who are interested in duplicating antique finishes still practice the ancient art of French polishing. Today it is used mostly on small items such as jewelry boxes and small tables or on the most expensive antique reproductions (**4–23**).

There are several methods of French polishing. The method I describe here works well for most applications. If you want a more complete explanation of French polishing, refer to my book *Classic Finishing Techniques*.

4-23 *A small table makes a good French polishing project.*

In its purest state, French polishing is done on wood that has no filler applied, but if you want to take short cuts, you can skip the process of filling the pores with French polish by applying a paste wood filler first. If you use paste filler, let it dry thoroughly; then brush on a thin coat of shellac. When the shellac is thoroughly dry, sand it with 400-grit sandpaper until it is perfectly smooth. If the wood is to be stained, use only water stain because the polishing process will rub off most other stains.

French polishing should be done in a warm, dry room. The temperature should be at least 68°F (20°C) and the air humidity should be relatively low.

MAKING THE PAD The first thing you need to apply a French polish is a set of pads. The pads are made from balls of raw wool—wool yarn cut up into small lengths, cotton balls, or wadded-up rags. The balls should be about two inches in diameter. Cover the balls with a piece or close-weave cotton or linen fabric (**4–24**). Gather the fabric together on one side of the ball and twist the fabric tight. Make three or more of these pads at once. Each pad is used in a separate step, and if it is kept in a tightly capped, air-tight container it will last for a long time.

Grip the pad like you would a baseball, with the gathered edges inside your palm. In use, the pad will develop a flat side where it contacts the work and the pad will comfortably conform to your hand.

In all steps of French polishing, the pad should be filled by pouring the shellac on the back of the pad; untwist the gathered material and pour the shellac directly on the back of the wool filling (**4–25**). Don't pour the liquid on the face of the pad or dip the pad into the liquid. The pad should just be damp, never dripping wet. After filling the pad, distribute the liquid evenly throughout by pressing the pad against the palm of your hand or a clean piece of cardboard.

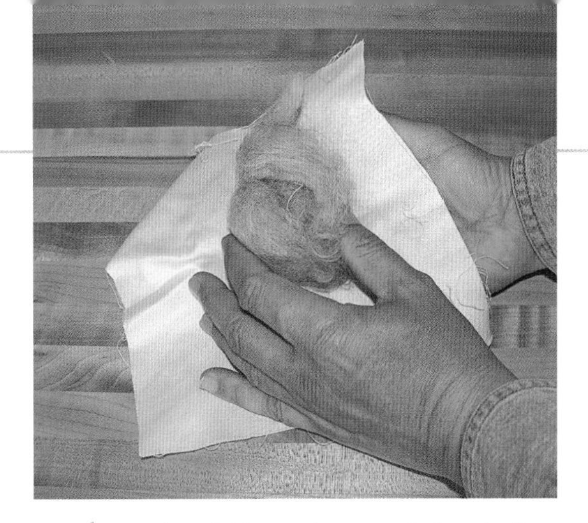

4-24 *French polishing pads are made from balls of raw wool, wool yarn cut up into small lengths, cotton balls, or wadded-up rags covered with a piece or close-weave cotton or linen fabric.*

4-25 *When adding shellac to the pad, pour it directly on the back of the wool filling.*

FILLING The first step in traditional French polishing is *filling*. If you have elected to use a paste wood filler, this step can be skipped. Pumice is used as filler in this step. Put some pumice in the center of a small square of open weave cloth. Gather the cloth around the pumice to form a little

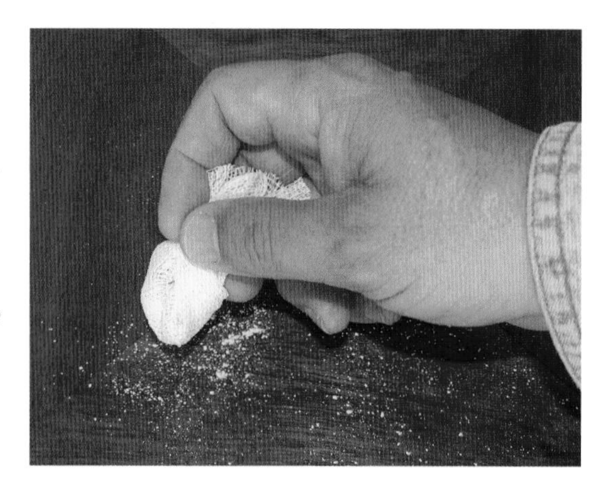

4-26 *To begin the process of filling the pores of open-grained woods with the French polishing process, sprinkle pumice from a bag made of open weave cloth. As you shake the bag, a fine dusting of pumice will fall on the surface.*

bag. You will use this bag to sprinkle the pumice on the work. As you shake the bag, a fine dusting of pumice will fall on the surface. The coarse cloth filters out lumps and lets you control the amount better than just spreading it with your fingers. It is better to start with just a fine layer of pumice because if you add too much it will clump up and leave lumps on the surface.

Choose a pad to be used exclusively for filling. Thin some one-pound cut shellac until it is almost as thin as the alcohol itself. Fill the pad with this thinned shellac. Rub the pad over the surface of the wood using a circular motion. Occasionally add a little thinned shellac to the back of the pad. Sprinkle a little fine pumice from the bag on the surface as you continue to rub the pad over the wood (**4–26**). The pumice will grind off fine wood dust as you rub; the combination of the wood dust and the pumice mixed with the shellac will be forced into the pores of the wood, filling them. Because dust from the wood itself is mixed with the filler, the color will match the surrounding wood closely.

After you have built up some polish on the surface, the pad will begin to stick. To prevent this, apply a few drops of mineral oil or raw linseed oil on the surface of the pad to lubricate the motion of the pad. A good way to estimate how much oil to use is to dip three fingertips into the oil, and then wipe the oil from your fingers onto the pad (**4–27**). Rub the pad over the surface in a series of small circles (**4–28**). Continue this process until all of the pores are filled.

4-27 *A good way to estimate how much oil to use is to dip three fingertips into the oil and then wipe the oil from your fingers onto the pad.*

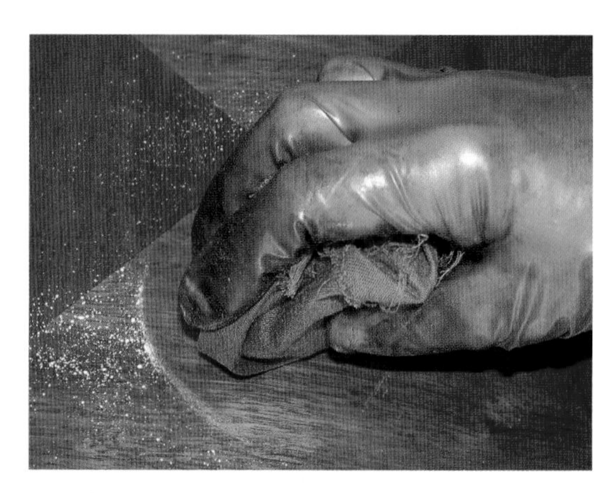

4-28 *To work the filler into the wood's pores, rub a pad filled with very thin shellac in a series of small circles over the surface that has been dusted with pumice.*

BUILDING UP A FILM Once the pores are filled, allow the filler at least 12 hours to dry before proceeding. Change to a new pad to be used for building up a film of shellac on the surface. This pad is filled with one-pound cut shellac. Apply two fingertips of oil to the surface of the pad before you begin. Work in quick circular strokes and keep the pad in constant motion (**4–29**). If the pad is left stationary on the surface even for an instant, it will stick and mar the work. Feed the pad from the back with more shellac as the pad dries out. After the surface has been coated in this manner, let the shellac dry about 12 hours before applying another coat. About four coats are needed to achieve a high gloss finish. For the final coat, thin the shellac with more alcohol and only use one fingertip of oil. This stage is mostly to polish the existing layer of shellac.

SPIRITING OFF Once you have achieved the surface buildup you are after, one final step remains. The oil used to lubricate the pad needs to be removed from the surface. This process is called spiriting off. Allow the last coat to dry for at least 24 hours. Change to a new pad and fill it with alcohol only; the pad should feel almost dry to the touch. As you progress, use less and less alcohol until you are using a pad that is almost completely dry at the last. Rub the pad with the grain across the surface of the work to remove the oil (**4–30**). Use very light pressure; don't go over one area too much or you will soften the finish. Let the finish "rest" for about one hour, and then go back and touch up any oily looking spots. This process should produce the characteristic sheen of a French polish finish.

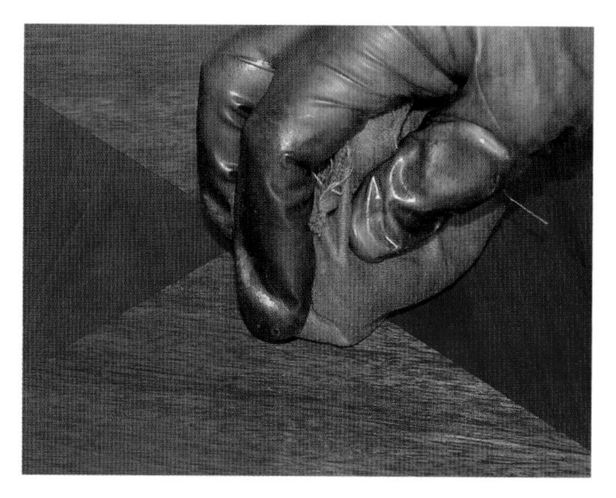

4-29 *To build up a film of French polish, switch to a new pad and fill it with one-pound cut shellac. Use two fingertips of oil to lubricate the pad.*

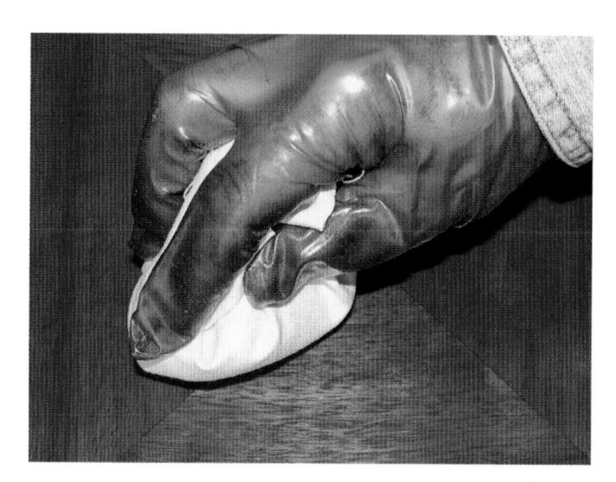

4-30 *Spiriting off removes the oil left on the surface. Use a clean pad moistened with alcohol.*

Although the steps involved sound relatively simple, the process is difficult to master because a lot of it depends on touch and judgment that can only be gained through practice. If you are willing to invest the time it takes to learn this art, you will be rewarded with beautiful finishes that everyone will envy.

Another form of French polishing is called *open pore French polishing*. This type produces a satin finish that shows all of the texture of the pores.

To produce an open pore finish, feed the pad with a one-pound cut shellac and always move the pad with the grain. No oil or pumice is necessary, and it is not necessary to spirit off the work at the end.

Professional Products

Two-Part Finishes

When certain resins are mixed with a catalyst or hardener, they harden chemically by a process called *polymerization*. These types of finishes are called two-part finishes because they consist of two separate components that must be mixed together before use. They can also be called *conversion finishes* or *catalyzed finishes*.

4-31 *Two-part finishes are often used by professional finishers on kitchen cabinets.*

Two-part finishes usually use amino, urethane, or polyester resin. These resins are useful as wood finishes, because once they are catalyzed they are extremely hard and resist acids, alcohol, and most common solvents. However, they have several disadvantages: they use highly toxic solvents (some emit formaldehyde as they cure); they have a short pot life; and they are difficult to repair. Because of their increased durability, two-part finishes are often used by professional finishers on kitchen cabinets and other commercial items that are subject to a lot of wear (**4–31**).

There are several types of two-part finishes, including conversion varnish, catalyzed lacquer, two-part polyurethane, and polyester finishes. Each manufacturer markets a system of compatible products to go with their conversion finishes. When you are deciding to start using conversion finishes, talk to the customer representatives from several companies and choose a system the best fits your situation.

Once you choose a system, use only those products to avoid problems later. If, for example, you use an incompatible stain under a conversion finish, it may look fine for a while, then the finish may start to peel or become cloudy looking. It's best to simply stay with products that you know are compatible. The customer reps are usually very helpful; if you have a need for a custom stain or have an unusual finishing situation, the rep can often help.

Since two-part finishes harden by a chemical reaction that takes place evenly throughout the film thickness, it is possible

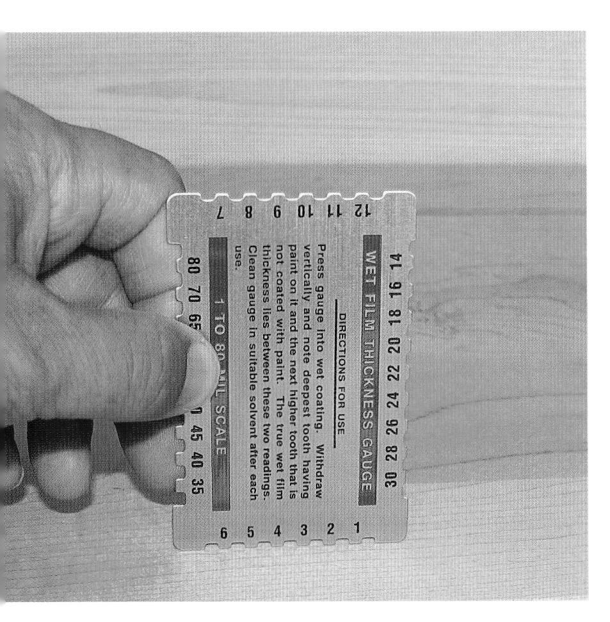

4-32 *A mil gauge measures the wet film thickness when you press the teeth of the mil gauge into the wet finish. The tooth with highest mil number that touches the surface of the finish indicates the film thickness.*

to apply very thick coats of the finish. Such a thick coat would be impractical with a finish that relies on evaporation of solvents to dry, because the top layer would dry before the inside of the film thickness could dry. Also, since no evaporation takes place in a catalyzed finish, there is no shrinkage, so this type of finish will fill surface irregularities and defects.

These finishes are referred to as *high solids finishes* because they contain mostly resins and not much solvent, and therefore form a thick coat. This ability to form a thick coat means that you usually only need to apply two coats of the finish. However, there is a downside to this property. It's easy to apply too much material and that can lead to crazing and other problems.

Applying the correct film thickness is very important with conversion finishes. You can use a wet film thickness gauge (mil gauge) to make sure that you are applying the proper amount of finish. To use the mil gauge, apply the finish to a test board and then press the teeth of the mil gauge into the wet finish (**4–32**). The teeth on the mil gauge are marked in mils. The tooth with highest mil number that touches the surface of the finish indicates the film thickness. Note that the mil gauge may leave tooth marks in the finish, so only use it on a test board or an inconspicuous area of the project. Once you have adjusted the spray gun and practiced the speed that you move the gun, you will be able to apply the same film thickness to the project.

Conversion finishes don't soak into the wood surface very much, so they rely on a mechanical bond with the surface. Because of this, you should stop sanding with 150 grit. This gives the surface enough tooth to allow the conversion finish to adhere. If you want to sand the surface with a finer grit, you can't apply the conversion finish directly to the wood. You must first apply a special sealer designed for the purpose. The sealer will soak into the wood to create a firm bond and it will create a surface the conversion finish can adhere to.

The catalyst should be added just prior to use, and only mix as much as you can apply during the pot life of the product. The *pot life* is the time that the finish will remain liquid. The pot life can vary from half an hour to eight hours. Follow the directions on the container for exact mixing instructions. The directions may give the mixing ratio in weight or volume. If the amounts must be

4-33 *When the directions give the mixing ratio in weight, place the measuring cup on a scale as you pour in the liquid.*

measured by weight, place the measuring cup on a scale as you pour in the liquid. An electronic postal scale works well (**4–33**). When the directions give the proportions by volume, use a graduated container to measure the amounts. Use a wooden stick to stir the mixture. Thorough mixing is of extreme importance. Work quickly, and frequently scrape the sides and bottom of the container to make sure that no pockets of unmixed resin remain there.

Conversion finishes usually should be applied with spray equipment. Be sure to follow the manufacturer's advice about thinning; some conversion finishes shouldn't be thinned at all. Conversion finishes have spraying characteristics similar to lacquer; however, they build the film thickness approximately twice as fast, so fewer coats are needed to achieve the desired film thickness.

If you apply second coat within a few hours (called the *recoat window*), you usually won't need to sand between coats. However, if you let a coat cure completely, you will need to sand off the gloss before applying another coat, because conversion finishes don't burn into previous coats like lacquer; instead they rely on a mechanical bond between coats like varnish. If you miss the recoat window and don't sand sufficiently between coats, you could have wrinkling or adhesion problems.

You must clean your spray equipment immediately after you are done spraying. If you let a conversion finish sit in your spray gun too long, it will harden to solid plastic and be almost impossible to remove.

Conversion Varnish

Conversion varnish is completely clear (water white). This can be an advantage when you want to accent the natural color of the wood, but sometimes the wood looks a little lifeless or plastic looking. Always test the finish on a sample of the wood before you decide to use a conversion product. The dry film thickness of conversion varnish usually should not exceed 5 mils. If you apply more coats past 5 mils, you run the risk of forming many small cracks called *crazing*.

Precatalyzed Lacquer

Most conversion finishes are too difficult to work with for a do-it-yourself finisher, and are usually only used in furniture factories and commercial shops. However, precatalyzed lacquer is suitable for small cabinet shops. Sometimes called *Pre-cat*, it comes pre-mixed, so you don't need to bother with mixing a catalyst before use. A special ingredient in the solvent keeps the catalyst from working until the solvent evaporates. This means that you can use a precatalyzed lacquer about the same way you would use ordinary lacquer. Precatalyzed lacquers have a short shelf life, so only buy as much as you can use immediately. This product is also available in aerosol cans so it can be used for touch-up work or small projects.

Postcatalyzed Lacquer

For a more durable lacquer-type finish, use postcatalyzed lacquer (*post-cat*). It is a two-part product that must be mixed before use. Many finishers choose catalyzed lacquer for furniture because its slight amber hue looks more like traditional finishes (**4–34**). The dry film thickness should be no thicker than 4 to 5 mils, to avoid crazing.

Two-Component Polyurethane

If you are after a "wet gloss" look, a two-component polyurethane finish may be the answer. Sometimes called *2K polyurethane*, this finish can be applied in very thick coats with no limit on the film build. After it is dry, it can be rubbed out or polished and it is extremely durable. On the down side it has a short pot life, a longer drying time and is very susceptible to incompatibility problems. Be sure to only use products from the same system designed for use with 2K polyurethane.

4-34 *Many finishers choose catalyzed lacquer for furniture.*

Polyester Finishes

For surfaces that will really take a beating, like bar tops, a polyester finish is best. Polyester can be applied in extremely thick coats and is the hardest of the two-part finishes. It can be used as a base coat for 2K polyurethane when you want to build up a thick coating quickly. Some polyester finishes include a third part called a *promoter*. It speeds up the curing time. This allows you to make adjustments for air temperature and humidity.

Paint

Paint is one of the oldest protective coatings. It was probably first used more for its decorative qualities and that is still the case in many instances, but ancient people soon discovered that paint could protect a surface as well as decorate it. The Barrier Canyon people who lived in what is now southeastern Utah around 4,500 B.C. used paint to make giant illustrations called *pictographs* on the face of sandstone cliffs. Many pictographs survive today, attesting to the durability of paint (**4–35**). But even though paint has such ancient origins, in the last

Solvents

There are many solvents used in wood-finishing products. Here is a brief description of some of the most common ones:

Acetone Acetone is a very strong solvent that evaporates quickly. It is too strong to use as a thinner for most conventional finishes. It can be used to thin some catalyzed finishes. It is most useful for cleaning up equipment that has been used with conversion finishes. It will attack many synthetic fabrics and plastics.

Alcohol Alcohol is the only solvent recommended for use with shellac and spirit stains. There are several types of alcohol, but the type to use with wood finishing products is denatured alcohol. There are two grades: pure denatured and solvent grade. The solvent grade is less expensive, and it works fine for shellac.

Glycol Ether There are several types of solvents in the glycol ether family. They all share one important characteristic: they are compatible with water. This makes them important in waterborne finishes, because they will dissolve resins and still mix with water. Glycol ethers are very toxic, but they are used in such small concentrations in waterborne finishes that they emit less toxic fumes than other solvents. You usually can't buy glycol ethers by themselves; they are only used to manufacture other products.

Lacquer Thinner Lacquer thinner is actually a mixture of several solvents. Be sure to use a high-quality lacquer thinner that is recommended by the manufacturer of the lacquer you are using. Lacquer thinner contains ketones and esters to dissolve the resins in lacquer; it may also contain some alcohol, toluene, and xylene. If the proportions of these ingredients aren't correct for the type of lacquer you are using, you won't get the quality of finish that you would get with the correct thinner.

MEK Methyl-ethyl ketone (MEK) is a strong solvent that is more aggressive than acetone, but it evaporates more slowly. It can be used to clean up equipment used with conversion finishes.

few decades it has probably changed more than any other finishing product. In fact, the paint industry is undergoing what could be termed a revolution.

Terminology is a major casualty of this revolution. In an effort to avoid confusing the public, paint manufacturers have applied traditional paint names to new products, but in some ways this has only added to the confusion. For example, at one time almost all quality paints were made with linseed oil. They were called *oil-based paint*. Today linseed oil has largely been replaced by other ingredients, but the name oil-based paint is still applied to new products. Until recently oil-

4-35 *The paint used to make these pictographs in southeastern Utah has survived for over 6,000 years.*

Mineral Spirits Mineral spirits is a petroleum distillate. It is a good general-purpose solvent. You can use it to clean brushes and thin oil-based paint or varnish. It evaporates slower and is more oily than naptha. It will dissolve wax.

Naptha Naptha is a petroleum distillate solvent. It is similar to mineral spirits, but it evaporates faster. It can be used as a thinner in most oil-based products. It is sometimes labeled VM&P Naptha. This is an abbreviation of Varnish Maker's and Painter's Naptha.

Paint Thinner Paint thinner is a petroleum distillate; it may contain mineral spirits or naptha. It is a good general-purpose solvent. You can use it to clean brushes and thin oil-based paint or varnish. It will dissolve wax.

Toluol Toluol (toluene) is chemically extracted from petroleum. It is a stronger solvent than mineral spirits or naptha. It makes an excellent cleaning solvent because of its strength, but it is too strong to use as a thinner for most oil-based paints or varnishes. Some specialty finishing material may specify toluol as a thinner.

Turpentine Turpentine is an extract from pine trees. There are two grades; the best grade, *gum spirits of turpentine,* is distilled from pine tree sap. The second grade is called *spirits of turpentine* or *wood turpentine;* it is distilled from pine wood. Turpentine is a good thinner for oil-based paint and varnish, but it is too expensive to use for clean-up. It is a stronger solvent than paint thinner. It evaporates faster than paint thinner. It will dissolve wax.

Xylol Xylol (xylene) is similar to toluol. It is chemically extracted from petroleum. It is a stronger solvent than mineral spirits or naptha; it makes an excellent cleaning solvent. It evaporates more slowly than toluol. It is too strong to use as a thinner for most oil-based paints or varnishes. It can be substituted as a thinner for finishing materials that specify toluol as a thinner.

based meant that the product had to be thinned and cleaned up with mineral spirits, but now there are some oil-based products that can be cleaned up with water.

Latex is another term that has changed its meaning over the past few years. It is a type of rubber that was used in the early water clean-up paints. The name latex stayed with water clean-up paints even though now they usually contain synthetic plastics like acrylic resins. Gradually the name latex came to mean any water clean-up paint, but now that distinction is blurred by the introduction of water clean-up oil-based paints.

Enamel is another paint term that has lost its original meaning. This was originally a single product that was made by adding colored pigments to varnish. The resulting paint was prized for its glasslike surface, toughness, and washability. At present, the term enamel is applied to a wide variety of paint products of varying composition. Generally, it means that the paint is more durable or washable than other paints.

Because paint has been in use for so long, there is a lot of folklore associated with it. The paint revolution has made practically all of the old folk formulas and methods of manufacture obsolete. There are dozens of old formulas for paint fortifiers that use linseed oil, white lead, turpentine and other ingredients. Don't use any of them. Modern paints are superior. You should also realize that they are made to be used straight from the can. The addition of any unapproved ingredients will degrade or ruin the paint.

An obsolete piece of folk wisdom about paint is that you can judge a paint's quality by how heavy the can feels. This is based on the fact that lead was a major ingredient of most paint formulas. More lead in the paint made it feel heavier, and therefore it was supposedly better quality. Since lead has been found to be a health hazard when used in paint, it is no longer included in paint formulas, so the weight of paint has nothing to do with its quality.

Today the only reliable source of information about a specific type of paint is the label on the can or literature provided by the manufacturer. Most paint cans have a list of ingredients on the label. By analyzing the ingredients you can get a better idea of what you are getting. The label will usually list the following basic categories of ingredients: pigments, extenders, resins, oils, and solvents. Resins, oils, and solvents together are known as the *vehicle*.

Pigments

Pigments are finely ground minerals or synthetic materials that give the paint its color. Some of the natural mineral pigments are similar to the pigments used thousands of years ago. Others have been developed very recently. The degree of fineness to which the pigments are ground plays a role in how smooth the resulting finish will be. The paints using the coarsest pigment are called *barn paints*. They are especially well-suited for rough lumber. House paints use finer pigments. The most finely ground pigments are used in interior paints formulated for use on furniture and woodwork.

Besides providing the color of the paint, pigments play a role in the hiding power of the paints and in the paint's durability. White pigments are used in all but the darkest colors of paint because some of the white pigments offer more hiding power than any other type.

TITANIUM DIOXIDE Titanium dioxide is a fairly new pigment. It has a very high hiding power and is extremely durable. It has taken over as the most widely used pigment. Each of its many forms is designated by a Roman numeral. The various types have different properties that make them suitable for different applications, but when choosing paint it is usually not important to know what type of titanium dioxide was used. What is important is how much was used.

Titanium dioxide is one of the most expensive pigments, so inexpensive paints will skimp on it. Generally, the higher the amount of titanium dioxide, the higher the paint quality. However, as with almost everything in the rapidly changing paint industry, this is not a hard and fast rule. Very dark colors won't use any titanium dioxide because its white color would lighten the paint too much. A high concentration of titanium dioxide is more important in an exterior paint because it offers more durability. Interior paints may not need as much.

LITHOPONE Lithopone is white pigment that is frequently used in interior paint when the durability of titanium dioxide is not needed.

ZINC OXIDE Zinc oxide is sometimes used in exterior paint to control mildew. It is not suitable for use in large proportions because it may cause the paint to crack, but in small quantities it can improve the paint's performance.

COLORED PIGMENTS In most paints, the colored pigments make up only a small volume of the total pigments in the paint. Most of the paint's properties come from the type of white pigment used. In very dark paints, pigments like burnt umber, iron oxides, or carbon black may be substituted for the white pigment.

Lead Caution

In the past, white lead was one of the most widely used paint pigments, but lead is poisonous and will cause serious health problems when its dust is inhaled or when particles are eaten. This is particularly a problem for young children. Lead compounds have been banned from paint for many years; however, you need to be careful when you are working on a surface that you suspect was previously painted with a paint that has a high lead content.

Wear a dust mask or respirator to avoid inhaling particles of the paint. If you scrape loose paint from the surface, use a drop cloth to collect the chips and dispose of them in accordance with local dump regulations. Don't allow chips of lead paint to fall into the soil around a house while you are working on an exterior paint job. Plants grown in the soil will accumulate high concentrations of lead. This is particularly bad if the area is used as a vegetable garden. Don't allow children to stay in a house during renovations if the house contains lead paint.

Extenders

Extenders are also called *suspenders* or *fillers* and are usually listed with the pigments on the paint-can label. Extenders are a necessary ingredient in all paints. They improve the paint's working characteristics and help suspend the pigments in the vehicle. However, when the extenders make up a large percentage of the total amount of pigments, the quality of the paint will be lowered. Some common extenders are silica, calcium carbonate, barium sulfate, calcium sulfate, aluminum silicate, magnesium silicate, and mica. Mica and magnesium silicate help to reduce cracking of the dried paint film. Mica is also added to some acrylic latex paints to make them more water repellent.

Resins

Resins glue the pigments and extenders together to form the dry paint film. They are sometimes referred to as *binders*. In modern paints the type of resin used is one of the most important considerations. The resin used determines what the paint is suitable for and how durable it will be.

ACRYLIC RESINS Acrylic resins, synthetic plastics, are one of the most popular resins for use in water-based paints. It produces a tough water-repellent film that adheres well to wood. Acrylic latex paints have two properties that make them very desirable as a wood finish. The paint film will keep out liquid water, but it will allow water vapor to pass through it. This property is called *breatheability*. Paints that breathe allow the wood to adapt to climatic changes without causing paint blisters. Acrylic paints are also very flexible, so the wood can expand and contract without cracking the paint film.

ALKYD RESINS Alkyd resins are also synthetic resins. Almost all modern oil-based paints contain alkyd resin. Alkyd can also use used in water-based paints, usually in connection with another resin such as acrylic. Oil-based alkyds produce a very tough, long-lasting paint film that is impervious to water. This makes them ideal for use in wet locations to prevent water from damaging the wood, but because they don't breathe, they are more likely to blister if the wood has a high-moisture content. Water-based alkyds produce a breathing film, so in that respect they are superior to the oil-based type for use on wood. An oil-based alkyd will adhere better to old, weathered paint, so it is sometimes preferred for repainting previously painted wood. However, the water-based type is constantly being improved in this respect.

POLYURETHANE RESINS Polyurethane resins are used in paints when an extremely tough abrasion-resistant film is needed. Polyurethane paint is much more expensive than alkyd or acrylic, but it will pay for itself through its durability in some situations. Polyurethane paints come in two types. The first comes as a single liquid just like most paint and can be handled like ordinary paint. The second type comes as two separate liquids. Once they are mixed together the paint will remain a liquid for about eight hours. After that it will harden into solid plastic even if it is in a sealed can. This type is tougher and more weather-resistant than the single liquid type.

EPOXY RESINS Epoxy resins are similar to polyurethane resin, only they are even tougher. Epoxy resins won't produce quite as glossy a finish as polyurethane. Like polyurethane, they are available as a single liquid or as a two-part catalyzed finish.

VINYL RESINS When flexibility of the paint film is of prime importance, vinyl resins are used. Vinyl is used mostly in water-based paints, sometimes in conjunction with one of the other resins.

BUTADIENE-STYRENE RESINS These resins are one of the first types used to make latex paint. They are low cost and yet still give a tough rubbery film.

A variety of other resins including polyethylene, polystyrene, polyester, and phenolics are also used, usually in connection with one of the other resins listed above. Each additional resin is included to add a special quality to the paint such as durability, water resistance, or washability.

Oils

Several types of oils are used in paint to add desirable qualities to the final film. They tend to make the paint film more durable and water resistant. They are desirable in paint that is used as a wood finish because they tend to soak into the wood and help preserve it. Although oils are mostly associated with oil-based paint, many water-based paints incorporate some oils into their formulas. Linseed oil was once used almost exclusively, but now a wide variety of other oils such as soya oil, tung oil, safflower oil, sunflower oil, and others are also used.

Solvents

So far all of the ingredients discussed have contributed in some way to the final paint film. The job of the solvents is different. They are meant to evaporate from the paint as it dries, leaving only the other ingredients behind. The solvents thin the paint to a workable consistency and make it easier to apply by helping it flow out to create a smooth surface.

By far the most popular solvent in use today is water because of its many advantages. It is inexpensive, makes cleanup easy, is nonflammable, is non-toxic, evaporates quickly, and it has no odor. The only major disadvantage of using water as a paint solvent is that it may raise the grain of bare wood.

Petroleum distillates are another popular solvent. Most oil-based paints use petroleum distillates like mineral spirits or naptha as the solvent. Paints that use petroleum distillates can be thinned with paint thinner. The main disadvantage of petroleum distillates is that the fumes are toxic and flammable.

Some paints like epoxies require special solvents such as acetone or MEK (methyl-ethyl-ketone). Pigmented lacquer should be thinned with lacquer thinner.

When it is necessary to thin paint, the thinner should be compatible with the solvents in the paint. Always use the type of thinner recommended on the paint can.

Primers

Primers are necessary whenever you are painting bare wood. Top-coat paints don't penetrate deep into bare wood, so they don't adhere well to it. Primers are formulated to penetrate the wood, thus helping preserve it and holding the paint film firmly in place. They dry with a slightly rough surface that is called *tooth* which makes a better bond between the primer and the top coat. Paint folklore has it that you can make a good primer by thinning the top coat 50 percent. This is no longer valid. If you try this method, you risk having the paint peel or blister at a later date.

Each manufacturer markets what is called a *paint system* that consists of several paint products, including primers, wall paint, exterior paint, and interior enamel, that are all compatible with each other. Once you have decided on a particular type of paint, stay with that system for all of the other products you will use on the job. That way you can be sure there won't be any problems of incompatibility between the products.

Most systems offer at least two types of primers for use on bare wood. One is usually an oil-based alkyd and the other is water-based. Water-based products will raise the grain of bare wood, so you should use the oil-based primer on surfaces such as interior woodwork or cabinets that need a smooth surface. For building exteriors, raised grain doesn't present as much of a problem because some wood texture is usually desirable aesthetically. So, if you can tolerate the raised grain, a water-based primer will perform better for exterior use because it produces a breathing film while the oil-based primer produces an impervious film. If you use an oil-based primer under a paint like acrylic latex, you lose some of the advantage gained by choosing the breathing paint because the primer won't breathe.

Some types of wood contain pigments will bleed through a paint film, creating a stain on the finished surface. Woods that are especially prone to bleeding are redwood, cedar, mahogany, and fir. Knots in other types of wood, especially pine, are very prone to bleeding. Bleeding stains can appear even after the paint has been dry for several months. Follow the recommendations on the paint can for handling bleeding problems. It will recommend one of the products in the same system that contains a sealer to prevent bleed-through. It may be one of the primers or it may be a separate sealer.

One product that is often recommended as a sealer is pigmented shellac. It is similar to the shellac discussed earlier, but a high hiding pigment such as titanium dioxide has been added. Usually pigmented shellac is an alcohol-based product like the other forms of shellac, but a new development is a water-based product called *pigmented latex shellac*. This product combines non-volatile shellac with acrylic resin and titanium dioxide. It can be used a primer and sealer.

What Woods to Paint

Choosing the type of wood you will apply paint to is as important as choosing the type of paint. The underlying wood plays an important role in how the final finish looks and how durable it is.

For exterior use and for use in wet interior locations, redwood and cedar are the top choices. Even though they have bleeding problems, they can easily be sealed to prevent this. Paint adheres to these woods very well and, because they are so decay- and rot-resistant, there isn't any problem of deterioration under the paint film.

When interior trim such as door and window casing and baseboards are to be painted, they are usually made of pine or fir, but other woods such as hemlock are also used. Finger joints joining several short pieces into one long piece of molding are usually unacceptable if the woodwork is to be stained and given a clear finish, but they don't present a problem if the molding will be painted—as long as the joints are well made so that no gaps are visible through the paint.

For strictly utilitarian interior cabinet work, fir plywood is acceptable, but it is not well-suited for fine work where appearance is important because the grain absorbs paint so unevenly that there is almost always some grain that shows through the paint.

Birch plywood is an ideal choice for fine cabinetry and furniture that will be painted. Paint adheres well to its surface and it absorbs paint uniformly. It is close-grained so very little texture shows through the paint and its subtle grain doesn't affect the final appearance of the paint. Also, because of its light color, there is no problem with bleeding or with coverage when using light-colored paint.

Manmade wood products lend themselves well to a paint finish. One of the best is *tempered hardboard*. Its super-smooth surface will produce very good results when painted. It is usually only available in 1/8-inch and 1/4-inch thicknesses. For thicker panels, you can use *medium-density fiberboard (MDF)*. MDF also has a very smooth uniform surface that accepts paint well. *Particleboard* is not as smooth as tempered hardboard, but the better grades have a smooth enough surface to accept a good finish. Some types of particleboard are available with a preprimed face that accepts paint very well.

Medium-density overlay plywood (MDO) and *high-density overlay plywood (HDO)* are specially designed to be painted. They have a plywood core like most plywood, but the face veneer is a manmade product rather than a wood veneer. The surface of these plywoods is very smooth and has no grain. They are often used for exterior siding, and make a good substitute for birch plywood in interior cabinetwork.

All of the manmade wood products should be primed with an oil-based primer if the smoothest surface is needed. Water-based products will cause the particles of wood to swell, creating bumps. Many of these products come preprimed from the factory.

Specific Applications

There are some specific applications for which a particular paint product is best. For exterior wood siding and trim, acrylic latex is the leading choice at present (**4–36**). Because it breathes and is flexible, it doesn't blister, crack, or peel. Of course, this is only true when applying the paint to new work. No product will glue down an old paint film that has failed. If a previously painted surface has blisters or is cracking and peeling, the old paint must be removed from those areas and the underlying problem corrected.

4-36 *Acrylic latex is a leading choice for exterior wood trim.*

For interior moldings, a semi-gloss acrylic latex enamel is a good choice. But use an oil-based primer on bare wood.

The type of paint used on furniture depends on the type of finish desired. Pine or particleboard unfinished furniture can be painted with semi-gloss acrylic latex enamel if an oil-based primer is used first. If the furniture will receive heavy use, consider polyurethane or epoxy. For fine furniture, lacquer is the a traditional choice.

Lacquer paint is similar to the clear lacquer discussed earlier. It possesses all of the qualities previously described and the pigments used are usually very finely ground to give the smoothest possible finish. You can rub out a lacquered surface with pumice and rottenstone, steel wool, or rubbing compound.

Lacquer is available in a wide range of colors. Black is frequently used to finish Oriental-style furniture. Lacquer should only be applied by spraying; it is available in spray cans for those who don't have spray equipment. Follow the can label closely regarding the use of primers because lacquer will lift most conventional primers. Some lacquers can be applied directly to bare wood. If you want to repaint a previously painted surface with lacquer, you may need to remove the old paint or apply a special sealer because lacquer is not compatible with most other kinds of paint.

Lacquer is a professional product and is more difficult to apply than most paints, but it will provide the best-looking finish on fine furniture.

For a wider selection of colors and special effects like metal flake, some wood finishers are turning to automotive paint. Although it is formulated for use on metal, it will work on wood. Be sure to use compatible primers. Like lacquer, this is a professional product that should only be applied with spray equipment. You will have to experiment to find the best application procedure, because the manufacturers don't give directions for wood.

Floors are subject to a lot of wear and abrasion. If you want to paint a wood floor, use a paint specifically designated as a floor paint. In very high traffic areas, you may need to use a catalyzed polyurethane or epoxy to get the most durable finish.

Applying Paint

Paint can be applied with a brush, roller, pad applicator, or spray equipment. The technique of brushing paint depends on whether the paint is oil-based or water-based. Oil-based paint should be brushed out to a uniform thin coat by going over the same area several times; otherwise, the paint film may be too thick and runs, sags, or wrinkling may develop. Water-based paint, on the other hand, is very slippery and overbrushing will result in a coat that is too thin. Stop brushing an area as soon as you have achieved a smooth covering. Either natural or synthetic filament brushes can be used with oil-based paints, but only synthetic filaments should be used with water-based paints.

Rollers and pad applicators work well with either oil-based or water-based paint. Pad applicators are especially well-suited for exterior clapboard siding. When applying paint to a large surface with a roller, roll over the same area in several random directions to prevent lap marks.

An important principle in painting is keeping a wet edge. Lap marks will occur if you don't observe this rule. Plan your work so that you can paint an entire surface in one step. This is more difficult on large surfaces like building exteriors, but you can usually find natural stopping places like doors, windows or corners. If you stop in the middle of a large wall and then resume painting after the paint has dried, there will be a noticeable line at the joint between the two applications of paint.

Spray equipment can be used to apply most types of paint (see *pages 75 to 91*). Some will require thinning. Follow the manufacturer's recommendations about what type of thinner to use. Water-based paints usually are more difficult to spray than oil-based paints. You need a different type of nozzle to spray water-based paint with some sprayers. Airless spray equipment can handle thicker paints better than types that use compressed air. However, small self-contained airless sprayers require that thick paints be thinned considerably.

Prepare new wood for painting as you would for any finish by sanding it if a smooth surface is desired. A rough surface is desirable for some types of exterior siding and, in that case, no special preparation is needed. When repainting an old surface, thoroughly wash the old paint to remove accumulations of grease, wax, or dirt that may prevent the new paint from sticking. Flat paint can be painted over without sanding, but gloss paint should be deglossed by sanding with 150-grit sandpaper. Deglossing liquid is an alternative that slightly dissolves the top surface of the old paint and makes it dull.

4-37 *If you want an antique effect, you can use the "dry brush" technique when applying paint to furniture.*

PAINTING FURNITURE AND CABINETS WITH A BRUSH Brush the first coat of paint in long, even strokes with the grain direction of the wood. Brush out the paint so it forms a thin even coat. Let the paint dry, and then rub it with a medium synthetic finishing pad. This will remove any dust that got trapped in the wet paint and will also dull the gloss so that the next coat will stick well. A synthetic finishing pad or steel wool works better than sandpaper, because they won't clog.

Next, apply another thin coat. If the second coat "hides" well enough, you can stop. If additional coats are needed, rub the surface again with a synthetic finishing pad and apply additional coats. If you want an antique effect, you can use the "dry brush" technique for the third coat (**4–37**). Use a different color paint for this coat and very little paint on the brush. After you dip the brush in the paintbrush, move it over a scrap or piece of cardboard until the brush leaves distinct brush marks. Now lightly brush over the surface of the project. This gives the effect of worn areas where a different coat of paint is showing through.

PAINTING PREVIOUSLY FINISHED WOOD

When repainting an old surface, thoroughly wash the old paint to remove accumulations of grease, wax or dirt that may prevent the new paint from sticking. Flat paint can be painted over without sanding, but gloss paint should be deglossed.

To clean the old finish, use trisodium phosphate (TSP) mixed with water to wash the old finish. Mix the TSP with water in a bucket. Wear protective gloves and eye protection. Soak a sponge in the solution, and then wring it out and wipe the project with the damp sponge. Avoid getting a lot of water on the surface, because the water can soak through the paint and cause the wood to swell. Frequently rinse the sponge in the bucket of TSP solution. After you've cleaned the surface, wipe it dry with a clean cloth.

For items that need heavy cleaning, you can use a medium synthetic finishing pad instead of a sponge. There are also special sanding sponges that can be used for this operation. It is a sponge that is coated with abrasives. Use a fine-grit sanding sponge or a finishing pad to clean the surface with the TSP solution. Rub the sanding sponge over the surface lightly and rinse it in the TSP frequently. This will clean the surface and degloss it is a single step.

Be careful not to rub too much. Avoid cutting through the finish to bare wood; if you do, you will have to sand and prime the area.

If the surface doesn't need much cleaning, you can simply degloss the paint. You can mechanically degloss the paint by rubbing it with a medium synthetic finishing pad.

You can also use a liquid deglosser to prepare the surface. A liquid deglosser slightly dissolves the top surface of the old paint and makes it dull. *Deglossers can be toxic, so wear plastic gloves and work in an area with adequate ventilation.* To use a chemical deglosser, moisten a rag with the deglosser and wipe it on the surface. As the rag gets covered with old paint, refold it to expose a clean section and add more deglosser. Only rub in one spot long enough to remove the gloss. You don't need to remove a lot of the old finish. Then let the deglosser dry as specified on the container before you paint.

If the old finish is sound, then one or two coats of paint are all that are needed; no primer is necessary, because the old finish has sealed the wood. However, if you are applying a water-based paint over an old water-based finish, the color from the old finish may bleed through the new paint. To prevent this, apply a stain blocker.

Whenever you will need more than one can of paint to complete a job, mix all of the paint together before starting the job. Mixing compensates for variations in color between the individual cans. You can avoid the messy job of mixing by buying paint in larger containers. Paint stores that cater to professionals usually sell paint in five-gallon containers, and some do-it-yourself-oriented stores are beginning to do likewise.

Paint Problems

If you follow the directions closely when applying modern paint to new wood, you are unlikely to have any problems. But when you repaint a surface that was painted with one of the older types of paint, you may encounter some of the following problems.

BLISTERING Blistering is most likely to occur on building exteriors (**4–38**). Moisture from inside the building (especially near bathrooms, laundry rooms, and kitchens) travels through the walls because the sun heating the exterior of the wall draws moisture out. When the paint applied to the wall is of the non-breathing type (or there are too many layers of it), the moisture can't escape, so pressure builds up behind the paint. Eventually the pressure loosens the bond between the paint and the wood and a blister forms. Modern buildings incorporate a vapor barrier in the wall construction to help solve this problem, but older buildings lack this feature.

When repainting a blistered surface, use a scraper to remove all of the blisters. Prime the bare wood below the blister with a breathing primer; then paint the area with a breathing paint like acrylic latex. Unless you remove all of the old paint from the surface, the blistering problem is likely to reoccur in the areas that weren't scraped. You may be able to reduce the chances of more blisters forming by installing small vents in the wall to let the moisture out. To be truly effective, the vents must be placed at the top and bottom of each stud cavity because fire bridging usually blocks the cavity in the middle.

PEELING AND FLAKING Like blistering, this problem may be caused by moisture, or it may be due to lack of flexibility in the old paint (**4–39**). Wood expands and contracts with climatic changes. If the paint is not capable of flexing with the wood, it will crack and eventually flake off. To correct this problem, remove all of the loose paint and prime the bare wood before repainting.

4-38 *Blistering.*

4-39 *Peeling and flaking.*

If recently applied paint peels from an old surface it is probably because the old surface was not adequately prepared before repainting. Thoroughly wash the surface to remove grease or dirt that may prevent paint adhesion and degloss glossy paint by sanding or using a liquid deglosser.

MILDEW Mildew is fungus that grows on moist surfaces. It is especially a problem in areas that have a climate with high temperatures and humidity, but it can occur in any climate if moisture is present on the paint film for long periods of time. Before repainting, thoroughly wash the mildew from the paint with a solution of one part liquid chlorine bleach mixed in three parts water. Tough spots may require a higher concentration of bleach. Rinse thoroughly with clear water. When repainting, choose a paint that contains a fungicide to prevent regrowth of the mildew.

ALLIGATORING When the surface of the paint cracks and pulls apart in a pattern that looks like alligator skin, the problem is called alligatoring (**4–40**). This problem can occur with new paint if the primer was incompatible with the top coat. It can also occur when new paint is applied over a glossy surface without first deglossing the surface. It also occurs when many layers of old paint dry out and become brittle. The only solution is to remove the old paint.

4-40 *Alligatoring.*

4-41 *Chalking.*

CHALKING As exterior paints weather, a dusty film develops on the surface. This dust is called *chalk*. Chalk is actually the residue of the pigments in the top surface of the paint that are left behind as the binders in the paint weather away. To a certain extent, chalking can be desirable. It makes the paint self-cleaning. Stains and dirt that have accumulated on the surface of the paint will wash away with the chalk during rainstorms or when the surface is hosed down. When chalking becomes extreme, it becomes a problem. Excessive chalking will create streaks and stains on foundations and sidewalks or on areas of contrasting color (**4–41**).

For this reason, contrasting trim should always be painted with a chalk-resistant (not "self-cleaning") paint.

Chalking makes repainting difficult because the loose chalk creates a barrier between the new paints and the old surface. When using latex paint over a chalked surface, you must completely remove all of the chalk by hosing the surface down with water and detergent and scrubbing with a stiff brush. Some oil-based primers and paints will soak through a chalked surface to bond to the firm paint below. If you use this type of primer first, you can apply latex paint over it.

Exterior Protective Stains

Exterior protective stains differ from the stains discussed earlier in that they form a protective coating on the wood as well as adding color. No additional top coat is needed when these types of stains are applied. They are primarily intended for building exteriors and fences, but they can also be used for outdoor furniture and woodwork (**4–42**).

There are two main categories of exterior protective stains: *semitransparent* and *opaque*. Semitransparent is the most durable of the two and is preferred when the stain will be applied to new wood. It also has the advantage of letting the grain of the wood show. Opaque stains are also called *solid color stains*. They totally cover the grain of the wood. They are most often used to restain wood to a color that is substantially different from the old stain. Opaque stains should only be used on vertical surfaces such as walls. Decks and other horizontal surfaces should only be stained with semitransparent stains, because standing water won't affect semitransparent stains as much as it will opaque stains.

Both types of stain are available in oil-based and water-based formulas. The oil-based formula usually contains a large percentage of linseed oil to soak into the wood and preserve it. The water-based stains may include an acrylic resin, or they may use linseed oil that has been emulsified in water.

To provide the most protection, these stains must be worked into the wood by brushing back and forth. If spray equipment or rollers are used to apply the stain, brush over the surface while the stain is still wet to work it into the wood.

4-42 *Porches, decks, and outdoor furniture can all be protected with outdoor stains. Use opaque stain on vertical surfaces like posts and trim. Use semi-transparent stain on outdoor furniture and decks.*

5 Mixing Stains

Although there are literally hundreds of different colors of stains available commercially, there comes a time when none of them exactly fits your needs. You may visualize a particular project with a unique original color, or you may be trying to match a new piece to an existing set of furniture. In any case, you will have to mix your own stain to achieve your goal (**5–1**). Sometimes it's possible to mix two or more commercial stains to achieve the desired result, but you'll usually have more creative control if you mix tinting colors to get the color you want.

In order to mix stains intelligently, you need to know a little about color theory. Colors are classified according to three main criteria; hue, value, and chroma. *Hue* is what most people call color—red or blue for example. Red, blue, and yellow are the primary colors of pigments; this means that all

5-1

When you just can't find exactly the right color in a premixed stain, you can mix a custom color stain. These cabinets have been stained with a custom red stain.

of the other colors can be made by mixing these colors in different proportions. For example, yellow and blue mixed in equal proportions make green. Yellow and red make orange, and red and blue make violet.

Value is determined by the lightness or darkness of a color. Value is altered by the addition of white or black. Adding white to a color lightens its value; the result is called a *tint of the original color*. When black is added to a color, the result is called a *shade*; it has a darker value than the original color.

Chroma is the intensity of the color. High-intensity colors are brilliant, while low-intensity colors are grayish. Every color has a complementary color that will decrease the chroma of a color when the two are mixed. Complementary colors are opposite each other on the color wheel (**5–2**). You can buy color wheels from finishing supply companies that will help you determine how to mix colors (**5–3**).

Mixing colors for stains is slightly different than mixing pure colors such as red and blue. The colors most often used for stains are earth colors that are derived from natural minerals. They are not pure colors, they are mixtures, tints, and shades of pure colors. But since they are naturally produced colors, they look better on wood where you're trying to achieve a natural look. Colors used for wood stains usually have a low chroma and a fairly dark value. Colors with a high chroma tend to look very artificial on wood and should be avoided unless you are intentionally trying for an unusual look.

If you are using conversion finishes, ask the customer rep about a computer stain-mixing program. Some companies offer a

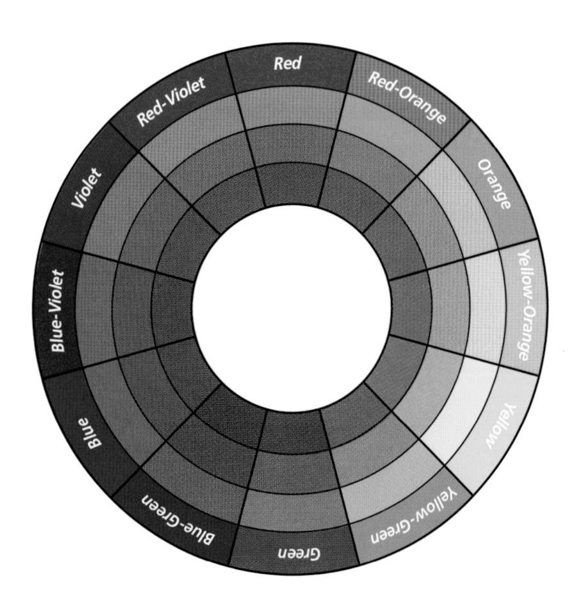

5-2 *You mix colors for stains using the same color theory artists use. The color wheel consists of twelve colors: the three primary colors—red, yellow, and blue—and the colors that result when they are mixed. Complementary colors are exactly opposite each other on the wheel.*

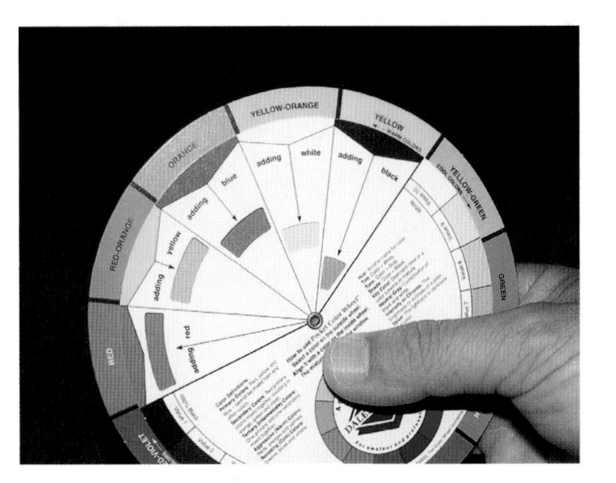

5-3 *When you align a color on the outer wheel with a color on the inner wheel of this commercial color wheel, it shows you the resulting color in the center window.*

program that you run on your own computer to create custom stain formulas. For stains used under conversion finishes, only use dyes and pigments recommended for the finish system you are using. Using a custom stain that contains incompatible materials can create problems later after the conversion finish is applied.

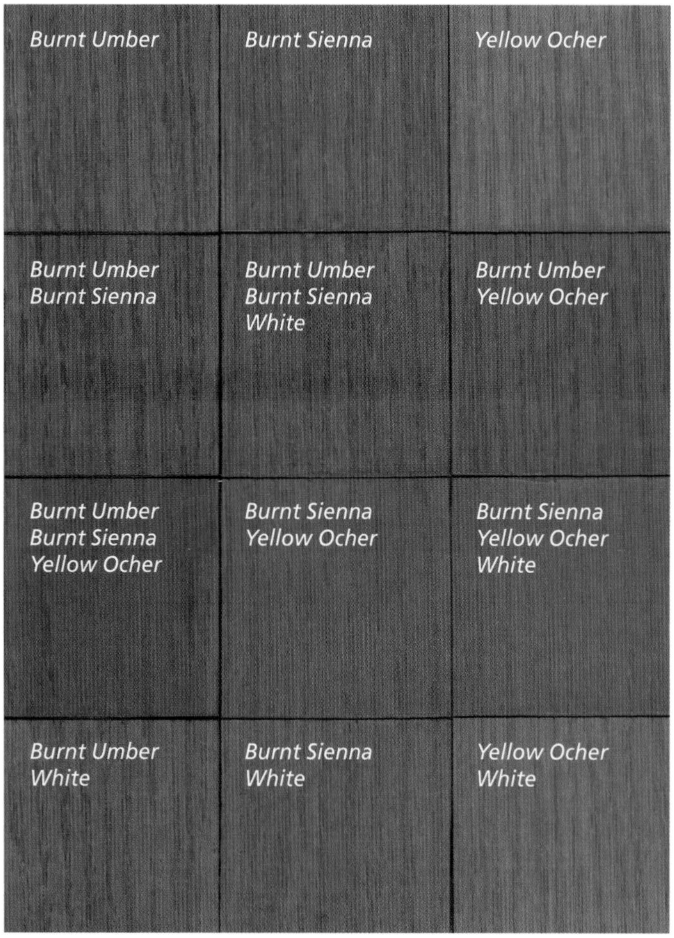

5-4 *A few of the many variations that you can make by mixing burnt umber, yellow ocher, burnt sienna, and titanium white.*

Tinting Colors

Tinting colors are pigments suspended in a liquid vehicle. They are classified by the type of vehicle used. There are three types of tinting colors: oil, Japan, and universal. *Oil colors* can be used to tint any oil-based product. *Japan colors* will mix with oil-based and lacquer-based products. *Universal tinting colors* will tint oil and water-based products. Of the three types, the universal tinting colors are the easiest to use to mix stains. They are more liquid, while the other two are a paste. The paste type is harder to mix completely.

Tinting colors are available in a wide range of standard colors that use standard names regardless of the type of vehicle or the manufacturer.

For small projects and touch up work, you can also use artist's oil colors or acrylics. To make a stain from oil colors, mix the colors with linseed oil. To make an acrylic stain, dilute the colors with water.

You don't need to buy a whole set of tinting colors to mix your own stains; in fact, 90 percent of the time you will only need four colors: burnt umber, yellow ocher, burnt sienna, and titanium white. Illus. **5–4** shows just a few of the many variations possible that you can make by mixing these four colors.

Burnt umber is a dark brown color. If you could only have one tinting color, it should be burnt umber. Almost all of the popular shades of brown stain can be made with varying amounts of burnt umber. When you buy your tinting colors, it's a good idea to buy a larger container of burnt umber because it will be a major constituent in almost all stains. Straight burnt umber is the color most commonly thought of as walnut stain.

Yellow ocher is a tannish yellow. Straight yellow ocher is the color of light pine stain. It is used to make light-colored stains or to add a yellow cast to darker stains.

Burnt sienna is reddish brown. It is used for mahogany-colored stains or, when mixed with yellow ocher, produces a pleasing orange color used on pine and maple.

Titanium white is used to lighten the above colors.

Pigmented Oil Stains

You can make your own pigmented oil stain very easily. If you are using traditional oil-based finishes, this will work well. Don't use this stain under conversion finishes or waterborne finishes. The formula is:

one pint paint thinner
7 oz. Danish oil
tinting colors as desired

Turpentine can be substituted for the paint thinner. Use a fast-drying Danish oil that contains tung oil. Any of the three types of tinting colors can be used, since they are all compatible with oil. The above formula will make about one quart of stain. The exact amount of stain produced will vary depending on how much tinting color is used.

To mix the stain, first pour about one cup of paint thinner into a container; add the desired tinting colors to the thinner and thoroughly mix. Now add the oil and mix completely. If the stain will be stored in the container for a long time, it needs an air-tight lid.

The stain is applied exactly the same as commercial pigmented oil stain. (See Chapter 3 for details.)

Varnish Stains

Universal tinting colors, oil colors, and Japan colors are all compatible with oil-based varnish, so you can use them to color varnish to any shade that you wish to create. Mix the tinting colors with a small amount of turpentine first; then add the mixture to the varnish. Universal tinting colors are compatible with water-based varnish; add the tinting colors directly to the varnish without thinning.

Lacquer Toner Stains

Lacquer can be tinted with Japan colors to produce a toner stain. Mix the Japan colors in lacquer thinner before adding them to the lacquer. Chapter 3 describes the uses for toner stains.

Water Stains

The dyes used to make water stains are not available as tinting colors, so to custom-mix true water stains you have to intermix commercially prepared stains. Mix the powdered stains with water before combining colors. Universal tinting colors are water compatible, so you can slightly alter the color of a water stain by adding a little universal tinting color. But remember that tinting colors are pigments while water stains are dyes, so by adding a pigment you are losing some of the clarity of the water stain.

You can make a water stain that is very similar in appearance to dye stains from transparent artist's watercolors. The colors come in tubes and are available from art supply dealers. Many of the colors use the same standard names as tinting colors, so you can easily choose the ones you want. Mix the colors together as they come from the tube; then thin them with water. Apply the stain the same way you would apply dye stain.

Color Mixing Formulas

The following formulas are meant to give you a general starting place in your search for your own individual color choice. By varying the proportions of the colors, you can considerably alter the resulting stain.

Color intensity is best altered by increasing or decreasing the amount of the colors listed. Adding white or black to the formula not only lightens or darkens the intensity, it changes the entire character of the stain. White tends to give the stain a pastel effect if used too extensively. Black is probably the most widely misused tinting color. Black is commonly added to stains under the misconception that it will darken the color. What actually happens is that the black pigment overpowers the other pigments and totally changes the look of the stain. Black pigments have a tendency to collect mainly in the pores or soft areas of the wood, greatly accentuating the grain. You will notice that none of the formulas listed contains black unless they are specifically a black or gray stain like ebony, silver-gray, or mission oak. Burnt umber is much better than lamp black for darkening a stain. You can add burnt umber to any of the brown stains to darken them without greatly changing their basic character.

The formulas include amounts that indicate approximately how much universal tinting colors should be used to make one quart of pigmented oil stain. This is just a starting place. Experiment with varying proportions to create the custom color you want. Start by mixing a small quantity using the same proportions and scale up to a larger quantity when are happy with the color. Other types of tinting colors may require different amounts, but the proportions should be similar.

The first group of formulas use only the four basic tinting colors discussed earlier. The second group of stains include other colors in addition to the basic four.

Stains Using the Four Basic Tinting Colors

5-5 *Walnut on walnut: 6 oz. burnt umber.*

5-6 *Red mahogany on mahogany: 6 oz. burnt sienna.*

5-7 *Brown mahogany on mahogany: 6 oz. burnt umber, 2 oz. burnt sienna.*

5-8 *Dark oak on oak: 6 oz. burnt umber, 1 oz. burnt sienna, 1/2 oz. yellow ocher.*

5-9 *Light oak on oak: 1 oz. burnt umber, 1 oz. yellow ocher.*

5-10 *Cherry on cherry: 4 oz. burnt sienna, 1 oz. burnt umber, 1/4 oz. yellow ocher.*

5-11 *Natural pine on pine: 4 oz. yellow ocher, 2 oz. titanium white, 1 oz. burnt umber.*

5-12 *Pickled pine on pine: 4 oz. titanium white, 1 oz. yellow ocher, 1/4 oz. burnt umber.*

5-13 *Antique pine on pine: 3 oz. burnt umber, 2 oz. yellow ocher, 1 oz. titanium white, 1/4 oz. burnt sienna.*

5-14 *Limed oak on oak: 6 oz. titanium white, 1 oz. yellow ocher, 1/4 oz. burnt umber.*

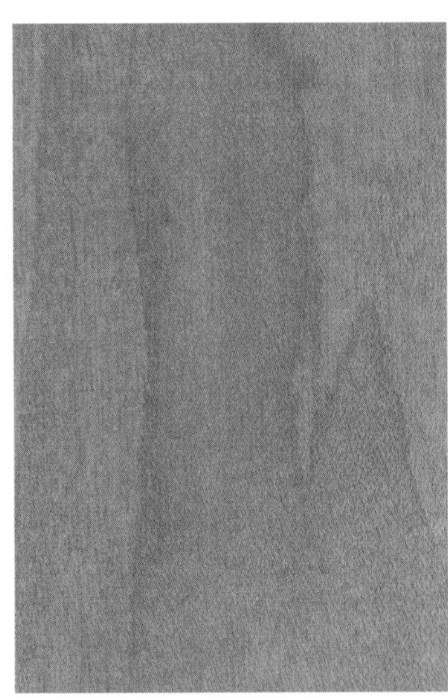

5-15 *Honey maple on maple: 6 oz. yellow ocher, 1 oz. burnt sienna, 1/4 oz. burnt umber.*

Stains Using Additional Colors

Medium Dark Walnut
5 oz. Vandyke brown
4 oz. burnt umber

Dark Walnut
7 oz. Vandyke brown

Bright Red Mahogany
5 oz. burnt sienna
1 oz. raw umber
1/2 oz. Venetian red

Dark Brown Mahogany
6 oz. Vandyke brown
1 oz. raw umber

Yellow Maple
3 oz. raw sienna
1 oz. raw umber

Honey Pine
4 oz. yellow ocher
1 oz. raw sienna

Light Cherry
3 oz. raw sienna
3 oz. burnt sienna

Mission Oak
3 oz. vandyke brown
1 oz. burnt umber
2 oz. lamp black

Ebony
8 oz. lamp black
1/4 oz. Venetian red
1/8 oz. Prussian blue

Weathered Silver Gray
2 oz. lamp black
3 oz. titanium white
1/4 oz. raw sienna

6 Finishing Problem Woods

Most wood will accept almost any type of finish with good results, but there are a few problem woods that are difficult to finish with standard methods. They are pine and fir, wood with uneven coloring, and wood with natural oils that interfere with some finishes.

Pine and Fir

Pine and fir are woods that are commonly used by do-it-yourselfers for projects and yet these are two of the most difficult woods to stain well (**6–1**). Pine in its natural state with only a clear finish is a beautiful wood with a very clear, subtle gain; but usually when it is stained, it becomes cloudy or muddy looking and the grain stands out much too prominently (**6–2**). Other soft-

6-1 *This pine cabinet was finished using techniques described in this chapter.*

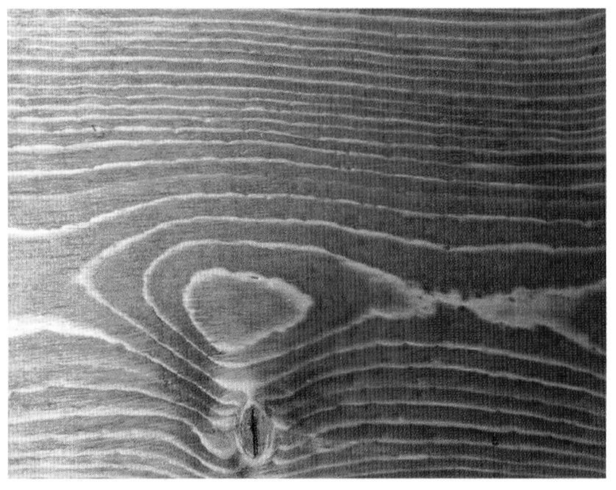

6-2 *This is an example of the muddy look that stained pine sometimes exhibits.*

woods such as hemlock, spruce, and cypress aren't as widely used, but they pose the same problems as pine for the wood finisher.

Some light-colored hardwoods, birch in particular, will sometimes look muddy when a very dark stain is applied. If you have a problem with this, try one of the remedies used for pine. Fir plywood is an even bigger problem, because the wood has been rotary cut from the log, resulting in a very wild, unnatural looking grain that stands out prominently when a stain is applied **(6–3)**.

Light-colored stains are not as big a problem as dark stains on these woods. Dark stains will stain the soft parts of the grain, but leave the harder parts practically the natural color. But even light-colored stains tend to have a muddy look.

There are several remedies to these problems. Water stains work better on fir and pine than oil stains do. Waterborne stain also seems to have an advantage (**6–4**). Probably the best way to treat problem woods is to apply a wood conditioner before staining.

6-4 *This pine sample was stained with a water-borne stain. It has accepted the stain fairly evenly, but there is still some splotchiness. Using a wood conditioner first would eliminate the splotches.*

Use the type of wood conditioner recommended by the manufacturer of the stain you are using. This will partially seal the grain and help the stain to be absorbed more uniformly (**6–5**). Gel stains don't soak into the wood very much, so you can even out the color by wiping to a greater degree than you can with stains that penetrate deeper.

Shellac can be useful when staining problem woods. In fact, you can use orange

6-3 *Fir that is rotary cut has a wild grain pattern that stands out prominently when a stain is applied.*

6-5 *This fir sample was treated with a wood conditioner before staining with a waterborne stain. Compare this with* ***6–3****. Both samples were cut from the same piece of plywood.*

6-6 *Orange shellac gives the pine the warm color of an antique.*

6-7 *This sample had a coat of clear penetrating oil applied before a coat of tinted oil.*

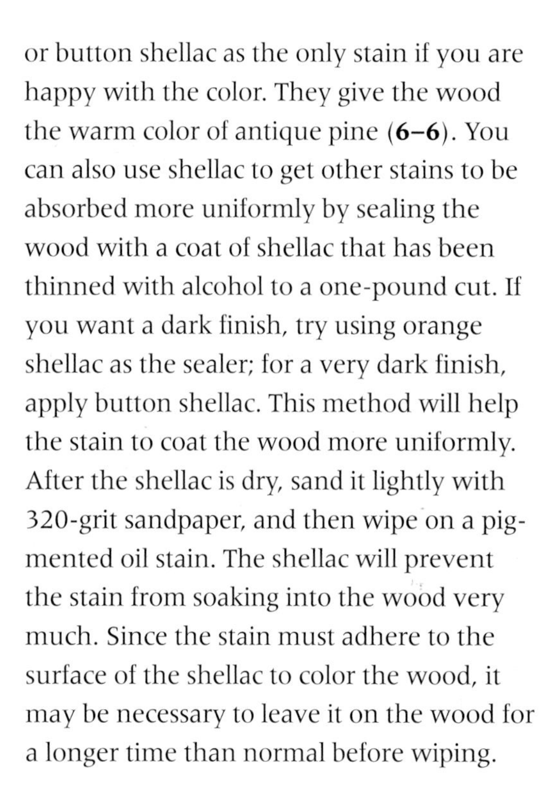

or button shellac as the only stain if you are happy with the color. They give the wood the warm color of antique pine (**6–6**). You can also use shellac to get other stains to be absorbed more uniformly by sealing the wood with a coat of shellac that has been thinned with alcohol to a one-pound cut. If you want a dark finish, try using orange shellac as the sealer; for a very dark finish, apply button shellac. This method will help the stain to coat the wood more uniformly. After the shellac is dry, sand it lightly with 320-grit sandpaper, and then wipe on a pigmented oil stain. The shellac will prevent the stain from soaking into the wood very much. Since the stain must adhere to the surface of the shellac to color the wood, it may be necessary to leave it on the wood for a longer time than normal before wiping.

Wipe the stain in long, straight strokes, not in a circular motion. The wiping is especially important on fir plywood, because you can help to hide some of the wild grain. Use a coarse cloth like burlap (hessian) and wipe lightly in long, straight strokes with the grain direction. The burlap will leave small lines in the stain that will tend to visually straighten out the wild grain patterns of the wood. Using orange shellac or button shellac as the top coat will even out the color further.

If you are going to apply a tinted penetrating oil finish, first apply a coat of clear penetrating oil. This will help seal the soft parts of the grain. You can wait until the clear oil is dry or you can apply the tinted oil while the clear oil is still wet. Experiment on a scrap first to see which method works better with the wood and oil you are using (**6–7**).

6-8 *A dark toner applied over a dark water satin will produce a uniform dark color on pine or fir, but it will hide most of the grain pattern.*

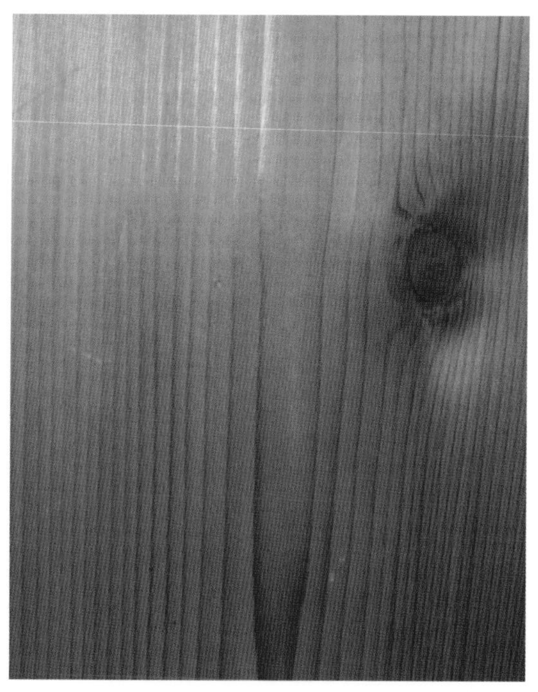

6-9 *A light toner applied over sealed wood will give the finish an inner glow when light reflects off the wood.*

Toners are clear coatings that have pigments or dyes added to color them (see Chapter 2). They can be used to even out the color of problem woods. One of the best ways to get a really uniform dark color on pine or fir is to stain it first with a water stain and when that coat is dry apply a coat of toner over it. This will produce a dark uniform color, but it will hide most of the grain pattern (**6–8**). Toners are useful for light colors as well; you can get a beautifully glowing light pine effect by sealing the bare wood with lacquer sanding sealer and then applying a light-color lacquer toner. Light will be reflected off the almost white color of the sealed wood. This will give the finish a very nice inner glow (**6–9**).

Sap Streaks and Color Variation

Other problem woods are those that contain sap streaks or wide variations in color (**6–10**). If the affected area is darker than the desired finish, you can selectively bleach the area first. If the area is too light, try applying a second coat of stain to that area only. If the color variation is not too great, you can even out the color by using a wiping stain and wiping the area more or less than the surrounding wood (**6–11**). When there is a difference in hue between two boards in the same project, you can bring them closer in color by adding some

6-10 | *This piece of walnut contains dark heartwood and light sapwood. Ordinary staining techniques will not even out this wide a color variation.*

6-11 | *This is the same piece of walnut after being stained using the techniques described in the text.*

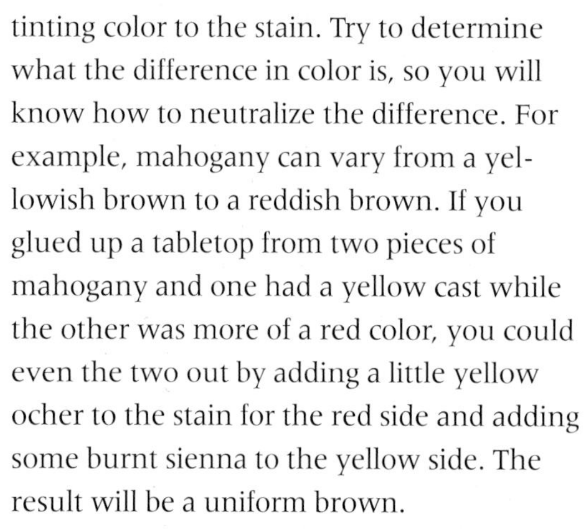

tinting color to the stain. Try to determine what the difference in color is, so you will know how to neutralize the difference. For example, mahogany can vary from a yellowish brown to a reddish brown. If you glued up a tabletop from two pieces of mahogany and one had a yellow cast while the other was more of a red color, you could even the two out by adding a little yellow ocher to the stain for the red side and adding some burnt sienna to the yellow side. The result will be a uniform brown.

You can see why this works by referring to the color wheel in Chapter 5. Red and yellow make orange; brown is a dark shade of orange. By combining the yellow ocher with the reddish color of the one side, the resulting color is brown. The burnt sienna is a reddish color, so it combines with the yellowish board to also make brown. You can use this technique with any combination of color variations; all it takes is some familiarity with the color wheel and an ability to judge what the actual color difference is. If two boards are about the same hue, but one is too intense of a color, you can try adding a little tinting color that is the complement of the color you want to tone down. Complementary colors are opposite each other on the color wheel.

When you are using wood with a large color variation and you want to achieve a very dark uniform color, you can use a chemical treatment to even out the base

6-12 *Left to right: A walnut sample with color variation, the sample after treating with potassium permanganate, and the sample after applying stain over the treated wood.*

color of the wood before applying a stain (**6–12**). This process uses potassium permanganate. *It is a hazardous chemical, so be sure to wear protective gloves and eye protection and follow all of the safety rules on the product's container.* The chemical reaction between the wood and the potassium permanganate turns the wood a dark brown color. Both heart wood and sap wood react to the chemical uniformly so the color variation between them is nullified. This process will make the wood much darker, so treat the entire project, not just the light areas.

To make the solution, dissolve 1 ounce by weight of the potassium permanganate powder in one quart of warm water. Experiment on a piece of scrap wood. If the color is too dark, dilute the solution. Be sure to wear protective gloves and goggles. Use a sponge, rag, or foam brush to apply the potassium permanganate solution to the wood. The wood will first turn a violet color but, it will gradually darken to a uniform brown. After the solution has dried, wash the wood surface with a damp sponge. Let the wood dry thoroughly and sand it lightly to remove the raised grain. You can now stain the surface using any type of stain.

Another problem encountered is that end grain will stain darker than the rest of the board. This can be corrected by applying a second coat of wood conditioner to end grain before staining. You can also seal the ends with a coat of dewaxed shellac.

Some pieces of wood, especially quartersawn varieties, will exhibit a quality called *grain reflection*. The amount of light that the grain reflects varies with the viewing angle and the angle that the light strikes the wood. This can make the wood appear lighter from one viewing angle and darker from another. Usually no attempt to compensate for this difference should be made because any attempt to hide the difference will simply make it more obvious from another angle. Normally grain reflection is regarded as a beautifying aspect of wood that emphasizes its natural character since it cannot be duplicated in man-made products, so simply enjoy this characteristic without trying to alter it. When the wood will remain in a fixed position and will be viewed under constant light conditions you may consider attempting to even out the differences. For example, a paneled wall that contains pieces with both vertical and horizontal grain may show all of the horizontal grain darker than the vertical grain. In that case, you may want to apply additional stain to the horizontal pieces to give the wall a more uniform look.

Oily Woods

Some of the more exotic woods such as teak, rosewood, cocobola, and lignum vitae contain natural oils that interfere with the finishing process (**6–13**). Sometimes varnish applied to these woods will refuse to dry and will remain tacky indefinitely. Lacquer may not adhere well to these woods. Conversion finishes are especially prone to adhesion problems when used on oily woods.

The best solution to the problem of finishing oily woods is to use a special penetrating oil finish formulated for use on these woods. This type of penetrating oil finish will combine with and harden the natural oils present in the wood. If you don't want to use a penetrating oil finish, you will have to create a barrier between the oily wood and the top coat with a sealer. First, remove as much of the oil as you can from the wood by wiping the wood with a rag moistened with alcohol or lacquer thinner. Change the rag frequently. After washing with solvent, let the wood dry and then apply a sealer coat of dewaxed shellac or vinyl sealer. When using polyester or 2K polyurethane conversion finishes, first apply a special "isolante" sealer. (Isolante sealer is a catalyzed polyurethane product that provides a barrier coat between oily woods and stains.)

From this point, you can finish the wood as usual. Another alternative is to first apply a penetrating oil finish. Let this coat cure for several days to a week, and then apply a sealer over the oil finish before you apply the top coats.

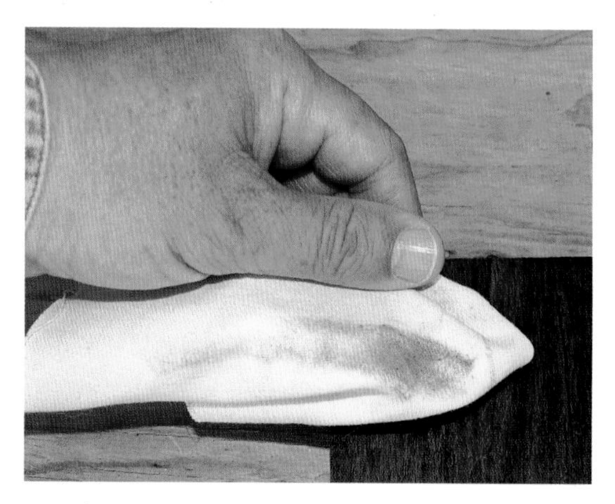

6-13 *This piece of freshly planed rosewood has so much oil on the surface that it leaves a stain on a rag wiped over the board.*

Rough Wood

Rough-cut lumber is a popular material for room paneling and rustic cabinet work. The rough texture can present a problem if you want to maintain the rough look and yet protect and color the wood.

Rough cedar is a popular material for interior room paneling. If cedar is left unfinished, it will darken with age. This may be desirable in some cases; but if you want to keep the look of fresh cut cedar without adding any color to the wood, you can spray a light coat of lacquer sanding sealer on the wood. Hold the spray gun farther from the work than is normal and set the gun to deliver a light dry spray. If the spray is too wet, it will soak into the wood and darken it. The idea is to get the sealer to dry almost as soon as it touches the surface.

In areas where rough wood will be touched frequently, it is desirable to apply a finish that will glue down the loose slivers to prevent them from getting into your skin. Waterborne varnish is one of the best materials to use for this. Because it is water-based, it will tend to raise the grain and accentuate the rough-cut look; and yet its thick glue-like consistency will firmly attach all of the loose wood fibers to prevent slivers. When you want to alter the color of the wood, you can use either a waterborne stain or one of the exterior oil stains especially formulated for rough wood.

Old barn lumber is especially prized for its acquired patina (**6–14**). In most cases, it should be left unfinished, to avoid destroying the natural weathered look. If a finish must be applied, spray lacquer sanding sealer in the manner described above. One problem with barn lumber is that any newly cut edges will not match the weathered surface. The best way to handle this problem is to design the work in a way that won't show any fresh-cut wood; use miter joints whenever possible. When it is impossible to hide the fresh cut wood, stain it with a custom-mixed stain that is as close as possible to the general color of the weathered surface.

6-14 *Old barn lumber is especially prized for its acquired patina. To hide exposed freshly cut wood, stain it with a custom mixed stain that is as close as possible to the general color of the weathered surface.*

Here is a recipe for a stain that will match most weathered wood: Pour about half a cup of paint thinner into a small container. Add enough zinc white and lamp black to make a silver gray color that is close to the general color of weathered wood. Add about two tablespoons of Danish oil to the stain. Now use some very thick oil colors. Add small chunks of burnt sienna, raw umber, and burnt umber to the mixture. Don't try to mix these thoroughly into the stain. The purpose of these colors is to create random variations in the color as the stain is wiped onto the wood.

Apply the stain with a rag to the cut edges of the barn wood. As a particle of the unmixed pigments reaches the surface, the rag will smear it into a long streak, simulating the variations found in the original surface. This technique requires some experimentation to find the correct color mix to exactly match a particular piece; but where the cut edges are not too conspicuous, it is only necessary to give the wood a general weathered look to sufficiently disguise it.

7 Hand-Rubbed Finishes

7-1 Rubbed finishes are most commonly used on flat surfaces like tabletops.

7-2 A hand-rubbed finish can produce an extremely flat surface free from defects that would disrupt the reflective quality.

It's difficult to find a finish that compares to the classic beauty of a hand-rubbed finish. It possesses a silky smooth texture and a fine sheen that can range anywhere from matte to high gloss (**7–1** and **7–2**). The traditional method of producing a hand-rubbed finish involves the use of two very fine abrasives, pumice and rottenstone, to smooth and polish the surface of the hardened top coat of finishing material. Rubbed finishes are most commonly used on flat surfaces like tabletops because it is difficult to rub parts with recesses, carvings, or intricate curves.

Not all finishes can be rubbed. If you intend to rub out a varnish coat, use a varnish formulated for rubbing. Rubbing varnishes are in the short oil category. Synthetic top coats like polyurethane and conversion finishes can be rubbed out; some are specially formulated for the purpose. Lacquer is well-suited to rubbing. Shellac can be rubbed out if water is not used as a lubricant.

Traditional Rubbed Finish

To produce a traditional rubbed finish, make sure that the top coat has had plenty of time to harden; then sand it smooth with wet-or-dry sandpaper (**7–3**). If the top coat is very smooth, you can use 600-grit paper; normally it's best to start with 400-grit paper to smooth out any dust nibs or surface irregularities, and then switch to 600-grit for a final sanding. Lubricate the sandpaper by sponging water on the wood surface or by pouring on a little paraffin oil. Paraffin oil is a mineral oil formulated for use in rubbing; it is also called rubbing oil. You can also dry sand the finish if you use an antiloading type sandpaper. After sanding, the surface should have a uniform dull matte look.

For the next step, you will need a solid block of hard felt. Wood-finishing supply dealers sell them specifically for rubbing (**7–4**). You will also need some pumice; it is available in several grades. "FFF" is the finest and most commonly used (**7–5**). Lubricate the surface to be rubbed with either paraffin oil or water. Paraffin oil is the traditional lubricant, but it has the disadvantage of being difficult to remove after the rubbing is complete. However, a rag dampened with paint thinner will usually remove any stubborn spots of oil. Paraffin oil also may react with some finishes, causing them to turn milky white; however, this is rare if you use a finish that is recommended by the manufacturer for rubbing. Water makes the pumice cut faster than it does with oil, and it

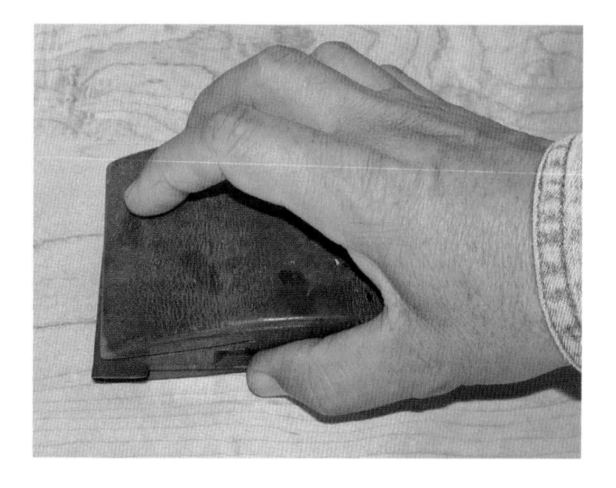

7-3

The first step is to sand the hardened finish. This will smooth out any dust nibs or surface irregularities. This is a crucial step; any defects that aren't removed now will show up after the final polishing.

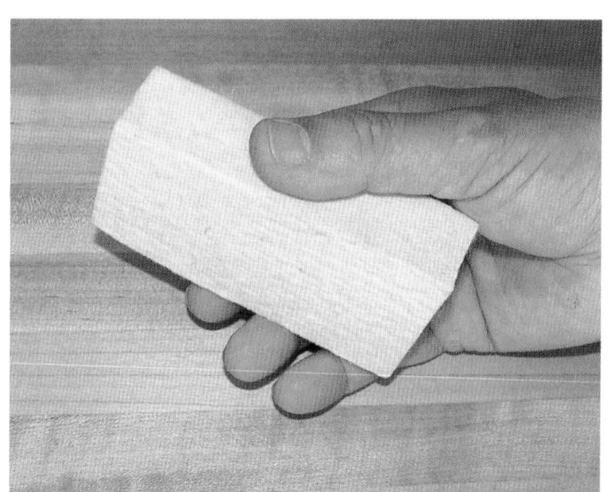

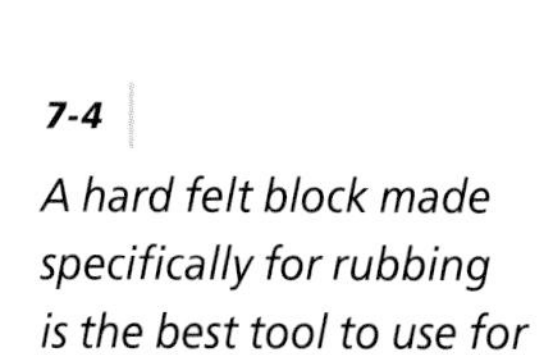

7-4

A hard felt block made specifically for rubbing is the best tool to use for a hand-rubbed finish.

7-5

Pumice is a natural abrasive of volcanic origin. The type used for rubbing a finish is a white powder.

7-6 *Sprinkle a little pumice onto the surface and use the felt block to rub it back and forth with the grain.*

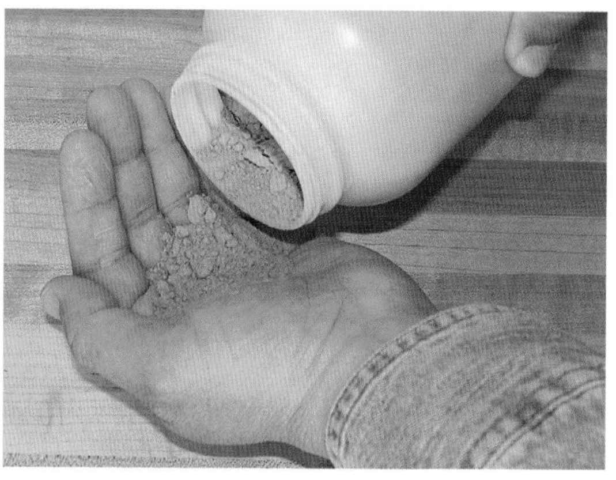

7-7 *Rottenstone is a dry powder made from decomposed limestone.*

leaves no residue on the finish, but it can't be used to rub shellac and it may make the pumice cut so fast that it is difficult to control. If you add a little soap to the water, it will behave more like oil and be easier to control; the soap will also retard evaporation so you won't have to add water to the surface as often.

Now sprinkle a little pumice onto the surface and use the felt block to rub it back and forth with the grain (**7–6**). Pumice becomes finer as it wears during the rubbing process. Because of this, it is best to sprinkle enough pumice onto the surface to do the entire job at once. As the pumice wears down, the finish it produces becomes progressively smoother; if you add fresh pumice in a particular spot, the finish in that area will be duller than the rest of the surface because the new pumice is coarser than the used pumice. If you need to add more pumice, be sure to run it uniformly over the entire surface. Occasionally wipe away the film of pumice and lubricant to check on your progress.

When all of the marks left by the sandpaper are gone, you are done. If you want a satin finish, simply clean off all of the residue left from the pumice and lubricant and apply a good quality paste wax to the finish. If you want a higher gloss, an additional step is necessary.

To achieve a high gloss by rubbing, switch to rottenstone (**7–7**). Use a different felt pad so that no trace of pumice will be left in the pad. Thoroughly clean all of the pumice from the wood surface. Then lubricate and rub the surface with rottenstone the same as you did with the pumice (**7–8**). Periodically wipe away the residue to see how the shine is progressing; when you've reached the shine you're after, wipe away all of the residue and apply paste wax.

This traditional method of hand rubbing has produced fine results for hundreds of years, but it is very time-consuming and laborious, so modern technology has developed several ways to achieve a rubbed effect with less work. You can buy premixed rubbing compound that contains its own lubricant.

7-8 *Use a felt block and rottenstone to polish the surface to a gloss. I prefer to rub in the direction of the grain to give the work a distinctive "hand-rubbed" look of fine parallel scratches. However, at this stage you can also use a circular motion to polish the surface to produce a look more like a machine-buffed finish.*

7-9 *Premixed rubbing compound contains its own lubricant. It is available in the paste form shown here or a liquid.*

These compounds were initially developed to rub out automotive paint, but they are equally good for rubbing out wood finishes.

Some wood-finishing companies now make compounds specifically for wood, but if you can't find this type the automotive type is readily available at auto supply stores. The compound comes in several grades: the coarse grades correspond to pumice, and finer grades perform like rottenstone. These compounds are used just like pumice and rottenstone, except that no additional lubricant is needed. The compound comes in a liquid or paste form (**7–9**). If it begins to dry out as rubbing progresses, a few drops of water will restore it to the proper consistency. The compound can be easily removed with a damp rag, leaving no oily residue.

A power buffer takes a lot of the work out of rubbing out a finish. The procedure used is the same as for hand rubbing, but the machine does most of the work (**7–10**).

7-10 *A power buffer can be used to polish a finish. Tilt the buffer slightly so that only the front half of the bonnet contacts the surface.*

7-11 *A synthetic finishing pad and rubbing lube can be used to produce a satin finish with the characteristic "hand-rubbed" look of fine parallel scratches. The lube prevents the abrasive from leaving deep scratches.*

Begin by sanding with 400- and 600-grit sandpaper; you can use a power sander if you want. Once all of the surface irregularities are sanded out, begin buffing. You can use pumice and rottenstone or special machine buffing compounds. Use a separate buffing bonnet for each step. Be careful when you buff close to an edge; it is easy to buff away all of the finish. If this happens, it is difficult to correct. You can try spot finishing the area, but usually you will need to apply another coat of finish to the entire surface.

Steel Wool or Finishing Pads

You can use steel wool or a synthetic finishing pad to produce a satin-rubbed effect. Use #0000 steel wool or the finest grade of synthetic finishing pad. Since the introduction of synthetic finishing pads I rarely use steel wool; the synthetic pads last longer than steel wool and they won't shed steel particles.

You can lubricate the surface with paste furniture wax, but the best lubricant is a special rubbing lube formulated for use with sandpaper, steel wool, and finishing pads. It is water-soluble and won't leave any residue (**7–11**). Rub the steel wool or finishing pad with the grain direction. The lube prevents the abrasive from leaving deep scratches. Keep rubbing until the surface has a uniform satin appearance, and then remove the lube with a clean, dry cloth. Finally, apply a coat of paste wax. Let the wax dry a while, and then buff the surface to a satin gloss.

Micro-Abrasive Sandpaper

Micro-abrasive sandpaper can produce a fine rubbed finish. To use this method, simply sand the surface with progressively finer grades of sandpaper. Lubricate the surface with water, oil, or the rubbing lube described above. Use paraffin oil for shellac.

After sanding with 600-grit, switch to 800-, then 1,000-, and finish with 1,200-grit sandpaper (**7–12**). For the ultimate in a smooth rubbed finish, use micron-graded or P-scale polyester-backed sandpaper.

Sandpaper graded under the CAMI standard can have a wider range of grit sizes on the sheet than the micron or P-scale standards allow. This means that the sheet of 1,200 grit sandpaper you are using may have a few pieces of grit that are closer to 1,000 grit. These larger pieces of grit can leave scratches that are deeper than the average, which makes them more noticeable. In most cases, the effect is hardly noticeable and you don't need to worry about it, but if you are after the ultimate rubbed finish, there will be fewer of these scratches if you use micron-graded sandpaper. You can use less expensive 400- and 600-grit sandpaper for the first steps, and then switch to 20μ micron-graded polyester-backed sandpaper. Progress to 15μ, 9μ, and 5μ if you want a glossier finish.

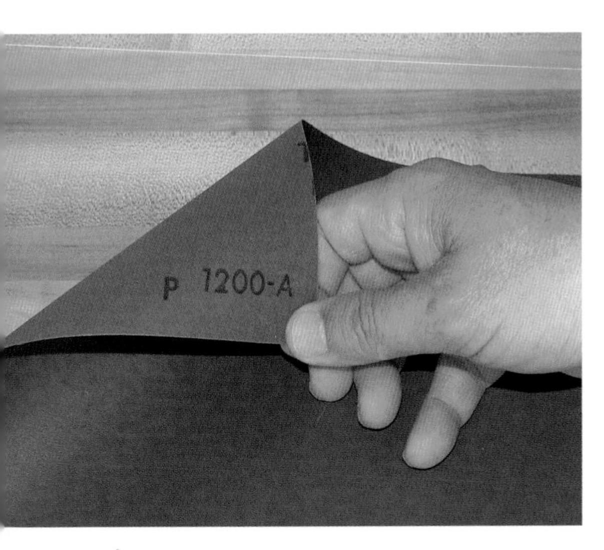

7-12 *Ultra-fine sandpaper can produce a fine rubbed finish. To use this method, simply sand the surface with progressively finer grades of sandpaper. You can use the same type of rubbing lube as shown in **7–10** for the final grades.*

Abrasive Foam Discs

Another way to achieve a rubbed finish is to use abrasive foam disks. These consist of silicone-carbide mesh laminated to 1/4-inch thick foam. ABRALON® is a trade name for these discs. They attach to a random orbit sander with a 6-inch hook & loop interface pad. Use a variable-speed sander for the best control. The pad's open cell design allows water or other lubricants to soak into the foam center and to be forced out through openings in the fabric face in operation. The foam center also provides cushioning to ensure an even pressure on the surface. To rub out the surface, spray the finish with water and wet sand using super-fine pad (1,000 grit). This will level the finish. Next, use a Micro-fine (2,000 grit) pad to achieve a satin finish. For a high-gloss finish, use a Mirror-fine (4,000 grit) pad. Always keep the surface damp when using pads.

8 Wood Graining

8-1 *The panel doors in Victorian homes were often originally wood grained. You can restore them to their original look by using the techniques described in this chapter.*

Wood graining is the art of duplicating the grain of an expensive wood on the surface of a less expensive substitute. The process is hundreds of years old. It experienced a major renaissance in the mid-1800s when the American pioneers went west. They found that the hardwoods they had become used to on the East Coast were scarce in the West, so they used wood graining to make the native red pine look like walnut, oak, maple, or cherry. After the railroads made transportation of lumber practical from one area of the country to another, wood graining began to die out. But recently there has been a renewed interest in wood graining.

Wood graining can be used to re-create the look of antiques and to restore Victorian-era homes (**8–1**). It can also be used as a method to hold down the cost of do-it-yourself projects. In almost every project there are some parts that can be made of a cheaper material if it matches the wood used elsewhere. The shelves and back of a bookcase are an example. By using MDF, hardboard, or particleboard for these parts, the cost of a project can be kept down.

8-2 *This inexpensive particleboard nightstand is a good candidate for wood graining.*

8-3 *After wood graining is complete, it's difficult to believe this is the same nightstand shown above in **8-2**.*

Wood graining will make it match the wood in the rest of the case.

A lot of inexpensive unfinished furniture is made of particleboard (**8–2**). Wood graining is a practical way to finish this type of furniture. You can achieve the look of real wood at a fraction of the cost of hardwood by graining particleboard (**8–3**). You can also use wood graining to salvage a piece of furniture that is too damaged to refinish with other methods.

Wood-graining techniques are also used to alter the grain of some woods like birch or lauan (Philippine mahogany) when these woods are used in a project along with other more prominently grained woods like oak or ash.

The first step in graining is to apply a ground coat of flat latex or oil-based paint. Use a paint that is the same color as the lightest part of the wood you are trying to imitate; you can use tinting colors mixed in white paint to achieve any ground color you want. Solid-color acrylic stains that are normally used for the exterior of houses make a good ground coat; they are available in a wide range of wood tones.

The direction of the wood graining is not dependent on the direction of the actual grain of the underlying wood, and man-made substances like particleboard don't have any grain direction, so before applying the ground coat, decide on the grain direction for each part and then apply the ground coat with all brush strokes in the direction of the grain. Usually the grain direction should follow the longest dimension of the piece.

A ground coat is not always necessary on hardboard or particleboard parts that won't receive close scrutiny. In fact, the small flecks of wood visible on the surface may enhance the appearance of the finished grain. Another instance where no ground coat is used is when you want to add a more interesting grain pattern to an otherwise uninteresting piece of hardwood. The lower grades of lauan are an example. Some pieces of lauan have practically no visible grain patterns; their only characteristic is a uniform pattern of pores distributed evenly over the entire surface. You can add interest to a board like this by using one of the graining techniques described later.

After the ground coat is dry, the graining stain is applied. The most important consideration is the consistency of the stain. It must be heavy-bodied or the grain pattern will flow together. Traditional wood grainers mixed their own graining stains, adding a thickening agent called *megilp* to make it the correct consistency; the modern equivalent is called *faux finishing glaze*. The glaze is a thick colorless liquid that will thicken and extend the working time of a stain or paint. For wood-graining purposes, pigmented waterborne stain is usually mixed with the glaze (**8–4**). There are several other products that can be used as a graining stain: gel stains, or heavy-bodied stains, will work well. You can also buy specially prepared graining stains from wood-finishing suppliers. You can use a waterborne stain over a latex ground coat, but don't use it on bare particleboard because it makes the particles swell, giving a bumpy surface.

The graining stain can be worked with special tools or applied freehand to achieve a number of different effects.

8-4 *Faux finishing glaze is a thick colorless liquid that will thicken and extend the working time of a stain or paint. For wood-graining purposes, pigmented waterborne stain is usually mixed with the glaze.*

Graining Tools

The old-time wood grainers used many tools to produce realistic grains. When I wrote the first edition of this book, wood graining was practically a lost art and graining tools were almost impossible to find, but since then there has been a renaissance in the field of wood graining and other faux finishes. Nowadays, you can buy practically all of the tools that were available to the old-time grainers.

One of the most useful wood-graining tools is called a *block cushion grainer*; it consists of a piece of rubber molded with semicircular ridges. The rubber face is attached to a block of wood (or a plastic form on modern ones) that holds the rubber in a

8-5 *The large graining tool on the left was made using the procedure described in the text. The smaller tool on the right is a commercial model.*

8-6 *The mold is made on a lathe. Cut V-shaped grooves with a skew chisel to cover the mold with concentric circles. Make all of the grooves the same depth to avoid high spots in the finished grainer that would make the tool difficult to use.*

curved shape. A handle attaches to the block. This one tool is capable of producing almost an infinite variety of realistic-looking grain patterns. This is one of the tools that is again on the market, but most commercial models are only about four inches wide, so I am still including instructions for making this tool in this edition. You can make your own grainers in any size you choose. Also, by varying the size and spacing of the grooves, you can alter the effects that it will produce (**8–5**).

To make your own grainers, you first need to make a mold for the rubber face. Cut a circle of 3/4-inch hardwood. The circle can be any size that will fit on your lathe. It's best to make a large mold because you can use it for smaller tools if you wish. Mount the circle on a lathe faceplate and, using a small skew chisel, cut V-shaped grooves 1/8 inch deep and 1/8 inch apart, until the entire face is covered with concentric circles (**8–6**).

An easy way to get the spacing for the grooves of your first mold is to touch the teeth of an eight-point saw to the face of the mold with the lathe running. Each tooth will make a scratch indicating the center of the groove. This will give you an average spacing that produces a grainer useful for most work. Later you can experiment with more or less spacing; closely spaced grooves make a grain that looks more like hardwood, while widely spaced grooves produce a grain that looks closer to pine.

It is important that all of the grooves be of equal depth; it is the bottom of the groove in the mold that produces the top point of the ridge on the gainer. All of these ridges must be equal in height so they will all contact the work uniformly.

After all the cuts are made, remove the mold from the faceplate, give the turning a good coat of penetrating sealer, and then wax with paste wax.

The grainer is made from silicone rubber caulking. You will need a lot of it, so buy a caulking gun cartridge of it rather than buying it in tubes. Cover the mold with a layer of silicone rubber caulking about 1/8 inch thick. (The full mold makes two tools, so if you want only one, cover half the mold.) Put a rag on top of the rubber and smooth it out. Rub over the rag to force the caulking into all of the grooves in the mold. Leave the rag on top of the caulking to form a reinforced backing. Let the caulking cure for at least 24 hours.

When it has cured, peel the rubber from the mold (**8–7**). Make a backing from a piece of wood about two inches square and as long as the diameter of the mold. Use a plane or a sander to round off one corner of the block so that it resembles a piece of quarter-round molding. Drill a half-inch hole in the center of each of the two remaining flat faces for a handle. Cut the rubber to fit the backing and glue it to the curved surface with contact cement. Fold it over the corners and staple for added strength. Cut a six-inch length of dowel for a handle.

8-7 *After the silicone rubber has cured, it can be easily peeled from the mold.*

8-8 *After the ground coat is dry, brush on a coat of graining stain.*

8-9 *While the graining stain is still wet, push the graining tool over the surface.*

To begin graining, apply a heavy coat of graining stain to the work with a brush (**8–8**). Push the graining tool across the surface, lifting the handle to rock the face of the tool (**8–9**). Wide boards require several passes with the grainer to cover the surface with a grain pattern. Overlap each pass slightly so there won't be any ungrained areas left between the passes. The larger homemade grainers will cover a wide board in one or two passes, while the smaller commercial models will require many passes to cover the same board. The effect produced when many passes are made with a small grainer looks like several narrow boards were glued together to make one wide board; the effect is not unnatural looking and may be sufficient for many types of work (**8–10**).

Combinations of forward and rocking motions produce a variety of results. Illus. **8–11** shows some combinations. Examples A and B were made by rapidly rocking the grainer while pushing across the board. To reproduce C and D, gradually and continuously raise the handle as you push the grainer across the board. The knot in E was made by rapidly raising and lowering the handle. Use a straight through motion on the rest of the stroke. Gradually raising and then lowering the handle will produce a grain like F. No rocking motion at all is used to make G. Slowly raise the handle while pushing across to reproduce H.

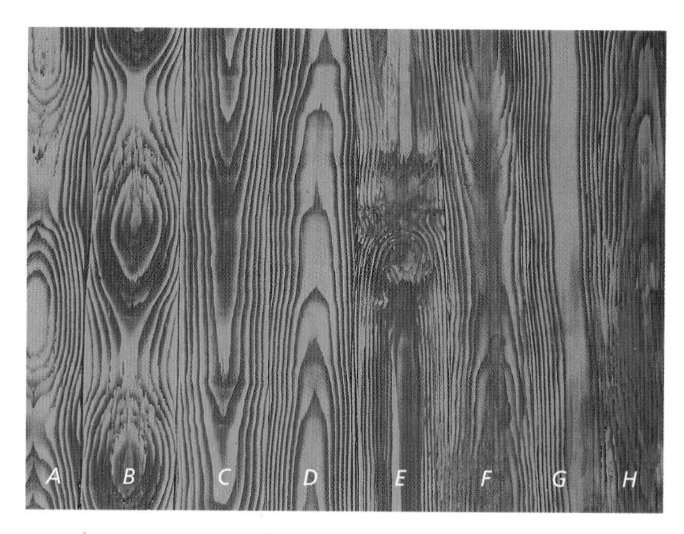

8-11 *Here are some of the many grains it is possible to produce using a block cushion grainer.*

8-10 *The smaller commercial graining tool must be passed over wide boards many times to completely cover the surface with grain.*

The purpose of having two handle positions is also illustrated in examples A through D. A and B were both made with the same motion. The only difference was the position of the handle. The same is true for C and D. For A and C, the handle was in the position closest to the large diameter half circles in the rubber. B and D were made with the handle next to the small diameter half circles.

If you aren't satisfied with the first results, simply pass the grainer over the same section again; you can make several passes over the same area before it is necessary to apply more stain. If the grain runs together after a while, the stain is too liquid; let it dry for a few minutes and try again.

You can make the graining look even more realistic by brushing over it with a dry brush. Brush in the grain direction to feather out the grain lines.

Graining Combs

Graining combs are another means of producing a grain on wood. Several companies now market specially made graining combs (**8–12**). Coarse-weave cloth such as burlap (hessian) or cheesecloth can be used in a manner similar to a comb; fold the cloth into

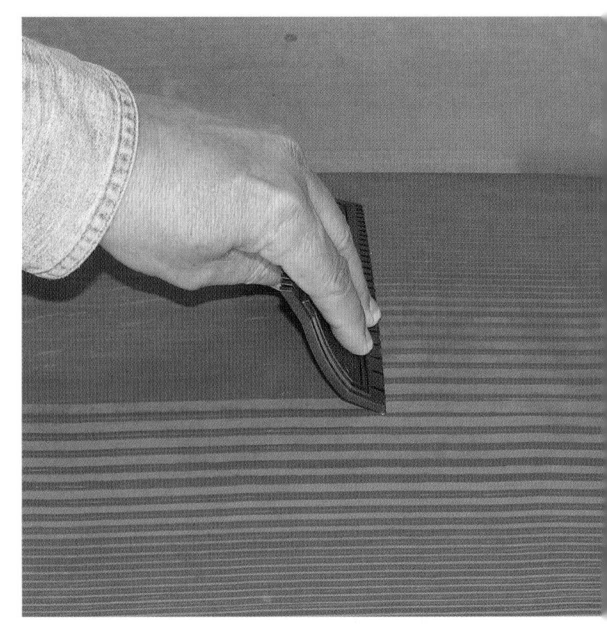

8-13 *The graduated tooth comb produces a very natural-looking grain because the spacing between the teeth gradually increases across the width of the comb.*

8-12 *Here is a sampling of the wide variety of graining combs available.*

8-14 *To produce a very natural-looking grain on wide boards, begin by making one pass in the center of the board with a small block cushion grainer.*

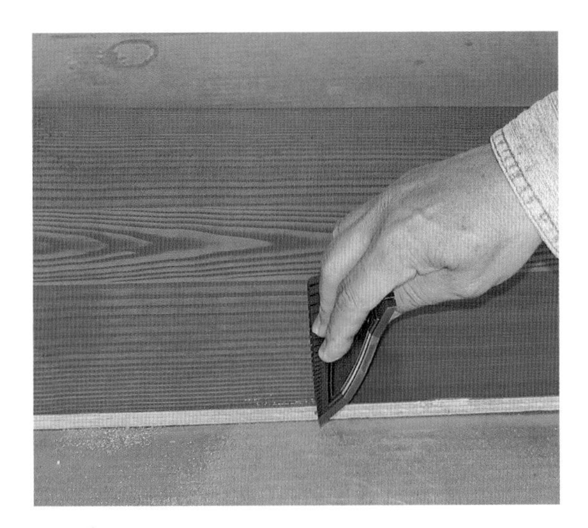

8-15 *Next, use the graduated tooth comb to add grain lines on either side of the pattern. Position the comb so that the wide spaced lines will be next to the pattern left by the block cushion grainer.*

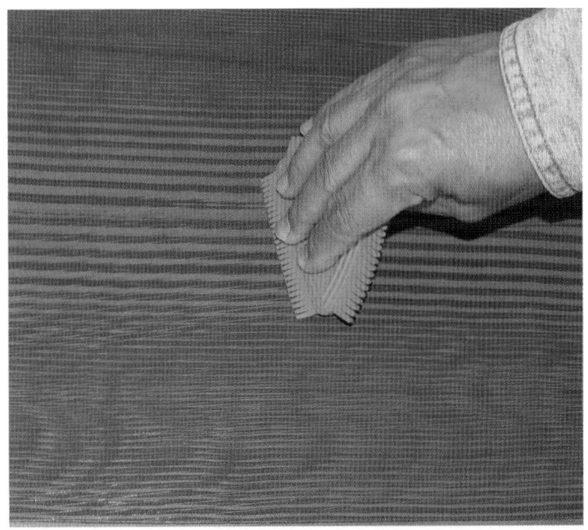

8-16 *To imitate the grain of quartersawn oak, first make a straight pass with a graduated tooth comb, and then make a second pass with a fine-tooth comb. Move the comb at a slight angle to the first pass so that the two sets of lines cross each other at a very shallow angle.*

a pad and use one edge just like the teeth of a comb. A piece of cardboard inside the pad will add some stiffness if you need it.

Use a brush to apply a thin coat of stain over the ground coat. Drag the teeth of the comb over the stain. The teeth will scrape the stain off of the areas they touch, making a lighter line. One of the most useful combs is the graduated tooth comb. The spacing between the teeth gradually increases across the width of the comb. This produces a very natural-looking grain (**8–13**). This type of comb can be used in conjunction with a block cushion grainer to produce a very natural-looking grain on wide boards. Begin by making one pass in the center of the board with a small block cushion grainer (**8–14**). Then use the graduated tooth comb to add grain lines on either side of the pattern. Position the comb so that the wide spaced lines will be next to the pattern left by the block cushion grainer (**8–15**). If you need to add more grain lines to fill the board, place the comb so that the closely spaced teeth will be next to the closely spaced lines on the edge of the pattern.

The grain produced by a comb is similar to the straight grain of quartersawn wood. You can heighten the quartersawn effect by dragging a fine tooth comb lightly over the first set of grain line. On this pass, move the comb at a slight angle to the first pass so that the two sets of lines cross each other at a very shallow angle (**8–16**). This technique repro-

8-17 *To imitate the look of the medullary ray pattern of quartersawn oak, use your thumb or a corner of a rubber comb to wipe irregular patterns across the quartersawn combing.*

duces the pore pattern of quartersawn oak. There is a tendency among beginning wood grainers to wave the comb back and forth, making a very wiggly grain, but if you look at a piece of quartersawn wood, you will see that the grain lines are really fairly straight.

When you want to imitate the look of the medullary ray pattern of quartersawn oak, use your thumb or a corner of a rubber comb to wipe irregular patterns across the quartersawn combing (**8–17**).

Ray Marker

If you look closely at a piece of plainsawn oak, you will see that the entire surface is covered with hundreds of tiny dashes. These dashes are the ends of the medullary rays (**8–18**). A ray marker is a tool that will reproduce these dashes. The ray marker has a set of wheels that rotate independently of each other on a common axle. Each wheel has a series of dashes embossed on its edge.

To use the ray maker, first reproduce a plainsawn grain on the board; then, while the stain is still wet, run the ray marker over the grain in straight parallel lines that run with the grain. If you want an even more realistic effect, let the stain dry, and then use a stain that is either darker or lighter than the stain used first. Dip a foam brush into the stain and hold it so that it touches the top of the ray marker wheels. Run the marker across the entire surface of the board in straight lines parallel to the grain direction (**8–19**).

8-18 *In this sample of plainsawn oak, the entire surface is covered with dashes that are the ends of the medullary rays.*

8-19 A ray marker produces small dash marks. Dip a foam brush into the stain and hold it so that it touches the top of the ray marker wheels. Run the marker across the entire surface of the board in straight lines parallel to the grain direction.

Freehand Graining

So far, all of the graining methods described have relied on some mechanical means of producing the grain; in freehand graining, you paint the grain on just like an artist paints a picture (**8–20**). The biggest requirement for freehand graining is an intimate knowledge of the wood you are trying to reproduce. Before trying your hand at freehand graining, study several samples of the wood you want to copy.

One of the most important tools for freehand graining is a type of artist's brush called a *sword striper*. This brush has very long, soft filaments usually made from camel's hair. It is the type of brush used to paint pin strips, but we will be using it to paint grain lines. You can buy this type of brush at an art supply store. You hold it at a very low angle to the work and drag it along so that the long filaments trail behind it in a straight line (**8–21**). Use the sword striper to draw in all of the grain lines; at first it may help to have a sample of real wood close by to determine how the lines should look.

At this point, the lines will look rather unnatural because of their uniformity; to remedy this, brush over the entire surface of the work with a fan-top graining brush or any regular paintbrush. Brush lightly in

8-20 An example of freehand graining.

8-21 A camel's-hair sword striper is used to paint in the grain lines in freehand graining. Notice how the brush is held nearly parallel to the surface.

8-22 *Fanning out the grain lines is especially important in freehand graining.*

straight lines with the grain. This brushing out will fan out and break up the grain lines (**8–22**). Freehand graining takes a lot of practice and study of wood samples, but it is useful when you want to produce special effects such as book-matched grain patterns, burl patterns, quartersawn ray patterns, or other patterns that can't be produced with mechanical grainers.

Graining Doors

The panel doors in Victorian homes were often originally wood grained. Over the years, these doors usually received several coats of plain paint covering the original wood graining. You can restore the door to its original look by applying a new wood grain over the paint. New homes often use steel doors. You can also use wood graining to make these doors more attractive.

The way to make a door look realistic is to use the appropriate grain pattern for each part. Don't overuse the block cushion grainer. It is more natural looking to include some areas of straight grain. For example, the door in **8–1** has a plainsawn pattern on the rails, but the other parts have a straight grain pattern. Another option is to use graining combs to produce a straight grain or a quartersawn look on both the stiles and

8-23 *This door has been grained using graining combs to produce a straight grain or a quartersawn look on both the stiles and rails.*

rails (**8–23**), but use a block cushion grainer or freehand graining to give the panels a plainsawn look (**8–24**). Use flexible combs to apply a straight grain to the moldings. In the smallest parts of the moldings, you may need to use a coarse rag instead of a comb.

Overgraining

Overgraining blends the grain lines produced either mechanically or freehand into a more uniform-looking grain. Although it can be used with mechanical graining, it is most important in freehand graining, because the grain lines that are painted on in freehand graining are so distinct from the ground color.

Let the first grain pattern dry, and then brush on a thin coat of stain; choose a color that is a little different hue than the original grain lines. Use a rag to spread the stain around, wiping some areas more than others to create a natural-looking variation in color (**8–25**). You can also use graining combs or a pad of coarse cloth to produce a second grain pattern over the first. This graining should be a subtle grain, usually just straight parallel lines.

8-24 *A plainsawn pattern adds interest to door panels.*

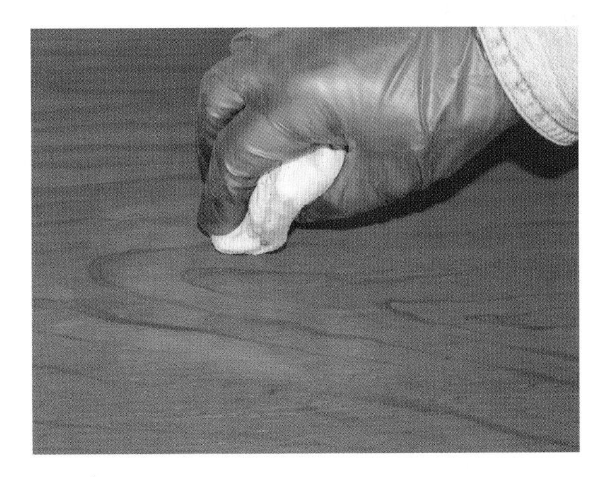

8-25 *Overgraining gives the completed grain a more natural look. Use a color that is a little different hue than the original grain lines and wipe some areas more than others to create a natural-looking variation in color.*

Finish Coat

After all of the graining coats have dried, you can apply any top coat that is compatible with the stains and ground coat used. A waterborne varnish is a good choice.

9 Chemical Stains

9-1 | *This oak ice chest was treated with ammonia fumes to darken the wood's color before applying the finish top coats.*

Wood is impregnated with hundreds of chemicals as it grows. The exact chemical composition of a piece of wood depends on the type of soil it grew in, the climate at the time it was growing, and the species of tree. Tannin is one chemical that is found to a greater or lesser degree in almost all wood.

The natural color of wood depends on the chemicals present in the wood. These chemicals will react with other chemicals to create new compounds of differing colors. This fact makes the process of chemical staining possible. Through experimentation over the years, wood finishers have found certain chemicals that will alter the color of some species of wood (**9–1**).

Quite a few woods can be stained by chemical methods, but the best results are obtained with woods that are high in tannin. Oak, walnut, chestnut, and mahogany are all high-tannin woods.

Chemical stains penetrate deeper into the wood than any other type of stain and they are the most permanent.

Chemical stains are not for the novice; they are often unpredictable and the chemicals are almost always dangerous, but for the

9-2 *Chemical stains have the ability to bring out grain details like these birds'-eyes.*

advanced finisher chemical stains offer some distinct advantages. First, they provide a clarity of grain that is even superior to water stain. This is because chemical stains don't add any color to the wood; they alter the existing color. Chemical stains have the ability to bring out grain details like bird's-eyes or crotch grain that may be obscured by other stains (**9–2**). Natural wood has slight variations in color from one part of the grain to another; ordinary stains tend to even out these color variations. If you want to keep that natural look, chemical stains are a better alternative because they won't conceal the color variations, and may enhance them.

Many of the chemicals discussed in this chapter will be difficult to buy; they don't have any household use, and so they are only available from chemical wholesalers. Sometimes they will only be available in large quantities. These chemicals are listed for the finisher who wants to experiment with them, but be prepared to do some extensive shopping to find them. It's easer to find these chemicals in small quantities now that you can search for them on the internet. Some online wood-finishing suppliers now sell chemicals in small quantities.

Most chemical stains involve a reaction between tannin in the wood and the stain. Since the tannin content of wood is not constant even within one species, the color achieved may vary from board to board. Because of this, you should plan ahead in the early stages of the construction of the project. Whenever possible, all of the boards in a project should be from the same tree; however, this is difficult to accomplish unless the project is a small one and can be built from a single board.

Before selecting the lumber to be used in the project, test small samples of each board with the chemical stain you plan to use. This way, you will be sure that the color produced is what you expected. Use the test samples to group the boards according to color, so you can match all of the boards used in the project. If you must use boards that vary widely in tannin content, you can add tannin to the boards that stain lighter. Use a diluted solution of tannic acid. Apply this with a sponge or brush on the board before applying a chemical stain.

Chemical stains will react with metal hardware to create undesirable dark stains in the wood around the hardware, so don't attach any metal to the project before staining. Even nails can react with the stain, but they usually won't be a problem if they are set below the wood surface.

Putty and wood filler will not be colored by chemical stains, so they should always be applied after staining and then colored to match.

Mixing Chemical Stains

The chemicals used to make stains usually come in three forms: liquid, powder, and crystals. Before they can be applied as stain, they all need to be diluted in water. The powdered chemicals are the most difficult to dissolve in water, so it's a good idea to mix them well ahead of time to give them plenty of time to dissolve. You can make a strong solution from the powder and then add more water at the time of use to dilute it to the proper level. Liquids can be kept in their original state until used and then diluted. The crystals usually dissolve quite readily, so they can also be prepared immediately before use.

Tap water is normally all right to use in making stains; but if your water is high in minerals, especially iron, it's best to use distilled water. Iron reacts with many of the chemicals to make a bluish-black stain.

If you want to be able to duplicate your results consistently, you should measure the amounts of chemicals and water that you mix. You can measure either by weight of dry chemical or by volume. A simple postal scale will be accurate enough for weighing the chemicals. To measure volume, you can use the disposable graduated measuring cups sold at paint stores and finishing supply companies.

A gallon of chemical stain will cover about 600 square feet of wood.

Safety Precautions

Almost all of the chemicals used as stains are either poisonous, caustic, harmful, or irritating in some way, so use them at your own risk and exercise caution when using them. Many chemicals once considered safe as wood stains have recently come under suspicion as being hazardous to your health. Some of the health and safety hazards associated with these chemicals are detailed in the list of chemicals used to make stains on *pages 194 and 195.* However, new information is constantly being uncovered, so it's a good idea to check with a knowledgeable source before using these chemicals. Don't use poisonous chemicals to finish children's furniture or for items that will come into contact with food.

Safety goggles and protective gloves are a must when working with chemicals; a rubber lab apron is also advisable when working with acids and other caustic chemicals. A respirator should be worn when using chemicals that produce toxic fumes; an air-supplied respirator is best. Always keep chemicals in their original containers and read and follow all cautions listed on the container. Keep the chemicals out of the reach of children.

Don't use chemical stains on wood that has been bleached with chlorine bleach; poisonous chlorine gas could result.

When working with acids, remember that to dilute an acid always add the acid to the water a little at a time. If water is poured into the acid, a violent reaction may take place that will spray acid out of the container. When you use any chemical stain for the first time, test a small sample of wood with a diluted solution of the stain to check for any unexpected reactions. It is best not to mix any of these chemicals together, because some may react violently when mixed. If you want to use more than one chemical on the wood, apply each one as a separate coat, wash the wood thoroughly, and let it dry before applying any other chemicals.

Applying Chemical Stains

Most chemical stains are dissolved in water and applied in liquid form. One exception is ammonia fuming, where the chemical is applied as a vapor. To avoid raised grain in the final finish, the wood should be wet-sanded first, as is done for water stains. Use a chemical-resistant brush to apply the stains. Nylon and polyester brushes are good for applying chemicals; of the natural filaments, tampico is probably the most chemical resistant.

Chemical stains must be applied evenly or streaks and blotches will appear in the finished surface. You can make it easier to get an even application by first brushing on a coat of clear water, and then applying the stain while the water is still wet.

Fuming

Ammonia produces very strong fumes, as anyone who has used it knows. When these fumes settle on wood that is high in tannin, they will darken the color of the wood. Fumed oak used to be a very popular finish. Most antique oak furniture you see probably has been finished by fuming.

The process of fuming is not widely used today, because it requires an airtight container large enough to accommodate the object being fumed and because ammonia is difficult to work with due to the strong fumes. However, fuming has several advantages. It produces an even color without lap marks, streaks, or brush marks. It stains every surface of the object in one operation; and the fumes will even penetrate some finishes, so it is possible to change the color of a previously finished article without removing the old finish. The vapors penetrate deep into the wood, producing a color change that is more than just a surface coating. During the fuming process, no liquid comes in contact with the wood, so there is no problem of raised grain as there is with other chemical stains or water stain.

9-3 *To fume a piece of furniture, make a fuming tent which consists of a framework of wood covered with plastic sheeting.*

To fume a piece of wood, you must enclose it in an airtight container. This is not difficult for small items, but it can pose a problem if the item being finished is large. Larger items require that a special fuming box or tent be constructed. A wood box or crate with all joints sealed with caulking or tape will work. A fuming tent consists of framework of wood covered with plastic sheeting (**9–3**). Seal all of the joints with duct tape.

The best type of ammonia to use is 26-percent industrial ammonia. Household ammonia is much weaker, but it will work. It will just take longer. Pour some ammonia into several saucers and put the saucers into the container with the object to be stained.

Seal up the container and let the ammonia fumes work on the wood for about 24 hours. The exact amount of time it takes will depend on the strength of the ammonia, the amount of tannin in the wood, and the color you want to achieve. The colors produced by fuming range from light yellow through dark brown; a medium honey color is the most common. The wood will darken slightly after it is allowed to air out. If there is a slight greenish cast to the color, you can neutralize it by applying a coat of orange shellac.

Note: *Wear a respirator when working with ammonia, and provide adequate ventilation.*

9-4 *An ebonized finish produced with chemical dyes has more depth than black paint would have because the grain is still visible through the black dye.*

Chemicals Used to Make Stains

The following list contains most of the chemicals commonly used to stain wood:

Tannic acid is the most basic ingredient in chemical staining. In woods like oak, walnut, and mahogany, the tannic acid or tannin is already present in the wood. Woods that are low in tannin require an application of tannic acid before some of the chemical stains will be effective. To make a solution for this purpose, mix five parts tannic acid with 95 parts water. Apply the solution to the work and let it dry before applying any other chemicals. *Tannic acid is toxic when eaten or inhaled. Recently, tannic acid has been suspected of being a cancer-causing agent.*

Ammonia reacts with tannin to produce a wide range of brown colors. Industrial strength ammonia produces the best results, but household ammonia can be used. It can be applied as a liquid or used in the fuming process. Ammonia has an advantage over other alkalis, because it completely evaporates from the wood. Other alkalis leave a residue that must be neutralized. *Breathing the concentrated fumes of ammonia may be fatal, so always provide adequate ventilation. There is a moderate fire danger if ammonia fumes reach a point of 16 to 25 percent of the atmosphere.*

Potash (potassium carbonate) produces results similar to ammonia. It comes as a powder that must be dissolved in water before use. It leaves a residue on the wood after it has dried. To remove the residue, wash with clean water, and then neutralize it with a wash of household vinegar. Finally, wash with clean water again. *Potash is a skin irritant.*

Caustic soda (sodium hydroxide) is similar to potash in effect and must be neutralized in the same manner. *Caustic soda will burn the skin and is poisonous if swallowed.*

Potassium permanganate produces a wide range of beautiful browns when applied to high-tannin woods or over a wash of tannic acid. It comes in crystal form. Dissolve 1 1/2 ounces of crystals into one quart of water for a medium brown. The solution will first turn the wood violet, but the color will change to brown as the wood dries. *Potassium permanganate should always be used in a dilute solution; this chemical may cause burns, and strong solutions can pose a fire risk.*

Potassium dichromate is similar to potassium permanganate except the color produced tends to be more yellowish. *This chemical is poisonous if inhaled or swallowed. It may cause skin burns, and strong solutions can pose a fire risk.*

Iron compounds are used to produce gray to black effects. Several coats may be necessary to make a deep black color similar to ebony (**9–4**). A light wash will give new wood the silver-gray color of weathered wood. The iron reacts with tannin, so low-tannin woods should be treated with tannic acid before applying the iron compounds. Iron sulfate and iron chloride are commercially available iron compounds, but you can make your own iron stain by putting iron nails or iron filings into a jar of vinegar. Let the iron remain in the vinegar for several days. If you used filings, strain the mixture before applying it to the wood.

Iron compounds will emphasize fancy grain patterns such as birds'-eyes and crotch patterns; if they are applied in a weak solution, the grain will be enhanced without changing the basic wood color too much. There will be a slight graying of the wood, but a coat of water stain will hide the gray and still let the enhancement of the fancy pattern show.

Copper sulfate also produces a gray or black color when applied to wood. *It is poisonous if swallowed.*

Chemical Stain Formulas

Chemical stains offer a wide variation in color, depending on the strength of the solution used and the chemicals chosen, so they give you the opportunity to exert a lot of creative control over the staining process. But in order to use that creative control, you will need to experiment before the final formula is decided on. Here are a few formulas for simple stains.

Color: Brown (**9–5**)
Woods effective on:
oak, walnut, chestnut, mahogany
Chemical used: ammonia

Brush or sponge the ammonia onto the wood. Let it dry. Repeat applications until color desired is achieved. The ammonia can also be applied by fuming. A top coat of orange shellac will warm the color.

9-5
Color: Brown
Woods effective on: oak, walnut, chestnut, mahogany. Chemicals used: ammonia.

9-6 *Color: Ebony*
Woods effective on: oak, walnut.
Chemicals used: vinegar, iron filings.

9-7 *Color: Light Brown*
Woods effective on: birch, maple, pine, fir.
Chemicals used: ammonia, tannic acid.

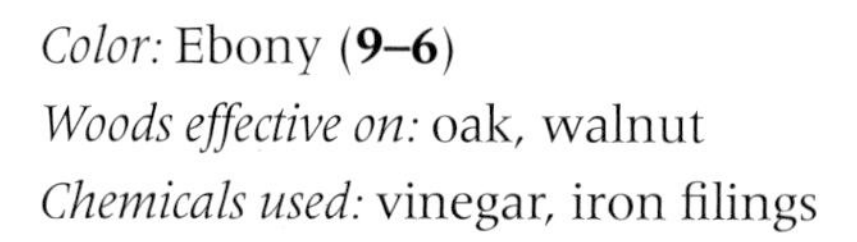

Color: Ebony (**9–6**)
Woods effective on: oak, walnut
Chemicals used: vinegar, iron filings

Add one ounce of iron filings to one quart of vinegar. The filings can be collected from a bench grinder used to sharpen tools. Iron nails can be used instead of the filings, but they may need to soak in the vinegar longer. Let the vinegar-iron mixture sit for about one week; it's ready when it looks gray and cloudy. Strain the mixture through a paint filter or several layers of cloth to remove the filings. Apply repeated coats of the vinegar mixture to the wood until a dark gray-black color is achieved; after a finish is applied, the color will be deep black.

You can use iron sulfate instead of iron filings. Dissolve one ounce of iron sulfate in one quart of water. Apply repeated coats of the solution to the wood until a dark-gray black color is produced. Wash the wood with clean water. After a finish is applied, the wood will be deep black in color.

Color: Light Brown (**9–7**)
Woods effective on: birch, maple, pine, fir
Chemicals used: ammonia, tannic acid

Mix three teaspoons of powdered tannic acid with 8 ounces of water. Brush the tannic acid onto the wood and let it dry. Apply ammonia to the wood either by brushing or by fuming.

9-8 *Color: Golden Brown Woods effective on: birch, maple, pine, fir. Chemicals used: tannic acid, ammonia, copper sulfate.*

9-9 *Color: Weathered Gray Woods effective on: birch, maple, pine, fir, oak. Chemicals used: iron filings and vinegar, tannic acid.*

Color: Golden Brown (**9–8**)
Woods effective on: birch, maple, pine, fir
Chemicals used: tannic acid, ammonia, copper sulfate

Mix three teaspoons of powdered tannic acid with 8 ounces of water. Brush the tannic acid onto the wood and let it dry. Apply ammonia to the wood and let it evaporate. Mix one teaspoon of copper sulfate crystals with one cup of water. Brush the copper sulfate solution onto the wood and let dry. Adding additional coats of copper sulfate will darken the color. Thoroughly wash off the copper sulfate residue with water.

Color: Weathered Gray (**9–9**)
Woods effective on: birch, maple, pine, fir, oak
Chemicals used: iron filings and vinegar, tannic acid

Brush tannic acid solution onto the wood and let it dry. Make the iron-vinegar solution described earlier and apply it to the wood. Apply additional coats of the solution until the desired shade is reached.

For more chemical stain formulas, see my book *Classic Finishing Techniques*.

10 Gilding and Stenciling

Gilding and stenciling are both popular methods of decorating wood. Either of these techniques can turn an ordinary-looking piece of furniture into something unique. Gilding is often used as an edge treatment or to accentuate decorative carvings. Stenciling is used to add decorative designs to the wood surface. The two techniques are used in combination to produce the gold stenciled designs commonly associated with Hitchcock chairs and Boston rockers.

Gilding

Gilding is the process of applying a metallic leaf or powder to the wood surface. The metal is usually gold or gold-colored, but silver- and copper-colored metals are also used.

In the past, entire pieces of furniture were gilded, but the trend recently is to use gilding as an accent to highlight a shaped edge or a decorative carving (**10–1**).

Gold Leaf

Genuine gold leaf is made from 23½ carat gold that is beaten into thin sheets. Each sheet is less than one-thousandth of an inch thick. Because gold is expensive, imitation gold leaf is available. The imitation gold leaf is applied in the same manner as real gold leaf and looks quite real. It is made from a bronze alloy.

Because each leaf is so thin, it is difficult to handle it without tearing it. To keep the leaves from being damaged, they come in books usually containing 20 sheets. Each piece of gold leaf is sandwiched between the paper sheets of the book to protect the leaf (**10–2**). A special brush called a *gilder's tip* is used to remove the leaf from the book and apply it to the surface. A gilder's tip is a flat brush with a very thin layer of bristles. The gold leaf is attracted to the bristles by static electricity.

Imitation gold leaf is a little more durable than the genuine gold, so it is sometimes possible to lift it by hand. Until you are proficient with the technique, it is best to prac-

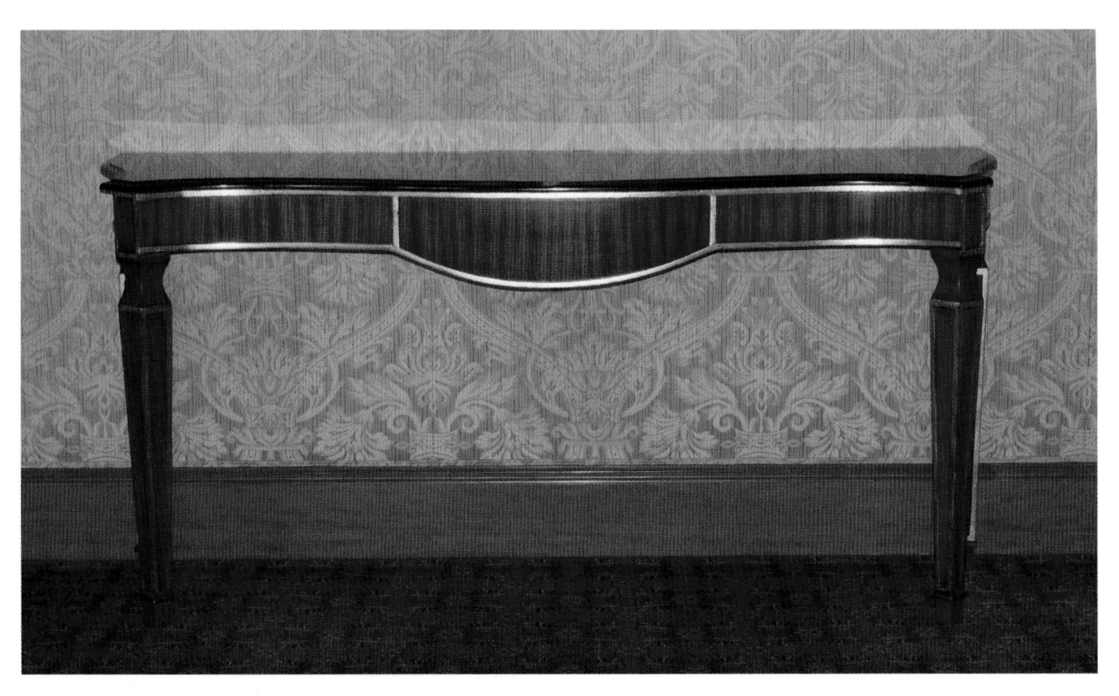

10-1 *This table has gilded accents.*

10-2 *Gold leaf comes in books with each piece sandwiched between sheets of paper to protect it.*

tice with the imitation variety. Some types of imitation gold leaf come attached to a plastic or paper backing. This type is very easy to apply because you can rub it on and then peel off the backing.

SURFACE PREPARATION The first step in preparing a piece of wood for gold leafing is to decide whether you want a smooth or textured surface. The trend today is to let some of the wood grain show through the gold leaf. If you want a smoother surface, apply a coat of a substance called *gesso*. The gesso is very thick, so it fills any surface irregularities and provides a smooth base for the gold leaf. The traditional formula for a gesso is rabbit-skin glue mixed with chalk powder. A more modern form of gesso uses an acrylic base.

Some people prefer to substitute a coat of paint for the gesso. This is especially true if an antique effect is desired. When red paint is used as the base coat, the effect is frequently called *Venetian gold*. When the leaf is applied, tears in the leaf are allowed to remain uncovered, showing the red base. Black and brown paint are also frequently

10-3 *Using a gilder's tip to lift a sheet of gold leaf from the book. Static electricity causes the leaf to cling to the bristles of the gilder's tip.*

10-4 *This leaf product is attached to a plastic backing. Press the sheet against the adhesive and rub it down, then pull off the plastic backing.*

used in a similar fashion to get an antique look. Gold paint applied as the base coat will help to hide any tears or missed spots.

After the base coat is dry, the area to be gold-leafed is given a coat of adhesive size. The adhesive size may be thin rabbitskin glue, varnish, or a polyvinyl adhesive made specifically for the purpose. The polyvinyl adhesive is the easiest to use and is the most popular among beginners. Allow the size to dry until it is tacky. The polyvinyl size will be milky white when first applied and will slowly become transparent; when it is completely transparent, it is ready for the leaf to be applied.

APPLYING GOLD LEAF Open the book of gold leaf to the first page and touch the flat side of the gilder's tip to the leaf. The leaf will cling to the bristles of the gilder's tip (**10–3**). Lift the leaf from the page and press it into place on the adhesive size. Continue to apply the leaf in this manner until the entire area is covered. Each leaf should slightly overlap the previous one.

To make the application process simpler, you can use a leaf product that is attached to a plastic backing. Press the sheet against the adhesive and rub it down, then pull off the plastic backing (**10–4**).

When all of the leaf has been applied, use a soft brush or a wad of soft cloth to press the gold leaf into all of the details of the surface. Next, burnish the surface by gently rubbing a soft cloth over the gold leaf. The cloth will remove any pieces of leaf that overlap or are not attached firmly, leaving only a single layer of firmly attached gold leaf. If tears or missed spots appear at this stage, you can repair them by pressing a small piece of leaf into the defect. Burnish the leaf again to give it a smooth polished surface. Professional gilders use a special burnishing tool tipped with a piece of highly polished agate stone to complete the burnishing process.

GLAZING When an antique effect is desired, a glaze is applied over the gold leaf (**10–5**). The glaze is similar to thick stain. Oil or Japan tinting colors thinned with paint thinner make a good glaze. Glazes are usually colored with burnt umber, burnt sienna, or raw umber. Brush or wipe the glaze over the gold leaf and then use a soft cloth to highlight the glaze by wiping it off of the gold, leaving more glaze in the low spots and removing most of it from the high spots. Glazing is especially effective on carvings, because it shows off the detail.

PROTECTIVE COATING The leaf should be protected with a coat of varnish, lacquer, or a protective coating made specifically for gold leaf. Apply the coating after the gold leaf is burnished and the size has dried. If you use a glaze, wait for it to dry before applying the protective coating. Make sure that the coating is compatible with the gesso or base coat of paint, adhesive size, and the glaze. For example, if varnish was used as the size, it should also be used as the top coat; if lacquer is used as the top coat, it will react with the varnish below. The polyvinyl size can be used with any top coat.

10-5 *A glaze applied over the gold leaf gives it an antique effect.*

Bronze Powder

Another method of gilding uses metallic powder to cover the surface. Although they are usually referred to as bronze powders, they are actually available in several colors that are made from different metals. Genuine gold as well as bronze, copper, silver, and aluminum are frequently used to make gilding powder. You should use the finest grade of powder that you can get. The best type for this purpose is called *bronze lining powder*.

APPLYING BRONZE POWDER The procedure for applying bronze powder is very similar to applying gold leaf. The surface should be sealed with a base coat of gesso or paint. Next, a coat of adhesive size should be applied. A special adhesive called *bronzing liquid* is available, but varnish or shellac are frequently used as the adhesive size. Let the adhesive size dry until it is tacky.

Applying the bronze powder at the proper stage in the drying of the size is of extreme importance. If the size is too wet, the powder will gum up and smear; if the size is too dry, the powder won't adhere well. To test the size, press your finger onto an inconspicuous place; the size is just right when you hear a definite snap as you remove your finger. Don't attempt to cover too large an area at once or the size will dry before you can apply the powder to the entire surface.

Dip a small brush into the bronze powder and use it to pat the powder onto the surface. Don't brush the powder around; just gently apply it to the surface with a patting motion. At this point it is not necessary to entirely cover the surface with the powder. Next, use a soft cloth to spread the powder around. Make sure that the surface has an even coat of bronze powder; then use the cloth to burnish the powder. Rub the cloth briskly over the powder to bring up a soft luster.

You can glaze bronze powder in the same way that was described for gold leaf.

The final step is to apply a protective coat of varnish or lacquer.

GILDING LIQUID Several companies market a gilding liquid or paint that consists of gold or bronze powders mixed with a thin paint base. This technique is especially useful on intricate carvings where it is difficult to get the gilding into the low areas. Gilding liquid is probably the easiest form of gilding available. To apply the gilding, simply paint it onto the surface with a brush (**10–6**). Let it dry; then burnish it with soft cloth to bring up a smooth luster.

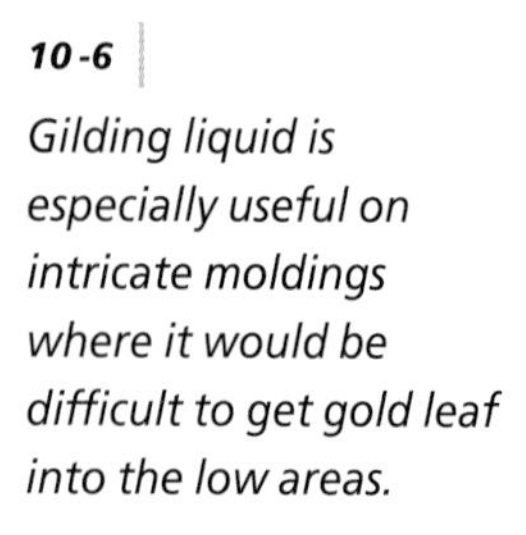

10-6

Gilding liquid is especially useful on intricate moldings where it would be difficult to get gold leaf into the low areas.

Stenciling

When stencils are used to apply a decorative pattern to a piece of furniture, even an ordinary piece can be turned into a showpiece. The stenciling procedure is a simple one, but the results can be dramatic. Stenciling is usually associated with antique designs, but there is nothing in the process that limits it to antique reproductions; many modern patterns can be adapted to stencils.

Stencils can be used either with paint or bronze powders. The bronze powder method is used to reproduce the look of old Hitchcock chairs; colorful paints are more often used for modern or Pennsylvania Dutch patterns.

Choosing a Pattern

The first step in stenciling is choosing a pattern that will harmonize with the furniture you will apply it to. You can draw your own pattern or copy an antique pattern. Craft stores sell precut patterns, and a trip to a museum will result in many ideas for antique patterns.

There are two main types of patterns: the *single-element pattern* and the *complex pattern*. Single-element stencils consist of only one element of a pattern, a leaf for example. Several single-element stencils can be used to make a design, or one single-element stencil can be used over and over to make repetitious design.

A complex pattern stencil combines all of the elements of the design in a single stencil. The complex pattern stencil is easier to use, but more difficult to make. The single-element stencil offers more creative freedom, because you can vary the elements in a particular design without making a completely new stencil. Generally, single-element stencils are only used with the bronze powder technique, because once the powder is applied it won't smear. Complex pattern stencils are used to apply paint, because the paint will smear if you keep apply the different stencils over the same area.

Reproducing a Pattern

When you have chosen the pattern you want to use, you will usually need to enlarge or reduce it to fit the item to which you want to apply it. You can use several methods to do this. The easiest method is to use a photocopy machine that has reduction or enlargement capabilities. Simply place the original in the machine and set the machine for the appropriate amount of reduction or enlargement.

If the pattern needs to vary more than about 50 percent in size, most copy machines won't do it in one step. To achieve a reduction or enlargement greater than the highest setting on the machine, simply make a copy with the machine set at its highest setting, remove the original, and replace it with the copy. Make a new copy with the machine set for reduction or enlargement as needed. If the new copy still is not the correct size, put it in the original position and copy it again. You can continue in this manner until you have achieved the correct amount of reduction or enlargement. You will lose a little copy quality each time you make a copy of a copy, but since you will trace the outline off later, you only need to have a recognizable outline to produce a good stencil.

You can use a computer with a scanner to scan in an image and then reduce or enlarge it using photo-editing software.

The grid method is another way to enlarge or reduce a pattern. It is more time-consuming and requires more skill than the photocopy or computer method. Start by drawing equally spaced grid lines over the original pattern, so that the pattern is covered with many small equally sized squares. Next, you will need a piece of graph paper, or you will need to draw second set of grid lines on another sheet of paper. If you want to enlarge the pattern, the second set of grid lines should be larger than the original ones you drew on the pattern. If you are reducing the pattern, the second set of grid lines should be smaller than the original. For example, if you want the final pattern to be half the size of the original, draw 1/2-inch squares on the original and 1/4-inch squares on the second sheet of paper.

To transfer the pattern, you must draw the portion of the outline of the original that falls into one square into the corresponding square on the second sheet of paper. This is not as difficult as it may sound. Because the squares are so small, the outline is broken up into very short segments that usually consist of straight or slightly curved lines. All that is necessary is to observe how that line is positioned in the square and draw it accordingly on the second sheet. If you are careful, this method will give you a faithful reproduction. The smaller the squares are on the original, the more accurate the reproduction will be.

The third method of enlarging or reducing a pattern uses a machine called a *pantograph*. The pantograph consists of several wooden or metal arms that are pivoted on each other. Many pivot points are provided. Changing the pivot points alters the amount of reduction or enlargement. The original is secured to the table under the arm of the pantograph that has a stylus attached. A blank sheet of paper is secured under another arm of the machine that has a pen or pencil attached. As you trace around the outline of the original with the stylus, the machine will automatically reproduce the pattern on the other sheet of paper, enlarged or reduced depending on how you set the pivot points. You can buy a pantograph at an art supply store.

If you want to copy the pattern from an antique, but it would be difficult to physically trace the pattern onto a piece of tracing paper, you can take a photo of the pattern using a digital camera. Hold the camera parallel with the surface the pattern is applied to. If the camera is held at an angle, the pattern will be distorted. Use photo-editing software to size the pattern and then print it out on stencil paper.

Cutting a Stencil

Once the pattern is the correct size, transfer it to the stencil material using carbon paper or print it directly on the stencil paper with your computer printer. Stencils can be made from several materials. If the stencil will be used with bronze powder, it should be made of architect's Mylar, which is available at drafting supply stores. Stencils for paint can be made of stencil paper, which is made specifically for that purpose, or they can be made from the heavy manila paper used to make file folders. If the manila paper is used, a coat of shellac on both sides of the finished stencil will increase the life of the stencil. If you plan to reuse a stencil repeatedly, drafting Mylar may prove to be more durable than either stencil board or manila paper. Stencils used for industrial production runs are usually made from thin sheets of copper, zinc, or aluminum.

To cut drafting Mylar, stencil board, manila paper, or acetate, you will need a razor knife. Almost any hobby knife will do, but for the best results, use a *frisket knife* or a *swivel knife*. A frisket knife is used to cut masks for air brushing and is ideal for cutting stencils. A swivel knife is especially useful for cutting designs that have numerous curving lines. The blade of a swivel knife swivels in the handle, so you can follow a curved line without constantly twisting the knife handle. Both types are available at craft stores or drafting supply stores.

Place the stencil on a cutting board made of hardboard, to cut out the openings. Some people prefer to work on a light table (a table with a glass or plastic top and a light source) so that they can see that the cut has been made all the way through the paper. You can buy a translucent plastic cutting pad for this purpose. You will have more control of the knife it you draw it towards you.

Continually reposition the paper so you can make all of the cuts in this manner. If you keep the knife sharp, very little pressure will be needed to cut through the paper, so there won't be much chance of slipping and cutting yourself. However, if you let the knife get dull, you will need to apply too much force and the chances of slipping and injuring yourself (or, at least, ruining the stencil) will be multiplied. You can keep the blade sharp by stropping it on a small piece of leather. If a little stropping won't make the blade acceptably sharp, replace the blade with a new one.

Any portion of the stencil that protrudes into a cutout area must be connected to the rest of the stencil. The connection is called a *tie* if it is connected at both ends, or a *wing* if it is connected only at one end. Wings should be avoided whenever possible, because they tend to lift up as the paint is applied and blur the image; also they're easier to tear off, so the stencil won't last as long. Take care as you cut close to a tie; if you nick the tie, it will be weakened and won't last as long.

Stencils made of sheet metal are cut differently. Sandwich the sheet metal between two pieces of 1/4-inch-thick wood. Secure the pieces together with nails or screws driven through waste areas. Transfer the pattern to one of the boards. Use a jigsaw or a coping saw to cut out the pattern. Drill an entry hole for the blade in each opening of the pattern.

Metal stencils can be designed exactly like paper stencils, but if you would like to eliminate all ties from the design, metal stencils offer an advantage. You can cut all of the portions of the stencil that would normally need to be attached with ties as separate pieces, and then use small pieces of wire soldered to the back of the stencil to secure them in their proper position. Because the wires won't touch the wood surface, the ties won't show in the final design. This method is especially useful for stencils that will be used with spray paint.

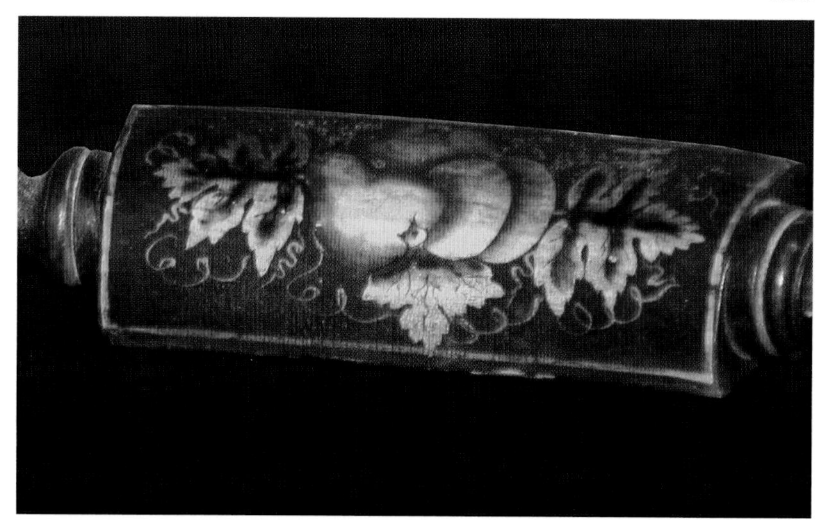

10-7 *Bronze powder stenciling can be used to reproduce the type of decoration seen on this chair.*

Bronze Powder Stenciling

Bronze powder stenciling is one of the most impressive types of furniture decoration, and it is a technique which offers you a lot of creative control. The famous original Hitchcock chairs that were made in the mid-1800s used this form of decoration (**10–7**).

The reason there is so much creative control with this technique is that the process allows you to blend different colors of bronze powders in the same stencil, and you can shade the design by varying the amount of powder applied to give it a three-dimensional quality. Single-element stencils can easily be combined into complex designs using this technique, so you can vary the design to suit the shape of the article it is applied to. In this way, several different pieces of furniture can be unified into a set by using common design elements, and yet the actual design can be varied to suit the individual piece.

To show off the bronze powder, the background must be dark; most original antiques were painted black, but the trend today is to use a dark stain so the wood grain will still show.

The first step in applying a bronze powder stencil is to give the area that will receive the stencil a thin coat of slow-drying varnish. Let the varnish dry until it is hard but still tacky. If you press your finger against the varnish and then pull it away, you should hear a sharp snap if the varnish has reached the proper stage of dryness. Also, there should not be a noticeable depression made in the varnish by your finger. It may take anywhere from ten minutes to one hour for the varnish to reach this point, depending on the room temperature and humidity; so test the varnish about every ten minutes.

Apply a commercial plastic stencil or a custom one made of drafting Mylar to the varnished surface. If the varnish is at the proper stage of tackiness, the stencil will stick to the surface and yet it won't leave a mark when it is removed. You need to work quickly at this point, because the varnish will continue to dry and will soon lose its tack.

Bronze powder comes in many colors. As you become more proficient with this technique, you may want to try many different shades; but at first you can achieve good results using the following colors: aluminum, pale gold, rich gold, and extra brilliant fire. A piece of velvet cloth glued to a square of cardboard makes a good palette for the powders. Fold the cardboard in half so it can be closed like a book for storage. Apply a small quantity of each color powder in a spot on the palette. Wrap a small piece of smooth soft chamois or cloth around your index finger and rub it into the color you desire on the palette; only a little powder is needed, so wipe the excess onto the palette.

Now rub your finger over the cut-out stencil area (**10–8**). Rub harder where you want a highlight, and apply very little pressure in the shaded areas. By using this procedure, you can give a three-dimensional look to the work. You may need to use a small artist's brush to apply the powder to very small details like leaf stems. Make sure that all of the bronze powder is rubbed into the varnish or removed from the area with a clean cloth, and then remove the stencil.

The same stencil can be reapplied in another area or a new one can be used to build up the design. If you use the same stencil over again, be sure there isn't any bronze powder clinging to it or it may leave a smudge when you reapply it. It's all right if the edge of a stencil overlaps an area that

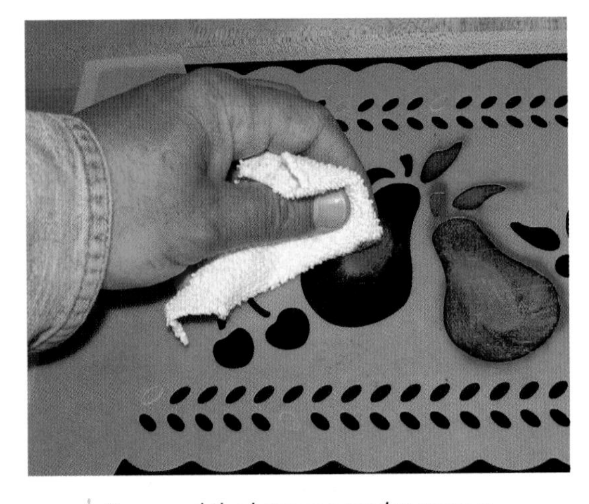

10-8 *To spread the bronze powder, wrap a piece of chamois or a soft cloth over the end of your finger, dip your finger into the bronze powder, and rub it over the area to be stenciled.*

has already been stenciled, because the powder won't smudge once it has been rubbed into the varnish.

If the varnish loses it stack before you finish, let it dry for 24 hours then revarnish it and continue working. Be sure to remove any stray bronze powder before you revarnish. Stray powder can usually be removed by washing the area with a mild soap solution; stubborn areas can be removed by rubbing with a pencil eraser. You can heighten the three-dimensional quality of bronze stenciling by applying a second coat of varnish over the first set of design elements and then applying more portions of the design slightly overlapping the first elements. The coat of varnish between the two designs will create a three dimensional appearance as the design is viewed from different angles.

When the stenciling is done and the varnish is dry, apply two coats of varnish over the design to protect it.

10-9
Cabinets and furniture can be decorated with colored stencil patterns.

Paint Stenciling

Sometimes cabinets and furniture are decorated with colored stencil patterns (**10–9**). Stencils used with paint are usually of the complex pattern type where all of the design elements are cut into one stencil; this is because it is difficult to apply several stencils to the same area without smearing the paint.

Painted stencils can be applied either before or after the last coat of finish has been applied. The finishing materials under the stencil should be completely dry before the paint is applied. Use masking tape to hold the stencil in place. Spraying is probably the easiest way to apply paint to a stencil (**10–10**). Aerosol cans work well; hold the can a little farther away from the work than normal and spray straight at the work, not at an angle. If you spray at an angle, the paint can be forced under the edge of the stencil. An air brush is an excellent way to apply the paint. The air brush gives you enough control to shade the stencil in a way similar to what you can do with bronze powder. Be sure to mask off any areas of the work that could be damaged by paint over-spray. You can produce

10-10
You can use spray toner to produce a stenciled design. The toner will let some of the grain show through in the stenciled area.

an interesting effect by using a toner instead of paint. The toner will let some of the grain show through in the stenciled area.

Paint can also be applied with a brush. Any thick-bodied paint will work. Cream paint that is designed for stenciling works especially well. A special stenciling brush is round and has short, stiff bristles that are cut square on the end. An old paintbrush can be adapted for use as a stenciling brush by cutting the bristles off so that only one inch remains.

Pour a small amount of the paint onto a flat plate and dip the end of the brush into the paint. Only the very tip of the brush should have paint on it. Tap the brush on a piece of newspaper to remove any excess paint; then, using a stippling motion, tamp the paint over the stencil, holding the brush square so that only the tips of the bristles touch the work (**10–11**).

If you want to use more than one color paint with the stencil, mask off all of the openings except those that will receive the first color. After applying the first color, mask off those openings and remove the masking from the openings that will receive the second color. Any number of colors can be added using this method. If you use cream paints, you can blend colors while they are still wet. Apply the first color to the entire area, and then blend in other colors by tapping the brush lightly in the desired areas (**10–12**).

After all of the paint has been applied to the stencil, hold your hand on the stencil to prevent it from moving and remove the masking tape with your other hand. Lift one corner of the stencil while holding down the opposite corner with your other hand. Peel the stencil off without any side-to-side movement that might smear the paint. Do this while the paint is still wet because the longer the stencil is in place, the greater the chance that the paint will bleed under the edge and create a fuzzy outline. If the paint is allowed to dry, the stencil will be glued to the surface by any paint that did bleed under the edge.

Clean the stencils with the appropriate paint thinner and save them for reuse.

10-11 *Apply the paint with a stenciling brush by tapping the brush in an up and down stippling motion.*

10-12 *You can blend colors while they are still wet. Apply the first color to the entire area, and then blend in other colors by tapping the brush lightly in the desired areas.*

Gold Leaf Stenciling

Gold leaf can be applied to a stenciled pattern. The process is similar to applying paint, only varnish is used instead. Remove the stencil and let the varnish dry until it is tacky. Apply the gold leaf to the varnished area in the usual manner; don't bother trying to follow the pattern, just cover the entire area with leaf. As you burnish down the gold leaf, it will only stick to the areas that received varnish through the stencil. Brush off all of the loose gold leaf and the original stenciled pattern will be perfectly reproduced in gold leaf.

Silkscreen Stencils

Silkscreening is a process commonly associated with printing, but it can be used to apply decorations to wood. The process uses an open-mesh cloth that is specially made for the purpose, stretched over a frame that is open in the center. A liquid similar to lacquer is painted onto the cloth to close the openings in the cloth and prevent paint from going through. The open areas of the stencil are left untreated. It is possible to produce very complex patterns using the silk screen method, and this method eliminates the need for ties and wings so the design doesn't have that characteristic stencil look; it looks more like a freehand-painted design. There is even a special emulsion that can be applied to the screen to make it light sensitive, so that designs can be applied photographically. With the photographic process, shading can be achieved by a process called *halftoning*, which superimposes a series of dots over the design. The dots are smaller in the light areas and larger in the dark areas.

Special silkscreen paints must be used with this process. A quantity of paint is poured into one side of the frame and then the screen is placed onto the work; a rubber squeegee is used to scrape the paint from one side to the other, forcing paint through the open areas of the screen and onto the wood. Then the screen is lifted from the work, and it is ready to be applied to another piece. This method is well suited for limited production runs, because the screen can be immediately reused without any cleaning between applications. Enough paint can be kept in the frame to do several pieces before additional paint is needed. At the end of a run, the screen can be cleaned and saved for reuse or the design can be completely removed with a special solvent and the screen reused for a different design.

The best way to get started in silkscreening is to buy a complete kit at a store that sells craft or drafting equipment. The kit will contain small quantities of all of the necessary supplies plus detailed directions; once you have become familiar with the materials in the kit, you will know which ones you use the most and you can buy them in larger quantities.

11 Reproducing Antique Finishes

As genuine antiques become scarcer and more expensive, there is an increasing demand for antique reproductions. There are many degrees of authenticity in reproducing antique finishes; in some cases, it is only necessary for the piece to have an antique look. At the other end of the scale is the exact duplicate which requires that the finish not only look old, it must be made of exactly the correct materials to correspond with the time period of the furniture style. Before attempting an exact duplicate, you need to thoroughly research the materials and techniques available at the time the original was built. Even the wood used is important; the best duplicates use old wood salvaged from old buildings or damaged furniture. However, in most cases an exact duplicate is not needed; you can use modern finishing materials as long as they are applied in a way that makes the piece look antique (**11–1**).

11-1 *This piece has been finished to have an antique look.*

Distressing

A genuine antique acquires a certain amount of damage during its hundreds of years of existence. If the damage is not severe, the marks left add to the piece's value because they denote its age (**11–2**). The process of purposely damaging a new piece of furniture to simulate these age marks is called distressing. The process has become a popular finish it its own right, and many new pieces of furniture are given a distressed finish. In many cases, there is no attempt to duplicate genuine distress marks. The surface is covered with marks that give it an interesting pattern, but bear no relation to the marks acquired over the years by a genuine antique (**11–3**).

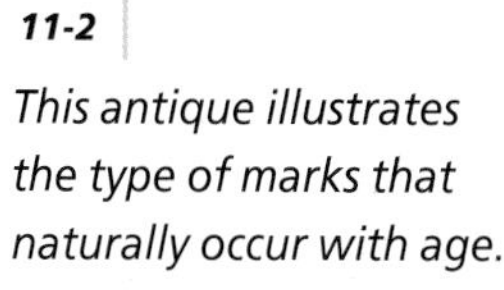

11-2

This antique illustrates the type of marks that naturally occur with age.

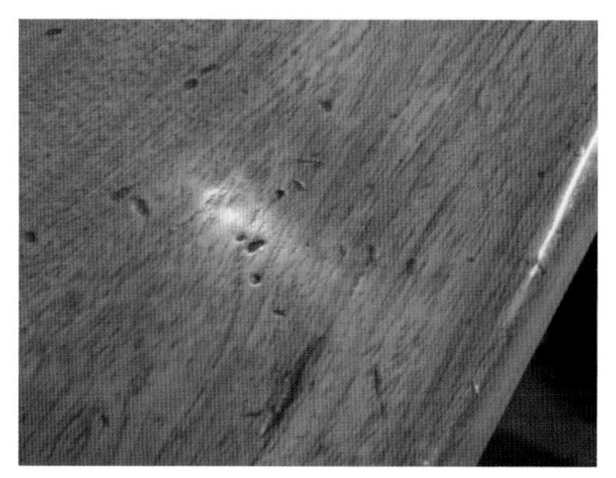

11-3

Distressing can be used to make marks that produce an interesting pattern. They give the impression of an antique, but they might not duplicate the marks acquired over the years by a genuine antique.

If you want to duplicate a genuine antique, you should study several and try to analyze how the distress marks occurred. For example, many old chairs have distinctive marks around the bottoms of the front legs. These marks were made by riding spurs on the boots of men who sat in the chairs. Once you realize that these marks were left by spurs, you can see that it would be uncharacteristic to make similar marks on the upper portions of the chair.

The writing surface of a desk may have many ink spots, but a cupboard probably wouldn't have any. Burn marks bear the shape of the object that made them; the marks should be consistent with the purpose the furniture was used for. Tables and cupboards used around a kitchen will bear the marks of hot pans, irons, or fireplace pokers; furniture used in other areas would be more likely to be burned by candles, lanterns, and cigarettes, cigars, and pipes. Since cigarettes came into widespread use fairly recently in the life of an antique, cigarette burns are not indicative of great age; an old clay pipe would be more appropriate.

There are two methods of applying distress marks: *physical distressing* and *surface distressing*. The most important thing to keep in mind when using either of these techniques is to make the marks appear random and naturally placed and not to overdo it. A little distressing can make a new piece look like a genuine antique; too much and it will look like a piece of junk.

Physical Distressing

To physically distress a piece of furniture, different objects are used to make actual dents, holes, burns, and scratches in the wood surface. If you are trying to make a close replica of a real antique, these marks should be applied after the finish is complete, as would occur in real use. The marks left should then be filled with accumulations of dirt and wax (rottenstone mixed with paste wax makes a good substitute). Normally, though, distressing is performed before the object is stained; this way, the marks accumulate more stain than the rest of the surface and show up darker, and yet they are the same color and so they blend with the finish better.

DENTS AND SCRATCHES The most common types of distress marks are dents and scratches; they are produced by hitting the wood with various metal objects. When you are trying for authenticity, you should use objects that would normally be found in a house of the correct time period to make physical distress marks. For example, use real spurs to make spur marks and use keys and kitchen utensils of the time period to dent tabletops. If you are only after an antique look, the process is simpler. Attach several different metal objects like keys, bolts, nuts, nails, and screws to a length of chain and whip the wood surface with it.

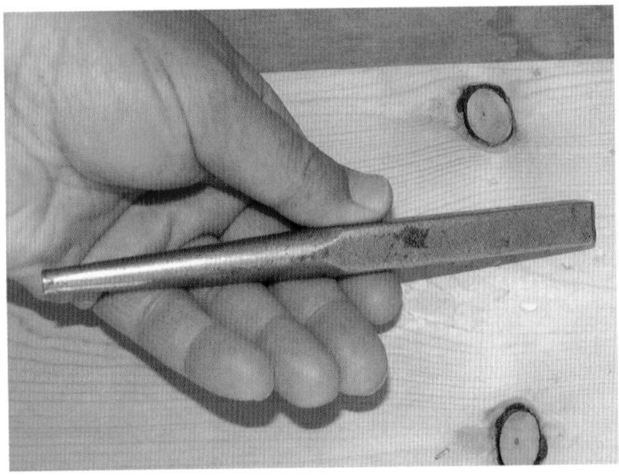

My favorite distressing tool is a large steel punch that has a round end and a square end (**11–4**). It will make a wide variety of marks, depending on how it hits the wood. Drop the punch on the wood at random. Distressing should be concentrated where it would naturally occur. Working surfaces and edges should get the most marks, while protected areas should get very few. The edges on a real antique receive many dents and nicks, so give them more marks than the rest of the project. You can use the punch to dent the edges. Hold the punch like a drumstick and hit it against the edges. Occasionally turn the punch end for end so that some of the dents are made by the square corners and others are made by the round shank. The punch works well for the small dents that are most common. Occasionally you may want to add a few larger dents. A smooth stone works well for making larger dents.

11-4 *My favorite distressing tool is a large steel punch that has a round end and a square end.*

WORM HOLES A variety of wood-boring insects attack furniture, leaving small holes in the surface. These holes are generally called *worm holes*. An awl can be used to simulate worm holes in the wood, but real worm holes don't taper like the hole left by an awl. A more realistic worm hole can be made by driving a small brad into the wood and then removing it or drilling holes with a very small drill bit. Worm holes usually are at an angle rather then straight in.

BURN MARKS A soldering iron or a woodburner can be used to make burn marks on the wood. Any metal object can be heated with a propane torch and then set on the wood surface to make a burn mark. Because of the danger of fire, propane torches should only be used outdoors. For authentic-looking marks, take into consideration how the piece was used and then choose an object that would be appropriate to burn the wood.

One characteristic type of burn mark is made when a coal oil lamp is placed too close to an upright part of a piece of furniture; the heat radiated from the glass of the lamp makes a burn that has no definite outline, but simply darkens the wood in a circular area. The best way to duplicate this type of burn is to place a kerosene lamp or a camping lantern in the proper position and let it burn the wood just as it would have happened a hundred years ago.

WORN EDGES Edges and corners receive more wear than other parts of a piece of furniture. You can simulate this wear by rasping and filing the edges round; worn edges naturally take on a highly polished look, so you should sand the rounded edges extremely smooth. Six-hundred grit sandpaper lubricated with a little paste wax will give the edges the proper polish. If you use wax, the sanding must be done after the finish has been applied. This produces a more authentic look anyway, because wear would normally remove the finish from the edges. If you aren't after authenticity but want to convey a rustic antique look, you can chamfer the edges in an irregular pattern with a belt sander or a chisel before you apply the finish (**11–5**).

11-5 *If you aren't after authenticity but want to convey a rustic antique look, you can chamfer the edges in an irregular pattern with a belt sander or a chisel before you apply the finish.*

ANIMAL MARKS Most antiques will have received at least a few scratches from the family pet over the years. These marks generally occur around the legs. If you have a dog or cat, you can probably persuade it to give the piece you're working on a few swipes with its claws, but if you can't, a piece of soup bone sharpened to a point will make realistic marks.

Surface Distressing

Surface distress marks are simply painted onto the surface of the wood; they are meant to simulate the spills and spots that accumulate over the years. Usually surface distressing is done after the stain is applied and before the top coats.

FLY SPECKS Whenever a fly lands on something, it usually leaves behind a small brown spot. In a normally well-kept house today, there aren't many flies, and so there are few noticeable fly specks on the furniture. In earlier days, however, flies were much more common in houses and antique furniture has had hundreds of years to accumulate flies, so most antiques are covered with a fairly uniform coating of small dots. Many people today don't even know what causes these spots, but they have become a trademark of an antique finish. Fly specks are easy to duplicate; although the real thing is brown, black paint is usually used to simulate them.

Spatter-distressing is a way to simulate the look of fly specks using drops of paint or stain spattered on the wood. The spattering is usually applied after the stain and before the topcoat is applied.

Use a 1-inch-wide nylon brush for spatter-distressing. Dip the brush into dark stain or thin, black or dark brown paint; then hold the brush in one hand and hold a wood stick below the brush in the other hand. Hit the metal ferrule of the brush against the stick of wood (**11–6**). This will send a shower of drops down onto the surface. The effect depends on the size and shape of the drops. Small spots look like fly specks. Larger, irregular splatters look like gouges or dents when viewed from a distance.

11-6 *Spatter-distressing is a way to apply distress marks using drops of paint or stain spattered on the wood. Use a nylon brush dipped in dark stain or thin, black or dark-brown paint. Hold the brush in one hand and hold a wood stick below the brush in the other hand. Hit the metal ferrule of the brush against the stick of wood to send a shower of droplets toward the wood surface.*

Practice spatter-distressing on a piece of scrap before you use this technique on a project. Varying the constancy of the stain or paint, how fully you load the brush, and how hard you hit the ferrule against the stick will create differing effects. With a little practice, you will soon find the effect you are looking for.

You can also use spray equipment or an aerosol can to make fly specks. Adjust the spray gun until it sprays out small droplets instead of an atomized spray. Usually you can accomplish this with a combination of low air pressure, thick paint, and a fairly heavy feed adjustment. If you press the valve of an aerosol can down only partway, it will sputter and spray out droplets that also simulate fly specks.

Of course, if you are after the ultimate in authenticity, only the real thing will do. Store the completed piece of furniture in a barn or stable where flies congregate. If there are enough flies, you can get several hundred years worth of specks in a few months.

INK SPOTS Desktops are usually covered with at least a few ink spots. Use India ink to make the spots. A drawing pen can be used to make small spots that simulate areas where ink soaked through a page or where the pen slipped off the paper. Ink spills are made by simply pouring a little ink onto the surface. If you would like something unique, draw an impressive-looking signature on a piece of paper with India ink. While the ink is still wet, place the paper upside down on the wood and rub it across its back. The result will be a reverse impression of the signature on the wood, as if a document was turned over on the desk without being blotted.

SPILLS Various types of food and drink spills can be duplicated by mixing a small amount of watercolor in water and pouring the water onto the wood. Let the water dry without disturbing it. If you want a glass ring, pour a little of the mixture on the wood and set a glass into the puddle; then leave it alone until the water dries.

RANDOM MARKS If you would like an antique looking finish without really duplicating any particular mark, you can achieve a good effect by daubing various objects into the wet stain as you stain the wood. Oil stain works best; wipe it as usual, but leave a little more wet stain on the surface than you normally would. Take a crumpled-up newspaper or a sponge and daub it into the wet stain. If you aren't satisfied with the marks, you can wipe them out with a rag and try again.

Stains

Any modern stain will provide satisfactory results if you aren't trying for an exact duplicate. Water stains and NGR (non-grain-raising) stains are especially good. Refer to Chapter 5 for directions on custom-mixed stains, if you are trying to match a particular color.

After the stain has been applied, a glaze is sometimes used to heighten the antique look. The glaze simulates years of accumulated wax and dirt. A glaze is similar to a pigmented oil stain; you can use a thick pigmented oil stain, thinned paint, or commercially available glaze. Usually the glaze is a shade darker than the first stain used. Apply the glaze to the entire surface; then wipe it off of all of the raised surfaces, leaving it only in the dents, cracks, crevices and in protected areas. The glaze can also simulate the accumulated oil and dirt from repeated handling; leave glaze around the edges of doors and work surface for this effect.

If you want to duplicate an antique finish, you have to use stains that were available to the finisher at the time the original pieces were built. Most antiques were stained with either vegetable stains or chemical stains.

Vegetable Stains

Vegetable stains are natural substances derived from various plants, roots, nuts, berries, bark, and leaves. Natural dyes produce beautiful clear colors, but most have a major shortcoming: they are not lightfast. This means that after prolonged exposure to sunlight the colors fade or change color. If you want total accuracy in a period finish, you can use natural dye stains and accept the fact that they will eventually fade. If you want to duplicate the original color of the period, but you want a more permanent finish, use a synthetic water stain. I'll tell you about a few natural stains here; for a complete discussion of natural stains, refer to my book *Classic Finishing Techniques*.

Most natural stains come from plants: roots, seeds, and pieces of wood are all used to make dyes. Many natural stains are sold as extracts. The extracts are easier to use, because they are concentrated and dissolve easily.

Most natural water stains can be used with a mordant. A *mordant* is a chemical applied to the wood to change the color or fix the stain, making it more permanent. Some mordants are applied separately to the wood, after the stain is applied. This results in a chemical change taking place inside the wood that locks the dye in place. Alum (potassium aluminum sulfate) and cream of tartar (potassium bitamate) can be used as a mordants with natural dye stains. Both are used in cooking and can be purchased at a grocery store (**11–7**). Some of the formulas below use ammonia as a mordant; in this case, the ammonia is mixed with the liquid stain.

Walnut husk stain is one of the easiest natural stains to make, and it produces a beautiful brown color (**11–8**). To make the stain, collect the fleshy outside husks of black walnuts. The husks start out green and gradually turn dark brown. Let the husks turn brown before using them to make stain. Place 1 cup of walnut husks in 1 quart of household-strength ammonia and let the mixture sit for several days. Pour off the liquid through a strainer.

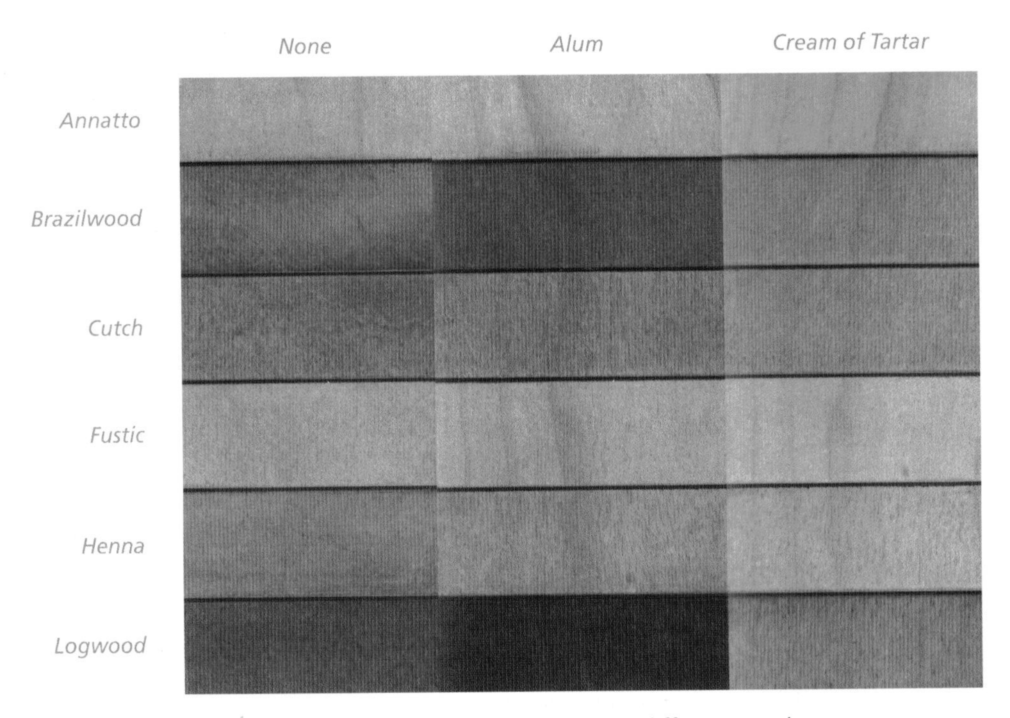

11-7 *Natural dye stains alone and with two different mordants.*

Walnut crystal stain produces a deep walnut color that is very natural looking (**11–9**). Walnut crystals are made from ancient peat beds found in the region around the city of Kassel, in Germany. They may also be called *Vandyke crystals* or *kassel extract*. To make the stain, bring 1 quart of water to a boil and remove the water from the heat source. Add 1 ounce of crystals and stir. Let the crystals dissolve overnight, and then pour the stain through a strainer. Add 1 cup of household ammonia. The ammonia deepens the color and makes it more permanent.

To prepare the stains listed below, bring 1 quart of water to a boil and remove the water from the heat source. Add 1 ounce of the dye extract and stir. Let the extract dissolve overnight and then pour the stain through a strainer. To prepare the mordant, add 1 ounce of alum or cream of tartar to room temperature water. Let the mordant dissolve overnight. First apply the stain to the wood. For an intense color, apply several coats. After applying the last coat of stain, brush on the mordant. You will see an immediate change in the color.

Annatto is sometimes used as a food coloring. It makes a reddish yellow or brown wood stain. If you are using seeds, crush them first and then boil them in water. Strain the liquid before using the stain. If you are using a mordant, let the stain dry before applying the mordant liquid.

Brazilwood stain can enhance the color of mahogany or dye other types of wood red. The dye is usually available today as Brazilwood extract.

Cutch is extracted from trees that grow in India. It is usually sold as an extract that can be dissolved in water. It will produce a variety of browns depending on the mordant used.

Fustic produces yellow colors. It is sold as an extract that dissolves in water.

Henna is a reddish brown dye. It comes as a powder that will dissolve in warm water.

Logwood extract is made from Campeachy wood. Its color can be changed to yellow, brown, black or gray by treating the dried stain with various chemical mordants such as alum, cream of tartar, ammonia, or iron and vinegar.

Some other natural stains are made from the following: dragon's blood (red), chestnut (brown), madder (purplish red), cochineal (red), yellowwood (yellow to olive brown), quercitron (yellow), Alkanet root (red), and chicory root (yellowish brown).

Chemical Stains

Chemical stains have been used for years. Chapter 9 gives complete directions for using chemical stains. Chemical stains were often used in conjunction with vegetable stains. Sometimes the chemical stain was applied first, and then a vegetable stain applied over it to deepen or alter the color. In other cases, a chemical stain was applied over the vegetable stain to alter its color. Since the vegetable stains are basically the same colorants found in natural wood, the chemical stains react with them in about the same way. So you can expect ammonia to add more of a brownish cast to a vegetable stain, while iron compounds will give the stain a gray or black look. Experimentation is the only way to determine the exact effect.

11-8 *Walnut husk stain.*

11-9 *Walnut crystal stain.*

Final Coats

After the piece has been distressed and the stain applied, the only thing left to do is apply the final coats of protective finish. For a really authentic looking job, you should use a finish that fits the period. Four popular finishes on antique furniture are wax, linseed oil, shellac, and varnish. Refer to Chapter 4 for detailed instructions for applying these finishes.

Wax

A wax finish is one of the simplest to apply, so it was widely used on antique furniture. Wax is not durable, so it is not as commonly used today. On open-grained woods, the wax will accumulate in the pores and eventually turn white. To combat this, the old-time finishers added lamp black or burnt umber to the wax. Black wax was frequently used over a fumed oak finish. The black wax in the pores accentuates the pore pattern (**11–10**).

11-10

Black wax was frequently used over a fumed oak finish. The black wax in the pores accentuates the pore pattern.

You can produce a similar finish that is more durable by using a modern paste furniture wax. Universal tinting colors can be added to this type of wax to produce black or brown wax.

Linseed Oil

Linseed oil has been used as a finish for years. The modern penetrating oil finishes are easier to use and are more durable. They look very similar, so in most cases you can substitute a modern penetrating oil finish. If you want to apply a genuine linseed oil finish, follow this old finishing adage: Apply the oil once an hour for a day, once a day for a week, and once a week for a year, and once a year for the rest of your life. What this adage is really saying is that it takes a lot of coats of linseed oil to make a good finish. Apply a thin coat of oil with a rag; then buff it off with a clean rag. Chapter 4 gives more details.

One of the advantages of a linseed oil finish is that it will darken with age giving the wood the mellow aged look of a real antique. The disadvantage is that this process takes several years (**11–11** and **11–12**). If you are impatient you can place the project in direct sun for several days. This will darken the finish, but the complete effect will still take several years.

Shellac

Shellac is a very old finish. Until recently, it was considered to be one of the finest finishes, so most good antiques are finished with shellac. The shellac was almost always applied by French polishing. (See Chapter 4.) White shellac is a rather recent development, so antiques should always be finished with either button shellac or orange shellac.

11-11 *This is what a linseed oil finish on pine looks like after it is first applied.*

11-12 *Here you can see the darkening that occurs after several years.*

Varnish

Today's natural-oil varnishes are similar to those used on antiques, so you can get a good approximation of an antique varnish finish by using them.

Varnish tends to darken over the years. To simulate this, you can add oil tinting colors to the varnish.

Sometimes old varnish becomes brittle and the surface becomes covered with thousands of tiny hairline cracks. This is difficult to duplicate, but there are several methods you can try. Craft stores sell a type of varnish that cracks as it dries; the cracks produced aren't exactly like the naturally occurring ones, but this is a sure way to get a cracked finish if you want one. You can experiment with some other methods, but the results are not always consistent. One way is to apply one coat of a long-oil varnish like spar varnish, and then apply a coat of short-oil rubbing varnish while the first coat is still tacky. If you're lucky, the top coat will dry to a brittle finish before the first coat is dry. As the first coat dries, it will cause the top coat to crack. Subjecting the finish to heat or cold may enhance the cracking. Another method is to apply water-based varnish over the tacky spar varnish.

The most realistic cracks can be produced by applying a coat of spar varnish and letting it dry. Then apply a coat of the hardest short-oil varnish you can find. Let the varnish dry and hope for the best. It may take several years for the cracks to develop. Subjecting the finish to changes in temperature and humidity may hasten the process.

Milk Paint

Most antiques that were painted received a coating of milk paint. Milk paint has a very characteristic look that doesn't resemble modern paints. The colors are usually muted and faded looking, because natural earth pigments were used (**11–13**).

Some manufacturers now make a powdered milk paint that follows the old formula. They use the same types of pigments originally used, so they look very authentic.

11-13 *Milk paint has a very characteristic look that doesn't resemble modern paints. The colors are usually muted and faded looking, because natural earth pigments were used.*

Making Milk Paint the Old-Fashioned Way

Commercial milk paints are usually the best bet: They look authentic, they are easy to use, and they give uniform results. Mixing your own milk paint is a little more difficult and the results aren't guaranteed, but if you want to try making your own milk paint, here is one formula:

For a small batch, mix two cups slaked lime (also called *hydrated lime)* with one-half cup water. Don't use quicklime; it generates heat when mixed with water. Let the lime soak up the water for several hours. Add one pint of plain cottage cheese to the lime and let is stand until all of the lumps are dissolved. Thin to the desired consistency by adding skim milk.

If you want a color other than white, be sure to use tinting colors that are compatible with lime; some types may produce a chemical reaction. Use dry powdered colors that aren't mixed with any vehicle. Here is a list of some colors that are compatible with lime: ferric oxide (Indian red), ultramarine blue, cobalt blue, precipitated yellow iron oxide, copper phthalocyanine green, sienna, ocher.

Commercial Milk Paints

To prepare the commercial dry-powder milk paint, mix the paint in a plastic, earthenware, or glass container; don't use a metallic container, because the metal can react with the paint and cause discoloration. Add water as directed in the instructions on the bag, and stir it thoroughly. You can use a wooden stick to stir the paint, or, to ensure thorough mixing, use a paint stirrer that mounts in an electric drill. After the paint is thoroughly mixed, it is usually advisable to strain the paint through a disposable paint strainer. This will remove any large lumps of pigments.

Mix only the amount you will use in one day. If you have some left, it will keep overnight if placed in the refrigerator, but the milk will go sour if you try to keep the mixed paint longer than two days. Keep unused powdered milk paint in a sealed glass jar or earthenware container to protect it from moisture. The powder will keep a long time if it is kept tightly sealed.

Applying Milk Paint

Use an inexpensive brush, because milk paint is hard on brushes. A nylon brush or the disposable foam-type brushes work well. Milk paint can also be wiped on with a sponge or rag. This results in a thin coat that is more like a stain than a coat of paint. There are several ways that you can apply milk paint. I will describe one method that works well for antique reproduction furniture.

Before applying the paint, wet the wood with a dampened sponge or cloth. This will help to keep the absorption of the paint even. Apply a coat of paint evenly over the surface and let it dry. When the first coat is dry, it will look terrible. It will be splotchy and uneven, but don't worry: the second coat will even it all out and give a uniform finish. Smooth the first coat by rubbing it with a medium synthetic finishing pad.

Next, apply another coat of paint. When this coat is dry, smooth it with a fine synthetic finishing pad. If you want a worn look, sand through the paint to bare wood at the edges and high spots or areas that would receive a lot of wear.

After the final coat of paint has dried and you have smoothed it with a synthetic finishing pad, wipe the surface with a rag dampened with linseed oil. The oil will soak into the paint and bring out the color (**11–14**). The oil will also give the paint a satin gloss. You can substitute a modern oil finish instead of linseed oil, if you want. The modern oils will dry faster and give the paint a harder surface.

For more information on milk paint, refer to my book *Classic Finishing Techniques*.

11-14 *Here you can see the effect of applying oil over the dried milk paint. The samples on the bottom have been coated with oil.*

Metric System

LENGTH

UNIT	ABBREVIATION	Number of Meters	APPROXIMATE U.S. EQUIVALENT
myriameter	mym	10,000	6.2 miles
kilometer	km	1000	0.62 mile
hectometer	hm	100	109.36 yards
dekameter	dam	10	32.81 feet
meter	m	1	39.37 inches
decimeter	dm	0.1	3.94 inches
centimeter	cm	0.01	0.39 inch
millimeter	mm	0.001	0.04 inch

AREA

UNIT	ABBREVIATION	Number of Square Meters	APPROXIMATE U.S. EQUIVALENT
square kilometer	sq km or km2	1,000,000	0.3861 square miles
hectare	ha	10,000	2.47 acres
are	a	100	119.60 square yards
centare	ca	1	10.76 square feet
square centimeter	sq cm or cm2	0.0001	0.155 square inch

VOLUME

UNIT	ABBREVIATION	Number of Cubic Meters	APPROXIMATE U.S. EQUIVALENT
dekastere	das	10	13.10 cubic yards
stere	s	1	1.31 cubic yards
decistere	ds	0.10	3.53 cubic feet
cubic centimeter	cu cm or cm3 also cc	0.000001	0.061 cubic inch

CAPACITY

UNIT	ABBREVIATION	Number of Liters	Cubic	Dry	Liquid
kiloliter	kl	1000	1.31 cubic yards		
hectoliter	hl	100	3.53 cubic feet	2.84 bushels	
dekaliter	dal	10	0.35 cubic foot	1.14 pecks	2.64 gallons
liter	l	1	61.02 cubic inches	0.908 quart	1.057 quarts
declitre	dl	0.10	6.1 cubic inches	0.18 pint	0.21 pint
centiliter	cl	0.01	0.6 cubic inch		0.338 fluidounce
millitre	ml	0.001	0.06 cubic inch		0.27 fluidram

MASS AND WEIGHT

UNIT	ABBREVIATION	Number of Grams	APPROXIMATE U.S. EQUIVALENT
metric ton	MT or t	1,000,000	1.1 tons
quintal	q	100,000	220.46 pounds
kilogram	kg	1,000	2.2046 pounds
hectogram	hg	100	3.527 ounces
dekagram	dag	10	0.353 ounce
gram	g or gm	1	0.035 ounce
decigram	dg	0.10	1.543 grains
centigram	cg	0.01	0.154 grain
milligram	mg	0.001	0.015 grain

Index

About the Author

Sam Allen has over 30 years of woodworking experience. He began experiments with new finishing techniques and little-used traditional methods at Brigham Young University, College of Industrial and Technical Education, where he was studying woodworking. These experiments continued after college while he worked as a carpenter and cabinetmaker.

His experiments with wood graining grew out of his interest in historic buildings in his native Utah. Many old buildings in Utah contain beautiful examples of classic wood graining, because the local mountains had no hardwood trees when the first settlers arrived. They used the native red pine for most of their woodwork, but they painted it to look like all of the hardwoods they left behind in the East.

Mr. Allen is a widely published free-lance author. He has had articles in *Popular Mechanics*, *The Woodworker's Journal*, *Fine Woodworking*, *Handy Andy*, and *Pacific Woodworker*. He has authored twelve books and contributed to nine others.